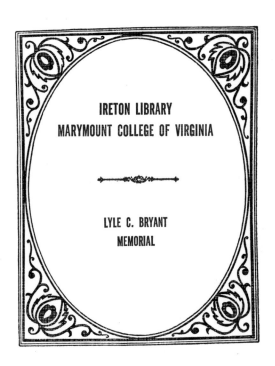

BUILDING THE STRATEGIC PLAN

Find, Analyze, and Present
the Right Information

BUILDING THE STRATEGIC PLAN

Find, Analyze, and Present the Right Information

STEPHANIE K. MARRUS

A Ronald Press Publication
JOHN WILEY & SONS
New York   Chichester   Brisbane   Toronto   Singapore

84410

Library of Congress Cataloging in Publication Data
Marrus, Stephanie K., 1947–
  Building the strategic plan.

  "A Ronald Press publication."
  Bibliography: p.
  Includes index.
  1. Corporate planning—Handbooks, manuals, etc.
I. Title.

HD30.28.M36   1984   658.4′012   83-17103
ISBN 0-471-86436-6

Printed in the United States of America

10 9 8 7 6 5 4 3 2

To

RICHARD LEE ROTNEM

Preface

This book about corporate planning has only one purpose: to simplify a complex and confusing topic so that you will not only understand the concept but will also know how to apply a specific set of techniques.

It is a book for the business professional—the practitioner—who has a job to get done and needs some help in deciphering the jargon, the theory, and the mystique. It is a how-to-do-it guide that can help you become a professional planner—or at least look like one. The graphics techniques explained here are the same ones used by some of the top consulting firms in corporate planning.

You will learn how to present business planning information by using graphics. Graphics are hardly new in business; the ubiquitous bar chart and trend line graph have been around forever. What *is* new is a graphic portrayal of corporate planning information in a unique way that conveys a large amount of data and much understanding of relationships in one glance. These techniques have impressed thousands of managers. They are powerful because they are well constructed and have tremendous visual impact.

Whenever I mention to a business colleague that I am writing a "how-to-do-it" guide on corporate planning, my pronouncement normally is greeted with one of four responses: (1) "You're crazy. Why would you want to write a book on planning?" (2) "Boy, do we need that! What *is* corporate planning anyway? I've never really understood it," (3) "Can you have that book ready by next month? We're just starting to look at planning and our guys could use something like that," (4) "I need that book. I've just been given responsibility for coming up with our first plan, and I'm not sure I even know what that means." I can empathize with this last comment. A number of years ago I was hired to set up a planning function in a company that had never done planning. Fresh out of a big-name consulting firm, I was supposed to know everything about planning, but I had never established a planning function from scratch and I was totally panic-stricken. I couldn't confide my uncertainty to my boss or any of my colleagues. That would destroy my image as the new "high-powered consultant," so I slinked off to the Harvard Business School library and read everything I could find on the topic of planning. When I returned to my office, I had two large folders filled with material I had gleaned from different planning books and I sat down to structure the planning format. But, alas, no book really told me *how* to do it. There were abstractions, theory, a few sample forms, and some case studies, but no explanation of what data to collect, how to collect them, and how to present them meaningfully.

This book was written for people in similar situations. It is for the business-person who is not a professional planner but finds himself or herself responsible for producing a plan, or providing the process for other people to produce a plan. It is also for planners who are comfortable with the planning process but would like to learn a set of techniques that provide a different perspective on the data. It will help the senior executive responsible for planning to become familiar with what is involved in developing a plan and what types of data are needed. Anyone concerned with competitive and industry activity also can benefit from these techniques. So can the functional manager who has been asked to provide data for the plan and needs to understand the importance of that information and where it fits in. The book is also for executives who have decided to hand the planning problem over to consultants but would like to understand what those consultants do.

But this book is not only for planners and those associated with them. There is another group of businesspeople who will find it useful—those who study industries. Wall Street financial analysts, government industry specialists, market researchers and marketing strategists within companies, advertising agencies, and consulting firms can all find value in the techniques.

Lastly, this book is meant for business students who are looking for practical experience in planning or who wish to do industry analysis.

We have talked about what this book *is,* not about what it is *not.* This book is *not* a theoretical tome on planning. Theory is addressed briefly in the early chapters and where applicable in the techniques chapters because you should know that there is an underlying empirical validity for the techniques. The relationships have not been drawn from thin air but have a solid basis in research. This becomes important when you see the stress given to a certain measure of the market that is new to you, such as relative market share, and wonder why it was chosen for this emphasis. However, this book definitely does not aim to give you a course in corporate planning theory. Many respected, high-caliber business academics have written excellent books on theory. The problem with these books is in the translation: how do you apply the theory to your specific business situation? It is assumed that you know how to do this or that you can hire a consultant to do it for you. This book makes the reverse assumption—that there is no one but you and your staff to do the planning, and you are all equally uncertain about methodology.

You will read about consultants at the end of the book, but a few brief comments are pertinent here. The consulting fraternity is a wonderful resource under the right circumstances—when management is receptive to their use,

when the corporate mentality approves of paying for outside expertise, and
when consulting is respected for its value—added as a supplement to internal
staff resources. Sometimes it is not practical or politic to bring in a consultant.
This book will enable you to perform the same analysis as a corporate planning
consultant. Then, the decision to use outside help will be based on criteria
other than analytical need. You may feel, after reading the book, that you do
not have the staff time, the resources, or the inclination to do the analysis in-
house even though you have the knowledge. You might prefer to bring in a
consultant. In this situation, you will be able to make a more informed judgment about the consultant's capabilities, and your expectations will be more in
line with the ultimate product if you have had the benefit of reading this book
first.

When I was first planning this book, I outlined the concept for a business
school professor and asked for his opinion. He specializes in sophisticated computer models, he has been published in all the proper academic journals, and he
teaches at one of the country's most prestigious schools. Coming from someone
with such impeccable theoretical credentials, his advice certainly impressed
me: "Keep it simple. If you do, it will be a best-seller. People are intrigued by
this stuff, but don't bore them by making it incomprehensible." I have tried to
follow his counsel.

STEPHANIE K. MARRUS

Weston, Massachusetts
February 1984

Acknowledgments

My thanks to several people who helped make this book happen: Len Lodish at the Wharton School for his encouragement and comments in the early going, Joe Kane at Atex for bailing me out of my mathematical dilemmas, and Janet and Bryan Marler for their help on the financials.

Contents

BUILDING THE STRATEGIC PLAN

Find, Analyze, and Present
the Right Information

PART **I**

What Planning
Is All About

Before we plunge into the graphics techniques for corporate planning, we must first gain some background in what corporate planning is, how a plan is developed, the concept of portfolio planning, and, finally, how the graphics techniques fit into this context. We will begin with a definition of corporate planning.

1

Demystifying Corporate Planning

WHAT IT IS, WHY IT'S DONE, AND WHAT MAKES IT WORK

Corporate planning has been around since the 1950s, but it still has a certain mystique. It is viewed as the realm of business school graduates, consultants and other super-bright people versed in the latest techniques who have mystically been initiated into the planning fraternity. Planners often have the ear of top management, and they gain entree to exclusive meetings attended by the CEO and other senior execs. They talk about PIMS, process, bubble charts, experience curves, top-down, bottom-up, adaptive, and integrative—a lexicon that intimidates the outsider. What is corporate planning really all about?

I went to business school relatively late in my career, after having spent more than a decade working in the business world. I did this for one reason: so I would no longer be intimidated by people with their MBAs. Three-quarters of what I took away from B-school was confidence in my ability to understand what was being said. No more would I dissolve in panic if someone suggested running a linear regression or told me that a change in depreciation methods had improved our financial results. Even if I did not know precisely what was meant, I had a book at home that could tell me. The same intimidation game goes on in corporate planning circles with its many buzzwords. Learning the vocabulary is the first step toward holding your own. Let's define a few terms up front.

WHAT IT IS

Corporate planning is the umbrella for a number of other planning terms. It means planning for the corporation as a whole. It is not market planning, or financial planning, or budgeting, but it entails making decisions for the whole company. One definition says:

> A corporate plan is a statement concerning the long-term *destiny* of a company. Now the destiny of any company, whatever its size, will normally depend upon two or three or four absolutely huge decisions. Corporate planning consists of identifying what those few decisions are for any given company and getting them right.*

Strategic planning derives from the military use of the word "strategy." It includes the definition of missions and objectives—how the company sees its purpose and where it wants to go—and determination of the best means to achieve those goals at a broad level. Strategic planning provides the basic direction and focus of the corporation, the so-called big picture. It is concerned with top management decisions about the company's businesses, asset acquisition/disposal, and product/markets. An assessment of the environment is needed, along with an appraisal of corporate strengths and weaknesses. Some of the company's basic strategic decisions might relate to questions such as: What business are we in? What business *should* we be in, now and in the future? What should be the geographic scope of operations? What are our research and development goals? How should products be sourced? What product or market is most vulnerable to competition? What should be the capital structure be? What is our distinctive competence? Where are we weakest? Should we diversify or prune our businesses?

Strategic planning is the top management decision process that focuses on the longer-range direction of the company and establishes the means by which that direction is reached.

Long-range planning gives the plan a time frame and can be used synonymously with strategic planning, which usually has a longer time horizon. A long-range plan should extend three to five years, as contrasted with a one- to two-year short-range time frame. Some companies, however, view three to five years as short-term and extend their long-range planning out 10 to 20 years. While this may be useful in a few industries that are subject to technological

---

* John Argenti, "Corporate Planning," *Director* (April 1979), p. 61.

obsolescence and must plan with long lead times for their continued existence, for the vast majority of companies it is unrealistic to anticipate that far into the future. An example from the recent past points to the fallacy of super-long-term planning. How many firms were able to anticipate one of the greatest shocks of business ever—the dramatic increase in oil prices in the 1970s that reverberated in a countless number of industries? If we were unable to plan for such an event in our three- to five-year planning, how could we ever guess 20 years in advance? Some companies have tried to answer this question by using scenarios, developing a plan around the most likely set of assumptions about the future environment and then playing "what if" games. What if inflation were 5% instead of 12%? What if interest rates were 25%? What if cars were forced to drive underground? And so on, until a series of scenarios for the future is developed ranging from best to worst and most likely case. Scenarios can be useful because they make you think out contingencies so you will not get caught with your pants down when your best case plan gets fouled up, but they are limited to the extent of your assessment of the range of alternatives. Do we really want a scenario in case the United States elects a Communist president? But, then, who foresaw high interest rates? At an 8% prime in the 1970s, a scenario for 15% must have seemed as ridiculous as the prospect of a Communist president.

Operational planning deals with the short term, the one- to two-year time frame. It should derive from strategic planning and is the next step in translating top management focus and strategy into a meaningful day-to-day guideline. The operational plan works with existing resources and today's situation; it provides a detailed blueprint for achieving near-term goals with the various functions of the company. An operational plan, sometimes called a tactical plan, might answer questions like: How many people should we add to the sales force this year, and in what regions? What should we spend on advertising and promotion? What steps should we take to increase our market share by two points? Where should we build a new plant? How should we finance it? How much longer should we give the R&D project now in existence, and how should we evaluate it? How should we respond to competitor X's new product entry? From where should we recruit personnel?

Notice the difference from the strategic questions we asked before. Operational planning questions are specific and short-term, and they require detailed answers. They are focused on today's operations, not five years out. Operational planning should be undertaken by the functional managers responsible for each area—market managers for marketing, personnel managers for human resources, manufacturing managers for manufacturing, finance managers for finance.

We can now compare the terms "strategic" and "operational" directly. "Long-range planning," a more ambiguous term, generally can be assumed to mean strategic planning.

	Strategic	Operational
Time frame	Three to five years	One to two years
Level of planner	Top management	Functional manage-ment
Specificity of plan	Broad	Detailed
Impact on corporation	Very high	Moderate, short-term

Budgeting is *not* planning. Despite the widespread acknowledgment of the existence of corporate planning, too many companies still confuse budgeting and planning. It is mind-boggling how many times I have listened to an executive proudly state, "Of course we have planning. We have a five-year budget that is updated every six months." Budgeting involves projecting the amount of profit or loss for the year, determining other sources of funds, and allocating them across the various functions of the corporation. It is a critical activity for any company, but it is only one element of operational planning and could certainly never be confused with strategic planning.

I recall my battles with an accountant during my first year at a planning job. Dave, who prepared the company's budgets very thoroughly, had taken the "Planning" title for himself and was none too happy with my appearance on the scene. A smart cookie, he knew there was more to planning than his group's number-crunching but he wasn't about to jeopardize his title by admitting it. No conversation took place between Dave and an executive without Dave putting in a plug for his "plans"—the annual budget. Dave was no more involved in real planning than the person on the manufacturing line.

Companies often get into planning through the budgeting function. Most (but not all) companies budget, and invariably someone will raise the questions: How do we know how much money to budget for this or that? Why do you want to increase advertising this year? Do we really need a new plant? Can't we buy those parts more cheaply than making them? Not surprisingly, budgeting leads to questions that point up the need for planning. When a company first decides it should get involved in planning, it typically gets its feet wet at the operational level, dealing with short-term, concrete issues. Strategic problems continue to be handled by top management intuition. Eventually, the business grows large enough and/or the environment becomes so uncertain that top management realizes that yesterday's gut feeling may no longer hold true and strategic planning finds its way to the executive suite.

WHY IT'S DONE

Why is corporate planning such a hot topic today? Perhaps the answer lies in a dissatisfaction with the way the old techniques have been working. Gut feelings may be great in a $1 million firm or a $10 million firm, but what about a $100 million firm? Once a firm goes public, it has a responsibility to its stockholders and is open to their scrutiny, a situation that didn't exist when the founders had control. The complexity of the external environment—with high levels of inflation, the oil crisis, and astronomical interest rates—requires new ways to deal with things. The speed of technological change makes certain products obsolete only a year or two after their appearance in the marketplace. On the opposite side of the coin, some decisions require a long-term commitment and won't see a payoff for a decade or more. In an era when capital is costly and uncertainty is high, people have a natural desire to reduce risk through planning.

It is an education to work for a small company that is trying to become big. When the company is small, top management knows everything that is going on. Management can talk to Bob the salesperson and find out how its product is being received in the marketplace. It can go into the labs and talk with the product designers. It can sit down with the accountant and worry about cash for the month. It can visit the plant and watch the boxes go out the shipping door. It knows all about the personal lives of company employees—when there's been a marriage, a new baby, or a vacation. Management knows *everything*. Employees and customers alike know the founders by first name and an informal camaraderie exists.

As the company grows larger, the founders are no longer able to manage everything. The first outsiders appear to take responsibility off the founders' shoulders. The founders concern themselves with key customers, new product development, and the bankers. They become farther removed from day-to-day activity. A new salesperson is hired but doesn't meet the founders for months. You can no longer just stop by a founder's office and get him or her to come along on a customer call. Customers who used to strongarm their way past the salespeople to the president for action on a complaint find that the president can no longer be reached by telephone.

More and more layers of management are added, and soon top management depends on others' judgments about the business. Management has lost total control. Suddenly, there is a need to plan to make certain that all elements of the organization are acting in accord and with agreement about the future. It may take years for a business to reach this point, but one day there will be the need to plan.

We have talked about growth as one cause of the requirement for planning, but it is only one among many. Some companies have had satisfactory performance for years and suddenly turn around, either for immediately obvious reasons or for less identifiable ones. Others are not facing a situation as serious as a reversal but may find that their former growth rate has slowed. A competitor may introduce a product or make another move that threatens a significant portion of products. There may be pressure to grow even faster than in the past, such as a buyout agreement predicated on certain financial goals. A major source of supply may become unavailable, or operations in a foreign country may be threatened by political instability. All of these situations cry out for corporate planning to help deal with the complexity and reduce uncertainty. Peter Drucker, an often-quoted management expert, says,

> The central fact about economic activity is that, by definition, it commits present resources to the future, to highly uncertain expectations.... While it is futile to try to eliminate risk, and questionable to try to minimize it, it is essential that the risks taken be the right risks.*

WHAT MAKES IT WORK

What has been the success of corporate planning? With all the attention it has gotten, from B-school courses to the cover of *Business Week,* does the stuff really work? More than a decade of academic research on the topic has produced many positive results. Companies that plan frequently perform better than companies that do not. There are times, however, when planning does *not* work. This can occur when (1) the CEO has not bought off on it, (2) the rest of the management team only gives it lip service, not real commitment, (3) the process does not fit the company, (4) results are not communicated properly to the organization, and (5) the plans are not properly implemented.

We have said that strategic planning is a *top management* exercise. It determines the direction and focus of the firm, decisions that can only be made by top management. If the CEO does not truly want corporate planning, effective planning will not take place. One CEO, writing about his experience with planning, warns that implementing a plan will disrupt the comfortable old ways of proceeding and cause great culture shock as people begin to feel insecure about their place. Without the CEO's strong, explicit support, the organization can kill the effort and reinstate the status quo, slowly but surely.

Sometimes you hear about a planning effort that was "grass-rooted" by a number of senior managers without CEO support. The hope is that the plan itself will convince the CEO of the worth of the effort. This is a big gamble; the plan may find its way to a bottom drawer of the CEO's desk and months of work go down the drain, or the planning committee may be eagerly embraced and taken off for a plush conference in Bermuda. It can go either way.

You will be one step ahead if you have the support of a group of senior executives who might persuade the CEO by sheer force of influence. When there is one lone executive who thinks planning would be a good idea, the chance of success is slim indeed. I was once brought in as a planner by a high-ranking vice-president of a company. When he was fired in a corporate power play, I went to my new boss, the CEO, and asked him which projects on my list he

---

* Peter F. Drucker, "Long-Range Planning Means Risk Taking," *Long-Range Planning For Management* (New York: Harper & Row, 1972), p. 6.

would like me to pursue. We went through the list of six projects and after each one he said, "No, let's drop it," until I was at the end of the page and had not received one "yes." So much for commitment to corporate planning!

Lip service to planning from the management team, a second cause of planning failure, may derive from the first cause, lack of CEO commitment. If the team does not perceive that planning is high on the CEO's priority list, it will generally resist attempts to plan at all costs. Planning is seen as an annoyance with no immediate payoff and can be threatening to the existing power structure. Why do it? Even if the CEO is solidly behind the effort, the management team will still need to be sold and shown how planning can help its *future*.

When examining planning in a company, you look at two things: the content of the plan and the process by which a plan is put together. The process needs to be compatible with the way the organization functions—the corporate culture. An organization that never writes memos and believes committing anything to paper is too formal will not respond to a requirement for a 30-page written plan. Managers get a message about the company's real interest if the process calls for two weeks to develop strategy and two months for the budget. The tightness of financial controls tells a lot about management's receptiveness to risky and innovative new product ideas. Group meetings with the CEO present may provide very different results from meetings held without the CEO, both positive and negative. Executives are adept at reading hidden meanings from overt actions and the process may communicate much more than was intended. When establishing planning, it is essential first to analyze the corporate culture, the external environment, and the desired objectives of the exercise before a proper process can be designed.

Feedback is critical in management, and yet it is a rare organization that is good at communications. In order for planning to work, the entire management organization must feel itself a part of the effort. There are too many closed-door, top-level meetings that never are summarized for the masses once meaningful direction has emerged. It remains a top management secret, and the remainder of the organization must play guessing games: Do they really want us to penetrate that market? If so, why aren't we given the funding and commitment? What are we going to do now that competitor X has entered the market? Should we sacrifice quality to make those profitability targets? Are we in that market for short-term profit taking or for the long term? What does that acquisition mean? The amount of management time wasted in second-guessing is a disgraceful loss of productivity.

The last reason for the failure of planning is the most obvious but the most overlooked—lack of implementation. It is easier to blame the planners for a "bad plan" than to blame line management for inept execution. Line managers know how to make the staff look bad when they should be taking the knock. *Business Week* wrote about the failure of AM International on its editorial page under the headline, "Planning is not enough."* The article's point was that even the best plan will not avert disaster if it is poorly executed:

> In many corporations, planning takes the lion's share of management's time and attention, with top salaries paid to people who work at shaping new strategies for growth. . . . Unless equal attention is given to expert execution of the plan, the company can be headed for disaster.

AM's "superb plan" failed because management ignored a few necessities, like production, sales, service, and financing. The lesson was that "even a plan built around the most sophisticated technological advances can lead to grief unless the company backs it with skill. Execution is the payoff."

* *Business Week* (January 25, 1982), p. 120.

2

Steps in Developing a Corporate Plan

A long time ago when I was a very junior analyst on corporate staff, I traveled with my boss, a corporate vice-president, to the head office of a division to meet with several of the senior executives to talk planning. This was my first trip into the field and I was excited about the prospect of high-level meetings even though my role was outlined as strictly to watch and listen. Over a drink at dinner the night before the meeting, my boss casually said, "By the way, I want you to take Bill and Dan through the outline of the planning process tomorrow." I nearly choked on my wine at the enormity of this request. Planning process? At this stage in my business career, I barely knew what planning meant.

That evening, I memorized something I've never forgotten: the elements of the planning process. I repeated them into the bathroom mirror the next morning, wrote them on my napkin at breakfast, and practiced them on the ride to the division office. By the time of the meeting when my boss said, "Now Stephanie will explain what we mean by planning," my patter was smooth as silk. I had learned five key concepts: situation, objectives, strategy, tactics, and control.

Corporate planners sometimes use different labels for the stages of the planning process and may even have different numbers of phases. Yet, these five concepts are the essence of all corporate planning, and we will use these terms here.

MISSION

Before we move into the phases of corporate planning, we need to think about our firm's purpose in life, a concept known as *mission*. On the surface, devising a mission statement may seem to be stating the obvious. ("We're in the computer business. Our mission is to sell computers and make money at it.") But, in fact, a careful consideration of mission can produce some surprising self-analysis that has implications for later strategy development. Is a railroad in the rail freight haulage business or the transportation business? The latter choice opens up other forms of transportation as alternatives. Is a book publisher in the book publishing business or the information business? The information business implies that all forms of information, including electronic, are fair game. Is a restaurant in the food business or, like Benihana of Tokyo, in the entertainment business? The mission statement forces top management to deal with the all-important issues of where it sees its fundamental purpose and what boundaries define the business.

The mission statement lays out the firm's view of its business in broad conceptual terms. The statement may include references to product, market to be served, desired market position, financial goals, method of doing business, distribution channels, and geography—but there is no requirement to include all or any number of these elements. Unlike other parts of the plan, the mission statement is not quantifiable and measurable. It may be a statement about today's business or where we would like the business to be in the future. There are fewer rules in writing the mission statement because its purpose is to express the corporate identity or philosophy, which varies greatly from firm to firm. The mission of a large city bank may have no resemblance to that of a small regional manufacturing firm, and different elements can be emphasized in each statement. For example:

Large City Bank: To provide a broad range of financial services to large corporations in the metropolitan area with specific emphasis on pension business.

Small Regional Manufacturing Firm: To produce average-quality home-building materials at low cost while providing employment for local residents.

The large city bank's statement includes references to product, geography, and market served. The manufacturing firm talks about product, a financial target (cost), and a social goal. Both of these are valid mission statements reflecting unique corporate character.

We can contrast the mission with an objective statement by using the manufacturing firm as an example. Remember that the mission talks about broad concepts; an objective is specific and quantifiable. We might rewrite the mission as broken down into three separate objectives:

1. Produce products that are perceived to be equivalent in quality to those of company X (an average-quality producer, measurable through market research).

2. Achieve a manufacturing cost of $3.10 per unit for product A, $1.80 for product B, and $0.24 for product C (low cost, measurable through accounting records).

3. Create 100 new jobs in fiscal 198X and fill at least 75% from Tompkins County (employment for local residents, measurable through personnel records).

Some additional examples of mission statements are:

To provide low-cost preventive health care to the local population (an HMO).

To be the dominant provider of up-to-date business information in the United States (a publisher and electronic information provider).

To market esthetically pleasing shelter projects to upper-income individuals in the metropolitan area in joint ventures with construction companies (a real estate firm).

The mission statement should be reevaluated during each year's planning cycle, but because of its broad and fundamental nature it probably will not change very much, if at all, in a given year. Since we are talking about the basic character of the business, we would not expect much change. Revising the mission in a significant manner is a *major* strategic decision. Events that might trigger such a reevaluation are generally cosmic, such as being acquired, death of the founder, new top management, recognition that the traditional market is dying, or inability to compete in existing businesses.

Developing the mission statement can be far more challenging than anyone expects and it has been known to take weeks of meetings before everyone is satisfied. Instead of wasting time, the issues raised and ensuing discussion can be among the most valuable activities the management team has ever undertaken. This is true of the entire planning process: the real value lies in the dialogue, not in the document. If the process gets the management group together to discuss critical issues facing the corporation and to reach agreement on direction and strategy, planning has done its job well. The least important output of the process is the 50-page looseleaf binder that fits nicely on everyone's bookshelf and collects dust. We all know the truth of this statement, yet it is so easy to give in to temptation and go for form rather than substance. A looseleaf binder both is easier and serves as tangible evidence of our efforts.

Now that we have defined our business, we are ready to move into the five phases of corporate planning.

SITUATION ANALYSIS

Situation analysis is also called environmental scanning, or environmental assessment. It describes where the company is today and what factors may be expected to influence it in the future. The "environment" being considered is both internal and external. Internally, it is important to look at the products or services offered, the company's financial resources, facilities, labor resources, and management depth. In looking at each of these factors, a candid assessment of strengths and weaknesses must be made. This is no time to be proud or to have blinders on; this is the time for soul searching and honesty. That will help management understand both points of leverage and vulnerabilities vis-a-vis the competitive world.

The second part of situation analysis is external: a look at the economy in general and those aspects of it which impact your markets, market characteristics, competition, technology, and political/social forces. Many people have difficulty relating to the broad measures of the situation—the economy and political/social forces. Because they are so macro in nature and uncontrollable, there is a tendency to gloss over these topics in planning, abstracting a few statistics on GNP or the coming election candidates' postures toward business just to show they have been covered. There are many businesses where these macro topics have real importance and should be given full attention. For example, insurance companies today are deeply affected by new social attitudes toward financial management and the widespread acceptance of money market funds as a way to save. This increasing consumer sophistication has hurt their business of selling low return policies as a means of saving, and some companies have market researchers dedicated to understanding future social trends. Another case is the real estate business. So exciting in the 1970s, it experienced a double whammy in the early 1980s from the poor economy and high interest rates. A planner in that industry had better understand some macroeconomics if he or she wants to forecast the future environment. Why is Detroit in so much trouble? One explanation is that the industry has been unwilling to recognize that economics and changing values have changed Americans' view of the automobile. Inflation, rising unemployment, interest rates, fuel prices, and a declining standard of living are all macroindicators that are also offered as ideas.*

The rationale for conducting the rest of the external situation analysis, the part dealing with markets, competition, and technology, is far easier to understand and critical to the graphics analysis we will be doing. The objective is to describe and analyze how our company is positioned within its markets and relative to the competition, how its markets/industries are structured and growing, and what technological changes there may be in the foreseeable future. Every company needs to tailor questions to its particular situation, but the following are some generic issues that apply across the board.

* "Why Detroit Is Not Selling Cars," *Business Week,* August 30, 1982.

Market/Industry

What market are we in?

How big is it?

What is its expected growth rate over the next year or two? In three to five years? How does that compare to GNP? (What is real, uninflated growth?)

What are the key factors for success in the business? What phase of maturity is the market in? Is it embryonic, on a growth curve, mature, or declining?

Is the technology dynamic or static? How fast does it change? How major are the changes?

How strong are the capital and technological barriers that would make it difficult for a new competitor to enter?

How stable is the market? Are competitors entering or leaving the business? How difficult is it to leave?

Is the market held by a small or large number of competitors? Is there a trend toward consolidation?

What is the basis of competition in the industry? Price? Quality? Other?

What is the industry's economics, the financial structure? Where is the most value added in the channel?

Your Company and the Competition

What is your market share today and over the last three to five years?

Who are your major competitors? What are their market shares and growth trends? What are the changes in their shares over the last few years?

What are their strengths and weaknesses? Where do they have leverage? Where are they vulnerable?

How do you compare to competition on the important factors in the business (price, quality, manufacturing, or other)?

What is your distinctive competence—the one thing you do better than anyone else?

What are your competitors' strategies?

Where will your sales and market share be in five years? What about your competitors?

How will both you and your competitors fund future business?

What is your financial health? How does that compare to theirs?

How much research and development are you doing relative to competition? What is your trend over time?

Where are you investing for the future? How about your competitors?

Answering all of these questions will give you an excellent feel for the market and competitive situation. The answers are not easy to get. Some will come from management discussions, others from original market research, and still others from published data. We have spent time on this portion of the planning process because it is a place where the graphics techniques can be of tremendous help.

OBJECTIVES

Authors and teachers of corporate planning always get hung up on the difference between objectives and goals when the distinction is not really very important. Both terms refer to a description of where the organization wants to go. To be precise, an *objective* is a broad statement of purpose, while a *goal* is specific and concrete, with measurable results and a stated time period. Notice the difference here:

Objective: Increase market share.

Goal: Gain three share points in the primary market over the next 12 months.

Objectives and goals, like the mission statement, serve a critical purpose in getting senior management to make explicit its targets for the firm. By communicating these to the rest of the organization, management ensures coordination of effort and common understanding about what is to be achieved. How many comments like the following have you heard?

A SALESPERSON: "I could write this business if I could just get some price concessions out of management. This is a big-name reference account and it would really give us an entry into this market. My boss says we want to be in this market, but I don't get any support; no one wants to give up a dollar of short-term profit. What does this company really want?"

or,

A FINANCIAL MANAGER: "They've told me to cut down on inventory, but as soon as I do it the marketing people yell that they can't ship fast enough and manufacturing yells because merchandising is on them. What do we want— sales or a clean balance sheet?"

or,

A MANUFACTURING MANAGER: "We're understaffed in Quality Control but Marketing and Finance are leaning on us to get the stuff out the door by the end of the fiscal year so we'll make our targets. I can move it out but it won't get inspected properly. Do we really want to damage our reputation in the field by shipping unchecked goods?"

This confusion may result from unclear or conflicting objectives. The bottom line is that it hurts the firm because people do not know what is expected of them. They are marching to the beat of different drummers, and the whole parade is out of step.

STRATEGY

We have talked about (1) how we see our business—the mission, (2) where we are now and what the future looks like—situation, and (3) where we want to go—objectives. Now we are ready to write the road map, to develop the strategy that will tell us how to reach our objectives. This is the most creative part of the process and also the most demanding, because it requires us to take the inputs about our current situation and the uncertain future, weld them together, and create a plan.

Strategy is a statement of the broad direction we will take to achieve our objectives. Suppose our objective is to grow by 20% a year for the next five years. Without a strategy to get there, this statement is no more than wishful thinking. It needs to be pinned down into some specific directions, such as:

Increase market share by 5% annually by reducing the shares of competitors *D* and *G.*

Penetrate the European market to reach a sales level of $30 million by 198X.

Provide better sales and service coverage in the United States, measurable by ratings equivalent to those of our major competitor.

Hold price at 5% beneath the market leader.

Each of these statements has two features: it provides general direction and a means for measurement. Measurement is not as critical in strategic statements as in objective statements, but it is always desirable in planning so that we'll know when we have achieved what we set out to do. Notice also that while the statements tell us *where* we want to go, they do not tell us exactly *how* to get there. How are we going to steal shares from competitors *D* and *G?* How can we penetrate Europe? Should we build a plant there or export and hire agents? How do we improve domestic sales and service? Should we fire our current personnel or simply add more? Do we hold our price by lowering overhead or by buying new equipment for the plant? Strategy doesn't give us these answers; it simply tells us in what direction to venture.

Looking at some real-life strategies used in the business world should make the idea clearer.

Calvin Klein, Gloria Vanderbilt, and Jordache announced entering the Brazilian market with their designer jeans to bolster sagging U.S. sales.

Xerox and its subsidiaries followed a price strategy to prevent the Japanese from taking away more market shares.

General Electric Credit Corporation changed its lending mix from consumer financing to commercial and industrial lending.

Good Housekeeping magazine sold subscriptions by direct mail instead of using outside selling agents (like the rest of the industry) to ensure a strong renewal base.

These statements all give us direction, leaving out details on how the objectives will be achieved.

Strategic development is risky. Popular business literature documents the woes of those who have blundered. Chosen at random, an issue of *Business Week* (May 24, 1982) had two pieces in its Corporate Strategies feature which described the misfortunes of those faltering. Panhandle Eastern Corporation, a gas pipeliner, gambled on a gas shortage in the early 1970s and based its strategy on that assumption. It set up costly programs to ensure supply and to gain new customers, only to find that the expected shortfall was a surplus. To quote the article, "Now Panhandle is running up against a harsh reality; long-term strategies work only if they are based on assumptions that hold up over time."

The second piece was on Milton Bradley, an also-ran in the hot electronic video game market. Milton Bradley executives in 1978 thought television-connected video games were a fad and never marketed the video game they had developed, missing a $1.2 billion market in 1981. Says *Business Week,* "That error shows how damaging one strategic blunder can be at an otherwise sound corporation." Earnings dropped 37% in 1981 as a result.

No one way to develop strategy ensures success. Some companies opt for offsite top management meetings, others use one-on-one meetings with an outside facilitator, some hire consultants to produce an end product, and still others do nothing special. Even companies that do not have formal planning processes have strategies, often based on gut feeling and perhaps unarticulated. Regardless of the method used, the development of strategy is a task for top management decision making and tradeoffs. It cannot be delegated to a bright new MBA who has learned all the latest techniques, because that person does not know what top management is thinking. Other management levels in the organization should be involved in the process, both for their knowledge and for the psychic benefits of participation that will accrue to the company in the next phase.

TACTICS

Tactics, also known as implementation or operational planning, are the detailed specifications of how strategy will be achieved. Recall the difference between strategic and operational planning and this will help you understand tactics. Tactics may be designed at lower management levels, are oriented toward short-term results, generally developed by functional area, and very detailed, specific, and structured. In contrast, strategy is a top management activity, long-term-oriented, cuts across the organization to affect many functional areas, is broad-based without much detail, and relatively unstructured.

Strategy left us hanging on the edge with a direction but no means to get there. Tactics give us the means. Tactics tell us what we are going to do to increase market share, how we will penetrate Europe, what actions we will take to improve sales and service coverage in the United States and how to hold price beneath the market leader.

Tactical planning will result in a series of concrete plans for each function or business group, depending on the company's organization. It is common to see separate plans for marketing, manufacturing, research and development, engineering, and financial and human resources that embody the strategy already developed. The plans will detail actions, timetables for their achievement, and organizational response. A properly phrased tactic might read like this:

Set up a distribution network in Germany and England by October 198X (Jim Hartwell).

Develop and execute an advertising campaign in those countries to hit by August 198X (Mary Kerr).

Make sales calls on 20 potential customers in the region by December, 198X (Lee Rizzo).

Of course, there will be a number of tactics in support of each strategic statement. A program might be developed to group tactics across organizational lines to achieve a particular strategic subset. For example, suppose a strategy involved the development of a new product, producing a series of related tactics in marketing, engineering, and finance. It might be advantageous to develop a program for product development staffed by a team from each of those functions to coordinate tactics.

We will contrast objectives, goals, strategy, and tactics in an example.

Objective: Increase market share.

Goal: Increase market share by three share points in the primary market over the next 12 months.

Strategy: Take business from competitor X in the midwestern region by undercutting their price.

Tactics: 1. Source components for our product in Hong Kong and reduce manufacturing cost by 10%

2. Buy two trucks for our midwestern region and make our own deliveries, eliminating the cost of the outside freight service. Pay back on the capital investment within 14 months.

3.   Price our products 20% below competitor X. Accept a 5% lower operating profit.

4.   Publicize our new pricing through six insertions in our trade journal and attendance at the midwestern area trade shows.

5.   Develop two promotional brochures and a sales presentation oriented toward our superior product at lower price.

6.   Make at least three sales calls on competitor X's major accounts by June 30.

You can see the very detailed, specific nature of tactics in contrast to the broad strategic statement that gave rise to them. Tactical planning should go as far as assigning responsibility for each item, a deadline for its occurrence, and a budget to fund the program. The cost of the tactic will be input to the budgeting process and used in resource allocation.

If the various tactical programs cost more than the total budget, priorities must be allocated and funding received by the highest on the list, or the various strategies should be reassessed. One of the most damaging responses to budget requests that equal more than the pot is to give everyone a little bit without giving anyone quite enough to do the job. We will overlook for the moment the budget games played in many corporations—asking for 10% more than is needed to get what we *really* needed—and assume everyone is straight. If we fund only half the sales coverage that is really required rendering the entire sales force impotent, we have done a far greater disservice than by eliminating something else from the program mix and putting the requisite dollars into the sales force. Resource allocation is a delicate balance and requires much judgment and insight into the business.

CONTROL

The last phase of the planning process is *control* or monitoring, ascertaining that the specified tactics are being followed and achieving their intended end. Control is where the gap between the plan and its implementation can be observed. If the plan goes on the shelf after the budget dollars are allocated and life goes on as before, planning has failed. We will know whether the plan is on target or just window-dressing through monitoring results.

Control may take the form of periodic reviews between top management and functional management to compare what we said we would do with what actually happened. Financial monitoring is the most commonly used method of control but is limited because it checks only one set of variables—the financial—and ignores issues relating to marketing, service, product quality, people, and the like. To be most effective, a series of controls must be designed to fit the situation, ranging from a check on actions taken internally to responses in the marketplace.

The importance of quantified statements can be seen in the control phase. If we are working with a strategy to "penetrate the European market," how do we measure success? Do three sales in England count as penetration? How about five prospects in Germany that are certain to sign next month? At what point have we satisfied ourselves and management that the strategy has worked? Our initial statement that set a $30 million European sales target by 198X gives us a way to measure our progress.

We have reviewed the five steps of the planning process (See Exhibit 2.1):

1. Situation   4. Tactics
2. Objectives   5. Control
3. Strategy

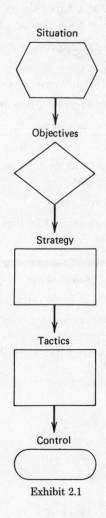

Exhibit 2.1

Much more could be said about each step, but the purpose here is to provide you with an overview so you can fit the graphics techniques about to be presented into a framework.

Why plan at all? The author of several books on planning gives us a laundry list of reasons, any one of which may make it justifiable in your company:*

It is indispensable to top management's effectively discharging its responsibilities.

It forces managers to ask and answer questions that are of the highest importance to a company.

It can simulate the future on paper, permitting a company to make better decisions about what to do now about future opportunities and threats instead of waiting until events just happen. It clarifies the opportunities and threats that lie ahead.

It's an effective way to look at a business as a system, thereby preventing suboptimization of the parts at the expense of the whole organization.

It stimulates the development of appropriate company aims, powerful motivators of people.

It provides a framework for decision making throughout the entire company.

It is necessary for the better exercise of most other managerial functions.

It's a basis for measuring the performance of the entire company and its major parts.

It flushes key issues up to top management and helps to establish appropriate priorities for dealing with them.

It is a superb channel of communication.

It helps train managers as managers. It facilitates quick and proper response to new events.

It provides an opportunity for people to contribute their talents to the decision-making process, giving them a sense of participation and satisfaction.

It pays off. Companies that do it have outperformed those that do not.

Success is more likely with strategic planning than without it.

* George A. Steiner, *Strategic Planning* (New York: Free Press, 1979), pp. 47–49.

3

Portfolio Planning and the Graphics Techniques

Corporate planning has come a long way since its early days. In the beginning, planning was done separately for every business or profit center, and an attempt was made at the top to blend it all together in a "corporate plan." The problem was that sometimes the elements didn't blend and the demand for corporate resources far exceeded supply. Someone had to make judgments about tradeoffs, and this was often accomplished in an arbitrary way: "Let's cut 20% off everyone's budget requests." Large, diverse corporations had the feeling there must be a better way.

Who came charging on their white horses to save the day? The consulting firms. These specialists in corporate planning introduced an approach called *portfolio planning*, a way for large corporations to manage diversity. The benefits of portfolio planning are significant and have been confirmed by research with firms using the technique:*

Portfolio planning allows companies to make better and more selective resource allocation decisions.

It yields higher-quality strategies.

It provides an overall framework that can be adapted to each individual business's needs.

* Philip Haspeslagh, "Portfolio Planning: Uses and Limits," *Harvard Business Review* (January–February 1982), pp. 58–73.

It gives companies a better ability to control strategy.

It gives corporate-level visibility to strategic performance of the individual business.

It allows management to give a different amount and type of attention to each business specific to its needs.

PORTFOLIO PLANNING DEFINED

Portfolio planning involves looking at a diversified company's businesses as a portfolio, analogous to a financial portfolio, to be managed and balanced to achieve certain corporate objectives. Each business's performance is to be measured against its own criteria but always viewed in the total corporate context.

Let us use the analogy of the financial portfolio for a moment. A financial portfolio might include stocks to allow you to realize benefits from the economy and inflation, bonds for a guaranteed return, and municipals for a tax shelter. The performance of each of these securities must be measured according to other securities of the same type. For example, did the bonds you bought offer as good a return as others available? Did you pick stocks that outperformed the market average? In addition, at the end of the year you want to evaluate the whole portfolio of stocks, bonds, and municipals to see if it met your overall objectives for return, tax minimization, and safety. How much capital did you gain or lose? What was the weighted overall rate of return? What was your tax rate? Based on these results, you make adjustments to the portfolio composition, adding to the percentage of stocks or enlarging your bond holdings, so the portfolio reflects your objectives for next year. The very same process occurs in corporate portfolio planning. The raw material is businesses, instead of securities; you adjust the mix of businesses to reflect corporate objectives. Within the chosen business mix, you develop strategies for the individual units to ensure that they are well positioned and performing according to expectations.

SUCCESS OF THE TECHNIQUE

Does this really work? When applied intelligently, you bet. A 1979 survey showed that almost half of the Fortune 500 companies were using the approach. Almost all of the managers surveyed said that the process had a positive impact on management. Some of the advantages were related to being able to communicate strategically in a common language, gaining a better understanding of the businesses, and having a real commitment to placing resources behind the plans.

Remember, it works *when applied intelligently*. That means two things: (1) the conditions in the firm must be right for acceptance of such a planning approach, and (2) the approach should not be followed blindly.

1. Conditions in the firm. As with all attempts at planning, portfolio planning will not work unless the CEO is committed both verbally and through actions, such as the amount of his or her own time put into the process. It is also important that the company have had some experience with planning in the past. Jumping into portfolio planning without laying the groundwork can be difficult at best. Line managers must be educated about the process and about strategic thinking. It is important to move quickly once you have gained agreement on the need so you do not lose momentum.

General Electric, one of the early leaders in corporate planning in the United States, was a good illustration of a company with the impetus that makes for commitment. A G.E. executive recalled the beginning of planning:

> When we decided to go into strategic planning, it was no toe-dipping decision; it was everyone-into-the-pool. Three hundred and twenty of the top executives were given a four-day offsite orientation in strategic planning. Four hundred and twenty-eight would-be planners were immersed in a two-week strategic planning workshop. And across the company, 10,000 functional and subfunctional managers received a day's worth of awareness training in strategic planning. The commitment was obvious, and commitment is essential to success.*

This was the way one major user of planning started the process. Unfortunately, not everyone has the corporate backing General Electric did when instituting its planning system.

2. Approach not followed blindly. The portfolio planning approach you will learn in this book is widely accepted and quoted. It is simple, it is easy to use, and it requires the least data among available approaches. But it is not perfect. If it is applied thoughtlessly, without consideration of the special features of your company or industry, it can lead to poor strategic decisions. Take it as a framework, as a universal discourse, as a starting point. If it makes sense to modify it after you are familiar with its benefits and limitations, by all means do so. The best approach is one that works well in your particular environment, not in a textbook or in someone else's company.

THE GRAPHICS TECHNIQUES

Once upon a time there was a company named the Boston Consulting Group (BCG). It was started in the 1960s by a former Arthur D. Little consultant, Bruce Henderson. The company rose to become the hottest corporate planning boutique in the 1970s. Henderson is responsible for a set of techniques used in

* Stanley Hoch, G.E. Corporate Planning Staff in Smith Barney Harris Upham report, *Strategic Planning and Management at G.E.* (August 27, 1981).

portfolio planning that have been dubbed "the BCG techniques." The most famous of these is the growth–share matrix that classifies businesses into stars, cows, dogs, and question marks, but the techniques extend beyond this into financial characteristics, cost curves, and overall market dynamics. The full range of techniques is covered here.

What makes these techniques so appealing, so much a part of the corporate planning lexicon today? There are three reasons:

1. The basic concepts are easy to understand.
2. The techniques are simple to use.
3. They graphically portray dynamics.

This third reason is especially important. There is a power in perceiving things visually that cannot be obtained from a table of numbers. You can see the *size* of the business and competitors, the *movement* over time, and the *position* relative both to competition and to the overall market. You can paste these pictures up and look at patterns. You can change some input data and see the result with your own eyes in the overall picture and trend.

It takes only one graphics presentation to make you a believer. There is nothing like sitting with a group of skeptical executives who are seeing their corporate portfolios displayed graphically for the first time and listening to the intake of breath as they see relationships they had never before understood. The power of *seeing* in a graph that most of your businesses are growing more slowly than the industry, or that only two of your 20 businesses are market leaders, or that you are the only company losing share in a market, is astounding. The executives had undoubtedly seen the numerical data before, but it had never had the impact of the picture in front of them.

The graphics techniques are hot because of their sheer force. They say things that the most dedicated planner could not get across verbally in a week of Sundays. Graphs are visual and instant. They are powerful.

WHERE THE TECHNIQUES FIT IN

One of the major strategic decisions of the firm is to assess the relative attractiveness of investing in each of the current businesses. This is determined by examining the overall portfolio, seeing if investment in those businesses will cause the firm to reach its overall objectives, and, if not, closing the gap by either developing new strategies for current businesses or adding new activities to the portfolio.

The graphics techniques can provide the basis for this analysis. They belong initially in the *situation* phase of the planning process, helping to define the competitive situation and the company's own internal balance. Once *strategies* have been devised, the projected results can be explored with the techniques.

Going back to our framework of the planning process, we view the techniques as useful at the two italicized stages.

Planning Process

1. *Situation*
2. Objectives
3. *Strategy*
4. Tactics
5. Control

WHY THEY ARE VALID

The graphs place a strong emphasis on the marketplace and competitive position. The reason lies at least partially with studies done by PIMS, a corporate planning acronym that stands for Profit Impact of Market Strategies. PIMS is a unique research project established more than a decade ago to identify the variables associated with business profitability. The project began at General Electric, was moved to the Harvard Business School, and finally became an autonomous institute in Cambridge, Massachusetts, known as the Strategic Planning Institute (SPI). More than 1,700 businesses contributed data on their strategic experiences over a five-year period, including information on the market environment, competition, strategy, and operating results. These data have given the business world a number of important findings on the keys to profitability, several of which confirm the market's importance.*

Business situations generally behave in a regular and predictable manner. The operating results of the company are not random but can be predicted by the "business laws of nature."

The laws of the marketplace determine about 80% of the observed variance in operating results across different businesses. This means that market characteristics, the business, and its competitors account for 80% of the reasons for success or failure, and management accounts for 20%.

Market position and growth of the market are two of the major influences on profitability and net cash flow. Market share, both absolute and relative to the company's three largest competitors, has a positive impact on profit and cash. Market growth is a positive influence on dollar profit but not on cash flow.

Product characteristics don't matter. The important thing in predicting operating results is the business's characteristics on market position, invest-

* SPI, Pimsletter #1, "Nine Basic Findings on Business Strategy" (1980).

ment, and productivity. Two businesses with different products but the same business characteristics will perform similarly in operating results. The converse is not true.

PIMS found that a difference of 10 percentage points in market share results in a difference of five points in pretax return on investment, strong evidence for the market's importance. PIMS suggests several reasons for this relationship*:

High-share businesses are more vertically integrated and therefore spend less on outside purchases. Manufacturing costs stay low because of the increase in efficiency of scale.

Marketing costs are subject to economies of scale and are lower for high-share businesses.

Market leaders have unique strategies and charge higher prices for higher-quality products than smaller companies.

The PIMS research is frequently cited as validation for portfolio planning techniques. By linking profitability and market share, PIMS has made an important contribution to business analysis, one that makes us comfortable with the underpinnings of portfolio planning. We can proceed with the graphics techniques knowing that the market relationship has been empirically justified.

* Robert D. Buzzell, Bradley T. Gale, and Ralph G. M. Sultan, "Market Share—A Key to Profitability," *Harvard Business Review* (January–February, 1975), pp. 97–106.

4

Defining Your Business

The first step in applying portfolio planning to your company is to redefine your business for strategic planning purposes. This is necessary because the existing operating structure may have little relationship to the strategic structure. There are examples of poorly defined businesses everywhere in industry, resulting in strategic problems for the company. Back in the early 1970s, Dart & Kraft, then called Dart Industries, had placed two companies in their direct selling group that were as different as night and day, except that they both used direct sales as their method of distribution. Tupperware sold plastic containers by the party plan, and Vanda Beauty Counselors sold cosmetics the same way. While it was true that both had common distribution channels, distribution was not the critical variable in the cosmetics business; fashion was. By grouping the two companies under one label, it was easy to overlook the strategic key for the cosmetics business and to focus instead on the distributor organization and the number of parties held, all the time missing the right product. Had Dart organized its fashion-oriented cosmetics business separately from its plastic container line, it might have been able to focus on the critical issues in each business and make a success of Vanda instead of losing money. Many other companies have made mistakes in business definition that brought them serious difficulties.

General Electric revolutionized corporate planning thinking with its concept of strategic business units (SBUs). The idea began in 1971 when G.E. realized that something had to give—its 1960s sales had grown tremendously but earnings had failed to keep pace. By redefining its businesses into SBUs, G.E. dramatically changed its planning process. The revolutionary concept it introduced was to define a business in strategic rather than operating terms,

29

allowing for planning and managing performance with a strategic focus. Independent product-market segments were identified, which held their own and could be managed separately. In practice, true independence from the rest of the firm was impossible because of shared manufacturing, marketing, and staff functions, but theoretically an SBU should have authority over each of its basic functions—engineering or design, manufacturing, marketing, and distribution.

A problem in SBU definition is developing a manageable number of units with which to work. A strict product-market definition could lead to hundreds of SBUs for a large, diverse firm, beyond a practical limit. Companies using portfolio planning/SBU approaches have recognized this difficulty and, on the average, have stoppped at 30 SBUs. G.E. managed to reorganize its $20 billion business consisting of nine groups and 48 divisions into 43 SBUs, many of which crossed existing organizational lines. Prior to the SBU concept, food preparation appliances were found in three separate divisions. These were reunited in a single housewares SBU.

Properly defining an SBU is a demanding but necessary task. The SBU is the fundamental planning unit, the starting point for all analysis, and it is worth spending time up front to make certain the right ones have been identified. One of the most comprehensible schemes to aid in SBU definition was developed by the Cambridge consulting firm Arthur D. Little (ADL). ADL has its own nomenclature for an SBU. They call it a strategy center, defined as a natural business with an independent marketplace for which one determines objectives and strategies. We will use the terms SBU and strategy center interchangeably.

Six clues help us identify a true strategy center versus one that belongs to a larger business in the corporation or is part of several businesses. In the multiple choice options, an *A* is a sign that the unit is acting like one strategy center, a *B* means it may comprise more than one strategy center, and a *C* means it may be part of another center. Take a business you know well through the test.

1. What is the effect of changing the price of one product in the unit?
    a. You must change prices on all other products in the unit.
    b. You must change prices on only some products.
    c. Pricing in another unit is affected.
2. How many sets of customers are there in the unit?
    a. A single set.
    b. A multiple set.
    c. Shares customers with another unit.
3. How many sets of competitors are there in the unit?
    a. A single set.
    b. Competes with different sets for different parts of its business.
    c. Competes against the same set as other units.

4. What is the effect of a change in the quality or style of a product in the
    unit?

    a. You must change the same parameters for all other products in the
        unit.

    b. You must change the same parameters for some but not all products
        in the unit; or the change has no effect on many other products in
        the unit.

    c. The change affects products in another unit.

5. May the products sold by the unit be substituted for each other?

    a. Yes.

    b. Some but not all products may be substituted.

    c. They may be substituted for products in another unit.

6. How great an impact would there be on the marketing/sale of remaining
    products if you dropped one product in the unit?

    a. Some impact.

    b. No impact.

    c. Impact on another unit.

Let us see how this works in a business situation. A company sells computer
systems with specialized accounting packages. It is organized into business
groups that sell to vertical end-user markets: one to banks, one to all types of
customers internationally, and a third to nonbanking customers in the United
States—manufacturing, law and engineering firms. We will place ourselves in
the domestic nonbanking group and take the test from that perspective.

Pricing.   A change in pricing in one market segment does not affect others in
the group because the customer sets are distinct, but a change in law firm
prices might affect prices in banks, a different group.   (*C*)

Customers.   Each of the domestic nonbanking markets has a different set of
customers.   (*B*)

Competitors.   There are different systems competitors in each of the markets, but some reach across markets in our group, such as (1) law firms and engineering firms, (2) engineering and manufacturing firms. Manufacturing firm
marketing faces many of the same competitors as in the bank market, a different business group, and international cuts across everything.   (*B, C*)

Quality/style change.   Each market requires different functions so changes
in one do not affect another.   (*B*)

Substitution.   Some functions of the product are common across markets
but many are specific to one market, therefore direct substitution is not always
possible. It is more possible to substitute between law firms and engineering

firms or between manufacturing and engineering firms than between law firms
and manufacturing firms. The manufacturing firm product could be substituted
for the bank product, another business group.   (B, C)

Impact of dropping one product.   Since each end-user market has a
slightly different product, there would be no impact within the business group.
If the manufacturing product were dropped, there would be some impact on
the bank market.   (B, C)

The test points to the need for a redefinition of strategy centers in this company. Consistent overlaps between manufacturing firms and banks and lack of
close correlation among law firms, manufacturing, and engineering firms suggest that the existing organization is not maximizing strategic management.
See Exhibit 4.1.

The fact that a business has been defined as a strategy center does not mean
that the organization must mirror it. There may be valid organizational reasons
for maintaining the status quo even though an SBU cuts across lines. It is certainly not advisable to put an organization through the trauma of change at the
same time as you are instituting a planning process. The key is to plan strategically for the proper entities, even if they are divided within the company.

SBUs are an important building block for corporate planning, but, by the
same token, they are not a substitute for corporate planning. It is not enough to
develop plans for each SBU, aggregate them, and call it a corporate plan. Corporate planning must be done at the top of the organization as well as at the
bottom. There is no substitute for top management synthesis and portfolio bal-
ance/tradeoffs in the process.

There are far more complex ways to deal with defining your business than
the one we just reviewed. Entire books have been written about just this one
aspect of planning. This has been a simple, useful way to start that, like all
methods, can be adapted to specific situations with your own criteria added.

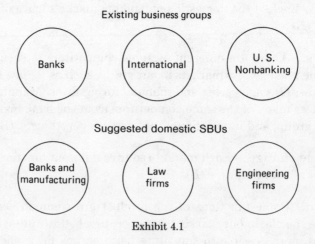

Exhibit 4.1

PART II

The Market Perspective

Now that we have covered the fundamentals, we must fine-tune a few of our tools to execute planning. One of the most important aspects is properly defining the business to be planned for. This topic is addressed in Chapter 4. Chapter 5 tells us where to obtain market data, the raw material for our graphs.

5

Where to Find
Market Data

The raw material for our analysis is data—data about competitors, our own company, and the industry as a whole. Few of us can go to a file cabinet and extract what we need. We must locate the data from secondary, already published sources, or we must create it ourselves by doing primary research.

The search for secondary data can be enjoyable. One of my favorite ways to spend a day is to go to a pleasant business library and browse among stacks of material, a welcome change of pace from the frantic office environment. There is something rewarding about coming away from the library with a briefcase full of information that was not in my possession at the start of the day, knowing there exists an answer to at least some of my questions.

I have spent years doing business research and have learned the hard way. Let me share a few "golden rules" that can save you time and heartache when doing a data search.

THE GOLDEN RULES OF DATA COLLECTION

1. Use a copier; don't copy by hand. I used to feel triumphant when I found the precious set of numbers I had been seeking, copied them by hand, and made my way back to the office with my treasure. Invariably, one of three things happened: (1) When I got involved in the analysis, I found I had failed to anticipate my need for the next number on the page, which I had not copied, (2) there was an asterisk next to a key number but I had not copied the footnote, or (3) my boss questioned the composition of the data because it did not fit with some other numbers we had, and I hadn't the faintest idea how the numbers had been developed (the information was in notes at the beginning of the source). These experiences taught me it is courting disaster to not photocopy the entire page or section from which the data came, as well as the portion on data collection and composition. Even if you are *certain* you need just one number, take the advice and photocopy the page.

2. Write the full citation on your copy, or photocopy the title page. You will need to know the author, title, publisher, volume, page, and date for every bit of data collected. Even if you are sure there will never be a reason to return for more data, copy the citation. You can never tell when the data are going to be so provocative that there are demands for more of the same, and hours can be wasted trying to reconstruct the source if you have not followed this counsel. In any event, the source should always appear with the data in any report or presentation to establish credibility and to give proper credit. Imagine a presentation where data appear on the screen showing Joe or Carol Executive in your audience that his or her business is going down the tubes. The executive's protective reaction will be, "Those data are wrong. I don't know where you got them, but there's no way that could happen in our market." You are on pretty thin ice if you cannot establish credibility by citing the source. Compare this response: "Those data came from the executive director of our industry association, to which we contribute sales information along with our six major competitors. The director feels the data accurately represent the industry situation." Now you have placed the onus squarely on an industry expert, a high-credibility outside source. Joe or Carol can take his or her protests to the trade association, leaving you out of the fray. The moral is, "Source all data."

3. Copy the name of the individual who prepared the data. Sometimes an individual is credited with the data preparation. This person's name may appear at the end of the report, as in some U.S. government reports, there may be a byline in a trade magazine report, or the name may be in the inside front cover. Copying this name is your protection when (1) you need more information than is printed, or (2) you need to resolve apparent inconsistencies in the data. During my investigation of the book publishing market, I came across two different sources that disagreed on the size of the market by thousands of units. I picked up the phone and called the individuals credited with the data in each organization, told them about the other source I had seen, and asked if they could explain the discrepancy. They both were extremely helpful and pleased to find someone else interested in their data, offering possible explanations based on different samples, methods of data collection, and industry definition. Without exception, I have received this type of friendly reception whenever I dig into data with the "author."

4.   There is always more to the data than you see. The U.S. government is a prime example of this phenomenon. The government crunches out reams upon reams of statistics that may never reach the hands of the public. Its Washington and Bethesda offices are filled with analysts who do nothing but collect and analyze data. The data perceived to be of most interest are published; supporting detail exists on computer runs sitting on a shelf somewhere. Whenever you see government data, assume there is a wealth of more information behind it. How do you uncover this gold mine? The best way is to go to Washington and walk into the office that puts it together. You will receive the most courteous treatment and you'll leave with more pamphlets, books, and printouts than you can carry. The data collectors exist to produce data and to help you. You can stop feeling guilty about using this tremendous resource when you remember that your tax money is paying for salaries, offices, and computers. If you cannot go to Washington personally, the next best approach is to call the analyst who prepared the information and tell him or her what you are looking for. The analyst can sometimes read the data to you over the phone or will be happy to put it in the mail. Remember that even if the analyst reads the data to you, also have him or her mail the source document. (That's the same as rule 1, don't copy by hand.)

5.   You can, and must, take it with you. Imagine that you have flown thousands of miles from home and find that the office of the Widget Trade Journal is rich with clipping files and back issues on your topic of investigation. After hours of digging around, you get the data that solidify your entire argument for the widget market. But, alas, the precious data in your hot hand are buried in a 30-pound oversized book. The nice person who has helped you find it says, "Look, let me put it in the mail for you. There's no point in lugging it all the way back to Hometown with all your other luggage." You heave a sigh of relief and surrender the data. That afternoon, you board your plane and return home. At least one of the following things happens:

1.   The nice person forgets to mail it. Two weeks later you are desperate for the data, which are still thousands of miles away.

2.   The nice person forgets to mail it *and* goes on vacation. No one knows what you're talking about when you call to track it down.

3.   The book arrives a month late, because of a mixup by the U.S. Postal Service. Your report was handed in a week ago.

4.   The book was sent but never arrived. It was the only copy in existence and is out of print.

Don't *ever* leave data behind. When you go on a data collection trip, pack accordingly and leave lots of room for material to travel home with you. If you absolutely, positively cannot hand-carry the data because you are proceeding directly to Western Africa for a month, personally mail it home. At least you will avoid possibilities 1 and 2 above, a 50% improvement.

6.   You will always get more from a personal visit. There is no way to quantify the difference in results between a phone call and a face-to-face communication, but the difference is major. Because you cannot develop a dollars-and-cents rationale, pity the poor junior executive who must justify a trip to the boss but can only plead, "I know I can get better information if I go in person." The only evidence I can offer is an example. While I was working on a study of the book market, I discovered that no data existed on the number of titles produced, the only meaningful measure for my purpose. All the data gave gross dollar sales but were impossible to convert to titles. I gave up until my boss said that we absolutely had to have the information. So I became more creative. I located someone in the industry who had prepared data on sales for many years (his name was on the published data), called him, and explained my problem. He sympathized and confirmed that data on titles simply did not exist. If I ever found some, I should let him know becuse he felt it would be a valuable asset. We chatted a while on the phone and I learned that he had been in the industry for more than 30 years, used to publish the major source of statistics, and had retired but still put data together on a consulting basis. On a hunch, I asked if I could visit him to discuss what I was doing. He was receptive to the idea and scheduled a meeting in his office, an hour's flight from mine. I spent two hours with this industry expert and came away with something I am certain no one else in the United States has—an estimate of the number of titles produced by type of book. It was all in his head, and he simply needed a little coaching to get it out. I could not have predicted success going in and I took a chance that the meeting could be a dud. His freely given information was worth many thousands of dollars, had I been able to buy the data.

People generally want to be helpful, and if you have a chance to build rapport face-to-face, you will get their best.

FINDING MARKET DATA

Business research books can be boring. They list hundreds of sources that have no relevance to your particular data search, and you must wade through all of them to identify the few that are applicable.

To spare you the same agonies, I will focus only on data to prepare the graphs, leaving out a lot of interesting but irrelevant collections you are welcome to look for on your own time if you have the inclination. Our search will be directed toward market and sales information. Financial information sources will be covered later in Chapter 11.

Some of the data you need on your company will come from internal records. This list relates to the information outside your company, usually found in already published materials. Since we generally want historical trends and/or multiyear averages, we will look for three to five years of data. Forecast data sources to predict industry trends will also be included.

We will concern ourselves with five categories of information providers:

1. The U.S. government
2. Trade associations
3. Data services
4. Trade publications
5. Directories

U.S. Government

Uncle Sam is the biggest publisher in the country. The statistics collected by the government are unparalleled in scope and value, yet few nonbusiness users have the foggiest idea that they exist. An entire industry lives off government data, repackaging it in more convenient or accessible form and charging a pretty penny for doing so. When you obtain data directly from the government, they are essentially free. You may have to pay a few dollars if you order them from Washington rather than visiting personally, but the price will never strain your budget.

The government maintains more than 1,200 depository libraries around the country, places you can visit in your city that contain copies of government publications. Depositories may be located in a regular public library, in a state government library, in colleges and universities, and in other special libraries. They are required to be open to the public during normal library hours for free use of the publications.

A second way to gain access to government data is to order them from the government, either from the printing office in your city or directly from Washington. You can establish a charge account with the Government Printing Office with a nominal sum of money against which your order is drawn. The present minimum account is $50. You can send a check made out to the Superintendent of Documents in Washington and receive an account number in one or two weeks, or you can open an account by visiting your local government bookstore and leaving them a check. After the account has been established, you can order materials through any of the 20 local stores or by calling the order desk in Washington. This is a great convenience for anyone who plans to make frequent use of government data, and it saves weeks of order processing time.

The address is:

Superintendent of Documents
Government Printing Office
Washington, D.C. 20402

The Washington order desk number that serves account holders is (202) 783-3238. The GPO also publishes a monthly catalog that details everything it has printed. You can pay $5.25 for one monthly copy, invest in a semiannual index for $12.00, or buy an annual index for $25.00.

The third way to get information from the government is to call the Washington analyst who prepared the data and request a specific item. The analyst will gladly send you the publication that includes the data you require or will photocopy the relevant pages.

There is one major problem with using government data—finding what you need. So much is produced and by so many different departments and sections that it is difficult to know where to start. If you find yourself in this situation, head for a directory. Washington Researchers, an organization that helps people find government materials, publishes an excellent set of directories to get you through the maze. Among their publications is the *Researchers' Guide to Washington Experts,* a directory that provides the names and phone numbers of thousands of data experts in the government. By looking up the name of the industry in which you are interested, you can get the name of the analyst, the department and bureau, the telephone number, and a list of all industries covered. A shorter version is *Industry Analysts in the Federal Government,* a listing of more than 100 specialists in the Bureau of Census and the Department of Commerce arranged by SIC code. A third source is the *Washington Information Workbook,* a publication that identifies information sources within the federal government and describes the type of information each collects along with phone numbers and contacts. Have you ever thought about contacting a legislative committee on Capitol Hill that is conducting an industry investigation? How about getting a World Traders Data Report that profiles a foreign competitor? The government will even do computer data base searches for a modest fee. *How to Find Information about Companies* gives you lots of helpful hints about hunting down elusive company information, a topic in which we are especially interested. It covers published sources, data bases, foreign firms, government sources, and the courts. A supplement to this book is a small case book called *Company Information,* which takes you through the paces of researching a closely held private company. Washington Researchers conducts seminars on how to tap Washington as an information source, a worthwhile investment if you are going to spend a lot of time seeking data and will do consulting or searches. Each publication costs less than $100 and is well worth the investment.

There is an easy sequence of steps to follow in searching for data with government sources.

1.   Identify the SIC code for your product or industry.   The Standard Industrial Classification (SIC) coding system was developed by the government to classify all business according to type of activity, and it is the key to unlocking government information. Codes include manufacturing, wholesaling, retailing, services, agriculture, construction, transportation, and public administration. The system is used universally by government agencies and many nongovernment data sources as well. It provides a means of communication with people who can help you find data because it precisely defines the industry or product you seek.

The SIC code bible is *The Standard Industrial Classification Manual,* revised periodically to reflect changes in economic composition by the U.S. Office of Management and Budget. It is available in any library that has government data, or it can be ordered for your own bookshelf for a nomimal sum from the U.S. Government Printing Office. The book has an alphabetical index in which you can locate your product or industry and determine its classification.

Each product or service is assigned a seven-digit code. However, not all data are available every year in the detail that seven digits provide. Each digit signifies a different level of aggregation; the more digits, the more detail.

Number of Digits	Level of Data
2	Major group
3	Individual group
4	Industry
5	Product class
7	Product

An industry example will give you a feel for the data. Our case example will be the book publishing industry, so we will look up its SIC code. As a manufacturing activity, book publishing is classified in division D, one of 11 broad divisions where all manufacturing resides. Book publishing's major group (two digits) is group 27, "Printing, Publishing, and Allied Industries." Group 27 is defined as including:

> Establishments engaged in printing by one or more of the common processes, such as letterpress, lithography, gravure, or screen; and those establishments which perform services for the printing trade, such as bookbinding, typesetting, engraving, photoengraving, and electrotyping ... [and those] engaged in publishing newspapers, books, and periodicals regardless of whether or not they do their own printing.

If we were looking for news syndicates, the book would tell us that they are not included in group 27 but are considered Service Industries.

The two-digit major group is broken down into three-digit individual groups such as newspapers, periodicals, books, and miscellaneous publishing. Choose the individual book group 273. The book group is further subdivided into two four-digit industry groups, one for establishments engaged in publishing only or in publishing and printing books and pamphlets, and the other for companies that print, print and bind, but do not publish. We want publishers, not printers, so pick industry group 2731, titled "Books Publishing, Publishing and Printing."

Many data stop at the four-digit level, not just within government publications but within data products sold by outside purveyors. Four digits may not give you a sufficiently focused definition for your product or industry, so it is critical to ask how many SIC digits a source can provide. The four-digit level is also as far as the SIC manual goes in detailing classifications, giving enough information to let you get started in the appropriate industry group. There are two further classifications used in the various censuses, a five-digit product class and a seven-digit product. To extend our example, let us suppose we went to the data to find product classes within the book publishing industry. We would see that industry 2731 is divided into:

	SIC #
Textbooks, including teachers' editions	27311
Technical, scientific, and professional books	27313
Religious books	27314
General books (trade)	27315
General reference books	27317
Other books, excluding pamphlets	27318
Pamphlets (5–48 pages)	27319

There is one last level of detail, the seven-digit product level. Let us look into one product class, general reference books (27317), and see how it is further broken down.

a. Subscription reference books:

Encyclopedias	2731721
Religious	2731723
Other	2731725

b. Other reference books:

Dictionaries and thesauruses	2731741
Atlases	2731743
Other	2731749
General reference books, not specified by kind	2731700

We have come a long way from data on the broad industry of book publishing to a product as specific as atlases. And the government has collected and published data on thousands of such products. In some cases, data will not be published at seven digits because there are too few producers and such publication would be tantamount to revealing one producer's sales. Or, the data may not be available in such a disaggregated form. The majority of products, however, can be seen in this fine detail.

We have spent a lot of time on SIC codes because they are the building blocks for government data research. The match between your product and the government's definition may not always be perfect, but it is probably close enough for your purposes. Once you have classified your product properly, you can proceed.

2. Find your product or industry in a Department of Commerce publication. The Census of Manufactures, published by the Department of Commerce, is the basic source for data on manufacturing in the United States. It contains data on every manufacturing plant with one employee or more. Starting with the establishment as the basic unit of analysis, it builds up data to industry and group aggregates. There are other economic censuses besides manufactures that cover different segments of the economy: retail trade, wholesale trade, services, minerals, and construction. We will use manufactures in this discussion because it is applicable to the majority of businesses. Keep in mind, however, that nonmanufacturing industry sources also exist.

The Census of Manufactures is conducted every five years (the last time in 1982), and it presents a set of statistics by industry, area, number of employees, type of ownership, and product specialization within plant. It takes two to three years after the Census is conducted before the data are published fully by state, by metropolitan area, and for the country as a whole. The Census is updated annually with the Annual Survey of Manufactures (ASM), based on a sample from the Census that includes about a fifth of all establishments, all of the large ones and a sample of smaller ones. A big distinction between the Census and the ASM is the number of SIC code digits presented, seven for the Census and five for the ASM. If you need the most detailed level for your product, using the ASM can be a problem. Data presented in the Census include historical sales for a 15-year period, industry operating ratios, statistics by geographic area, number of employees, and raw materials used in the manufacturing process.

Where do we look in this mass of data for the information we need—market growth over a historical time period? There are several places, depending on the desired level of detail. If you can be happy with the four-digit SIC code level, Table 1a of the Census provides "Value of Shipments" for 15 years up to the latest census. Value of shipments refers to the dollar value of product sold by the manufacturer to the next link in the channel of distribution and reflects the manufacturer's selling price. Not all data are shown at the seven-digit level, though, even in the Census. We can locate shipments for the book publishing industry (four digits) but not for atlases (seven digits). Another table (6c) does not give as many years of data but does provide more detail on the product (five digits). A third table (6a) only has two Census years of data but goes all the way to seven-digit product categories. You have to determine which of these is most useful for your purposes.

The Census distinguishes between product class and industry in its data. Product class, which refers to the primary product of an industry regardless of whether it was made by a company focused in the industry, is a better measure for our purposes.

3. Use the U.S. Industrial Outlook for a profile of your industry. This Department of Commerce annual publication summarizes recent trends and roughly a five-year outlook for more than 200 industries. It discusses changes in supply and demand, domestic and international markets, price changes, employee trends, and capital investment. The *Outlook* is well worth its nominal price for someone who has occasion to research a number of industries. One of its most valuable features is the signature of the analyst who prepared the material, an excellent route into the government labyrinth for more information.

Forty-eight major classifications are covered, with subclassifications at the four-digit SIC level included in the major chapters. Book publishing, SIC 2731, is found in the chapter on printing and publishing along with sections on newspapers, periodicals, and printing. The two-page section on books presents very current data on shipments from Census estimates (the 1982 *Outlook* has 1981 data, unheard of timeliness compared to the Census), a discussion of industry dynamics in 1981, developments foreseen in 1982, and a longer-term five-year forecast. Additional references are cited, and the analysts who prepared the sections affix their signatures.

Suppose the Census does not describe your industry properly, perhaps because it is too new to have been picked up by the 1977 Census or because the categories are a poor fit. What now? There are plenty of other places to look for information.

Trade Associations

An invaluable reference source is the *Encyclopedia of Associations,* published annually by Gale Research in Detroit. It is available at any business library or online through the Lockheed Information Systems data base. The *Encyclopedia* lists more than 15,000 trade associations and related organizations, indexed by subject along with name, address, purpose, and contact.

If you were looking for a trade association for books, you would find "Books" in the index, see a listing of associations that identify with that industry, and turn to the individual names for descriptions of their activities. After scanning the listing for the American Book Producers Association, the American Booksellers Association, the American Medical Publishers' Association, the Antiquarian Booksellers, and the Association of American and Antiquarian Booksellers' Center, you would come to the true industry force for book publishers, Association of American Publishers (AAP). This trade group collects industry statistics, possesses a complete library, and has scores of members who are experts on book publishing.

A word of caution: Don't expect every trade association to welcome you with open arms. Associations exist to serve their members, not to accommodate outsiders looking for data. Be prepared with a convincing argument to explain why you want the information without being in conflict with members' interests. Some associations will sell their information to outsiders so it helps if you can open your pocketbook.

I was able to convince the AAP that I had a legitimate business interest in book publishers and that my work could be beneficial to their membership. They were kind enough to make their library available. The use of this extensive collection of studies on book publishing saved me months of time and thousands of dollars.

Data Services

One of the best sources for profiling an industry is a service called "Industry Surveys" provided by Standard & Poor's. The surveys are published in parts, the most complete being the Basic Analysis produced about once a year, followed by Current Analysis roughly three times a year, and irregular special reports. The most recent Basic Analysis on the communications industry included the areas of publishing, broadcasting, and advertising. A four-page section on book publishing included a review of sales by category, a projection for this year's sales, 10 years of statistics on textbook sales, school enrollment statistics, distribution systems, and industry structure—a tremendous amount of useful information in a small space. Sources are cited so that you can search the original for additional information. Thirty-three major industries with subdivisions are covered. At the end of each report is a 10-year summary of financial information on major public companies in the industry and a comparison of critical financial ratios. Subscription cost is steep, but you can find the surveys at a good business library.

There are many data services besides Standard & Poor's, such as Moody's, Value Line, Funk & Scott, and others. The Industry Surveys are a great place to start, because of both their coverage and their references to other data sources.

Trade Periodicals

Several directories can help you identify the major periodicals in your industry. The *Standard Periodical Directory* by Oxbridge Communications provides data on almost 67,000 periodicals in the United States and Canada by category. The brief listings contain the most essential information: publisher, address, phone number, editor, circulation, and a one-to-four-line description of the publication.

Standard Rate and Data's *Business Publications* volume is used by agency media buyers to price space, but it is also useful for us in identifying the publications within an industry. We found the book industry in a classification called "Books and Book Trade." Individual magazines are listed with detailed information on the publisher, address and phone number, a description of editorial focus and target market, editorial content, and names of the publisher and editor. The remainder of the information is oriented toward the media buyer. New issues of Standard Rate and Data are produced monthly by McGraw-Hill.

A less direct method is to use the *Business Periodicals Index.* Look through a few recent issues of periodicals cited for your industry to get a flavor for the type of information they provide and the likelihood of uncovering market information. If the periodical looks like it has the right orientation, call the editor and explain what you are seeking. The editor may lead you to the writer who compiled the statistics or to the publication's librarian. If you find an article with statistics in a particular issue call the author directly. This is the technique that uncovered my industry expert on books.

Directories

Don't overlook the directories. These can save you a lot of work by listing in one place all the information sources associated with an industry. *The Encyclopedia of Business Information Sources,* published by Gale Research, lists trade associations, periodicals, other directories, statistics sources, price sources, financial ratios, handbooks, bibliographies, and general works. Ballinger publishes a *Directory of Industry Data Sources* that lists sources by industry divided into market research reports, investment banking reports, industry statistics reports, financial and economic studies, forecasts, directories and yearbooks, special issues of periodicals, numeric data bases, monographs and handbooks, dissertations and working papers, and conference reports.

We have focused on places to find historical and current industry data. What if we want to use an industry forecast in our analysis? Some of the sources already mentioned would be useful, like the *U.S. Industrial Outlook,* trade associations, periodicals, and Standard & Poor's. Another place to look is *Predicasts,* a quarterly published by Predicasts in Cleveland that summarizes forecasts from periodicals, government reports, and special studies by SIC code. When you have found a forecast in Predicasts, you can locate the source document for a fuller description.

All of the information we have covered thus far will help you find market size and growth rate data. You may also need to locate competitor sales.

Competitor Sales

Public companies record their sales in many places. You can go to a directory that lists public companies, one of the most popular being Dun & Bradstreet's *Million Dollar Directory,* and simply copy the number off the page, or you may get the company's annual report or 10K, an SEC filing. The search becomes more difficult with private companies, since they do not have to report their sales. However, industry sources generally have a pretty good idea about the size of competitors, so estimates by trade periodicals or associations are a good bet. A directory called *The Top 1,500 Private Companies,* published by Economic Information Systems (EIS) in New York, lists private companies along with sales estimates developed from EIS's data base. Companies are listed alphabetically and by sales volume so it is necessary to search for companies in your industry by name or by two-digit SIC code through the listing. The best way to get information may be to corner an industry expert and use his or her impressions of the competition. Washington Researchers' books on finding company information may help here.

A general source for company information is Funk & Scott's *Index of Corporations and Industries,* published by Predicasts. You can search the index by company name or SIC code and end up with citations for articles in business, industry, and financial periodicals. Brokerage house research is another place to look for information on public companies and may be a way to get a reading on business unit sales. The *Directory of Securities Research* by Nelson Communications tells you which stock analyst is following which company.

6

The Growth–Share Matrix

The growth–share matrix has been called "the most significant contribution to strategic planning over the last two decades." It was the brainchild of the Boston Consulting Group (BCG), and its cows and dogs have become a part of business vocabulary. Other firms have used the growth–share matrix as a starting point and have gone off to make "enhancements," yet today the original BCG technique still stands on its own. Its wide use can be attributed to its simplicity and its relatively minimal data needs compared to other techniques. Applied intelligently, it is a powerful tool for corporate planning.

The growth–share matrix focuses on the primary problem of a diversified firm: how to balance cash flows between products that need cash and products that supply cash. BCG has made two simple statements about cash flows:*

1. "The use of cash is proportionate to the rate of growth of any product." Cash is needed to finance added capacity, working capital, cost-reducing equipment, and advertising to gain market share.

2. "The generation of cash is a function of market share because of the experience curve effect." We will discuss the experience curve in a later chapter, but the idea is that the more a company produces, the more its unit costs decline. A high-market-share company will have produced more cumulatively than a low-share company and, therefore, the high-share company has lower costs and higher profits.

BCG recognized that nothing lasts forever. The product life cycle says that growth in each market will eventually slow as the market matures. When ma-

* Bruce Henderson, "The Experience Curve Reviewed IV" (BCG, 1973).

turity is reached, cash generated must be reinvested in growing products to provide for the corporation's future.

WHAT IT IS

The growth–share matrix positions individual businesses on two dimensions, one a surrogate for profitability (market share) and the other a measure of market attractiveness (growth rate). The relationship between market share and profitability has been empirically established in the PIMS research mentioned earlier. Growth is of strategic importance to a business because it allows a company to reach economies of scale, reduce its unit costs, and improve competitive position.

The completed growth–share matrix looks like Exhibit 6.1, with the various businesses of a company positioned properly in the matrix.

Stars

Characteristics. These are the high-market-growth, high-share businesses. Because they are growing rapidly, they use large amounts of cash. They may also generate large amounts of cash because of their market leadership position. Stars are normally about in balance in net cash flow, but they may be cash users if investment to foster growth is especially high. The growth rate is expected to slow over time, and if the star remains a leader it will move south into

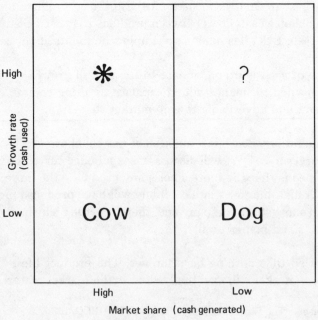

Exhibit 6.1

a cash cow position as investment requirements decline. If growth slows and the star loses its market leadership at the same time, it may find itself in the dog category.

Strategy. Maintain leadership. Invest as necessary.

Examples. McDonald's hamburgers, Digital Equipment Corporation's mini-computers, Litton Industries' microwaves, RCA's Hertz car rental.

Cash Cows

Characteristics. Cash cows are former stars whose market growth has slowed. They won their market leadership when the market was rapidly growing and maintained that position as the growth tapered off. Cows are now reaping the rewards for investing to keep their market leadership. Because they have lower costs and higher profits on what they produce than competition, and they no longer need to invest large sums in a growth market, these businesses are cash rich.

Strategy. Reinvest only enough in the cow to protect its current position. Use the excess to pay for R&D, dividends, corporate overhead, debt service, and, most importantly, to invest in other businesses that can become future cash cows.

Examples. Gillette's razor blades, BIC's stick ball pens, Binney & Smith's crayons, A. H. Robbin's Chapstick, Dart & Kraft's Tupperware.

Question Marks (Problem Children)

Characteristics. These high-growth, low-market-share businesses may be the next stars or the next dogs—they're a real gamble. Given enough cash and clever marketing, the question mark may move leftward into the star category as it grows. It eats up cash in excess of what it generates to maintain share, and it needs even greater amounts to buy share. These cash traps can easily become liabilities unless they transform themselves into market leaders. Question marks may become dogs if they are not properly funded or if they lack market viability. Most companies cannot afford to fund all of their question marks aggressively. One of the most common mistakes is to sprinkle limited resources among every question mark so that no one is properly capitalized.

Strategy. Choose a small number of question marks that offer the best potential and throw all developmental resources at them. Prune the remaining question marks so that they do not use up needed cash.

Examples. Exxon's word processors, G.E.'s 1960s computers, SCM's copiers, Texas Instruments' digital watches.

Dogs

Characteristics.   These are slow-growth, low-market-share businesses that neither generate nor use significant amounts of cash. They may report a profit but generally are net cash users, needing to reinvest cash generated from operations and a modest amount of additional cash to maintain market share. The greatest number of businesses fall into this category, given that most markets are mature and only one competitor can be the market leader. There are few opportunities to grow since there is little new business available, and the dominant competitor will resist attempts by others to gain share in a mature industry.

The cash cost of maintaining a dog business is just one type of cost. There is also the opportunity cost of diverting operating management resources from higher potential businesses and the disproportionate amount of top management time that must be spent on the large number of problems with a dog. Managers and employees of a dog business may suffer low morale from being associated with a loser. On the other hand, there may be hidden benefits from the dog, such as absorption of costs for another business, increased experience on parts needed elsewhere in the corporation, providing a source of supply for other SBUs, or protecting another SBU from competition. Certain types of managers may actually enjoy running a dog business and getting the best value in divestment. Research has shown that each type of business is run by a different type of manager whose personality traits are suited to the strategy. The benefits of a dog are generally outweighed by the negatives, but all aspects should be examined carefully before action is taken. Recent research has indicated that some dogs are significant cash generators rather than cash users.

Strategy.   Divest, harvest, or redefine the market.

Examples.   Chrysler's passenger cars, BIC's panty hose, Falstaff's Pickwick Ale.

Once we have plotted the corporation's businesses on the matrix, we should look at the following items:

1.   Balance.   A good corporate portfolio should be balanced among stars, cows, and question marks. A firm needs some stars to mature into tomorrow's cash cows. The more cash cows, the better; these provide the cash to fund other businesses. There should be some but not too many question marks because the corporation cannot fund everything. It would be nice not to have any dogs, of course, but that rarely occurs.

2.   Trends.   We should compare today's portfolio with the portfolio three or five years earlier so we can see the progress of each business over time. From this analysis, we can gain understanding of whether today's snapshot is a long-standing condition or one that developed recently, and we can see if our past strategies have been successful in encouraging the progress of the businesses. We should also project the growth–share matrix forward three to five years to see where the businesses will position themselves if present policies are kept. Last, we can show our ideal portfolio target in charts.

3. Competition. We should understand the portfolios of our major competitors as well as our own. It is important to know if we are attacking a competitor's cash cow, which it will defend to the end with plenty of cash resources, or a weak and vulnerable dog business. Strategies to gain share in a low-growth market make sense when we are roughly on a par with the market leader or when we are gaining rapidly already. It is useful to know if a competitor is strapped financially because of an overabundance of question marks and whether it is short of management resources because it is dealing with too many dogs. Information on competitors can be more difficult to obtain from the outside but should still be sufficient to make inferences at the business line level.

HOW TO DO IT

The growth–share matrix combines three measures on one graph:

1. Market share
2. Market growth
3. SBU or line of business (LOB) size

This three-dimensional quality is one of the reasons graphs are such a powerful visual tool for communications. Market share is represented on the horizontal x axis and market growth on the vertical y axis. The other two axes are drawn to make a rectangle and then divided into four parts. SBUs or LOBs are plotted on the matrix according to their position along the two dimensions. (See Exhibit 6.2)

We would ideally like to show SBUs in their true strategic sense on each of the graphs developed in this book. Unfortunately, it is only rarely that we are able to obtain SBU data for competitors because we are normally limited to publicly reported data. Companies report business lines, lumping together diverse SBUs under one aggregate label that presents their businesses in the best light. In recognition of that fact, we will use the term "SBU" only when referring to our own company and the term "LOB" or "business unit" when referring to competitor companies for which we do not have true SBU data.

We will examine each element of the matrix in turn and learn how the element is constructed, starting with market share.

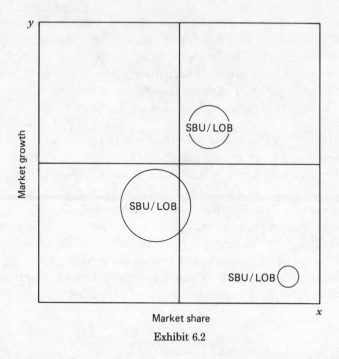

Exhibit 6.2

Relative Market Share: The Horizontal Axis

The horizontal x axis of the matrix represents a special measure of market share known as *relative market share*. Relative market share is different from regular market share because it factors in industry structure; it is your company's market share relative to that of the largest competitor.

Suppose your company has a 15% market share in an industry that looks like this structurally:

Market leader	20% share
Your company	15% share
Company C	5% share
Others with less than 5% each	60% share

Your small share of 15% still places you close to the dominant factor because of the market's fractionation. Contrast this with another market structure in which you have a 15% share:

Market leader	60% share
Company B	25% share
Your company	15% share

Here you are at the bottom of the pack, number three in a three-competitor market. The market share statistic of 15% alone would not distinguish between the two industry structures.

Relative market share is the ratio of your sales or share to the sales or share of the largest competitor in the market. Your position is measured as a percentage of the market leader's position. If you are the leader, the ratio is reversed: your sales or share is divided by the sales or share of the next largest competitor so that your lead is shown as a percentage above the second company.

Applying this concept to the example, we find a relative market share of 0.75 in the first case and a relative market share of 0.25 in the second, showing the company's much greater strength in the first case.

	Case 1		Case 2	
	Percent	RMS	Percent	RMS
Market leader	20	1.33	60	2.40
Your company	15	0.75	15	0.25

Relative market share of the market leader is calculated by dividing:

$$\frac{\text{Market leader share}}{\text{Second largest company's share}}$$

Relative market share of all companies other than the market leader is calculated by dividing:

$$\frac{\text{Other company share}}{\text{Market leader share}}$$

Our example of relative market shares are calculated as follows:

	Case 1	Case 2
Market leader	20/15 = 1.33	60/25 = 2.40
Your company	15/20 = 0.75	15/60 = 0.25

A competitor with a relative market share of more than 1.0 is the market leader by definition, with a share of exactly 1.0 it is tied for dominance with another company, and with less than 1.0 it is a follower. Research has shown that a relative market share of 1.5 is more strongly linked to a high return on investment than one of 1.0, so we will look at the 1.5 boundary as the indicator of highest profitability.* The matrix is divided horizontally by drawing a vertical line at the midpoint of the x axis, designated as a 1.0 relative market share. We will draw a second vertical line to the left of the 1.0 line to show the 1.5 relative market share position (Exhibit 6.3).

* Donald C. Hambrich and Ian C. MacMillan, "On the Product Portfolio and Man's Best Friend" (unpublished paper, Graduate School of Business at Columbia University, January 1982), page 5.

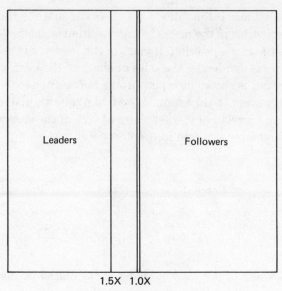

1.5X   1.0X

Relative market share (RMS)

Exhibit 6.3

Relative market share is calculated most accurately with unit sales rather than dollar sales. The most recent year of the historical period is the appropriate year for the data. If you are doing a forecast growth–share matrix, relative market share should be for the base year of the forecast. Some people prefer to use a three-year average relative market share instead of one year's data on the theory that an average counteracts any one-year aberrations in share. Using an average is indicated when an industry is volatile or when major structural changes have occurred recently. If you are using dollar volume for your calculations, be certain that each year's data have been deflated to exclude the effects of inflation. See Appendix 6A on deflators.

We will reiterate the steps to calculate an SBU's relative market share and use a company example to clarify things. We have chosen the book publishing industry as our case study and will examine "company X" in detail. Company X has several lines of business that are clearly identifiable with categories used by the industry and therefore lend themselves nicely to analysis. While far from being the largest book publisher, the company is still a significant factor in the market. It is a public company whose stock is actively traded, meaning that data can be accessed through published information. All of the data used here are from public sources.

There are pluses and minuses to using data structured for public purposes. On the plus side, at least some data about the company are available. Locating financial information on private companies is a major challenge. On the negative side, public data are rarely presented in a suitable way for analysis. This is well exemplified by the statements of one book publisher, Macmillan. Macmillan has a business line called "Distribution" that includes Gump's (the San Francisco department store), Macmillan Electronic Media (a distributor of educational and other films), Macmillan Book Clubs, and Brentano's (a retail bookstore chain). Every business on this list should comprise at least one SBU, but we are presented with financial performance for the "Distribution" business as a whole. For this reason, we will refer to the different businesses of a corporation as presented in public data as lines of business (LOBs), not SBUs. Data for your own company should be available in SBU form or you should be able to reconstruct them into SBUs.

We have rounded company X's data to the nearest million dollars for purposes of disguise. If we were not concealing the company's identity, we would use greater precision and show data in thousands of dollars instead of millions.

STEP 1. List your company's most current year's sales by SBU or LOB. If company X were really our company, we should be able to divide sales into true SBUs. Since we are at arm's length from the company and working with public data, we will have to be content with the data presented in the annual report and whatever the company is willing to tell us in a direct inquiry to supplement the data.

Company X reports its sales in three LOBs: educational texts, general books, and professional books. Book publishing industry data do not correspond neatly to those categories, so we must make adjustments to fit the two together. Combining our reading of the descriptive part of the annual report that details operations and our conversations with the company to clarify some discrepancies will produce a better cut on sales than we started with. The Professional Books group contains mainly medical books and journals, with a smattering of data base publishing. We have estimated that 95% of the group is in the medical area and have taken 95% of reported sales for our number. Three different numbers are reported for General Books (trade books), and we chose the appropriate one after a conversation with the company treasurer. The other categories were straightforward.

Company X Fiscal Year 1981
Sales in Millions of Dollars

College texts	$33
Elhi (elementary/high school) texts	25
Trade books	64
Medical books	36 estimated

STEP 2. Determine the largest competitor in each SBU or LOB. If you are the largest competitor, note the second-largest competitor. List the competitor's sales in that line of business.

LOB	Competitor	1980 Sales in Millions of Dollars
College texts	Prentice-Hall	$120 estimated
Elhi texts	SFN Companies	178
Trade books	Random House	95
Medical books	Saunders	40

STEP 3.   Assuming you are not the market leader, divide your sales into the leader's sales. If you are the leader, divide your sales by the second-largest competitor's sales. The result is your relative market share. Market shares can be substituted for sales in these calculations.

$$\text{Relative market share} = \frac{\text{Company sales}}{\text{Market leader sales}}$$

College texts: $\dfrac{\text{Company } X \text{ sales}}{\text{Prentice-Hall sales}} = \dfrac{33}{120} = 0.28$

Elhi texts: $\dfrac{\text{Company } X \text{ sales}}{\text{SFN Companies sales}} = \dfrac{25}{178} = 0.14$

Trade books: $\dfrac{\text{Company } X \text{ sales}}{\text{Random House sales}} = \dfrac{64}{95} = 0.67$

Medical books: $\dfrac{\text{Company } X \text{ sales}}{\text{Saunders sales}} = \dfrac{36}{40} = 0.90$

Remember that the growth–share matrix displays one corporation's portfolio of businesses. Each SBU's relative market share depicts its position against the leader in the SBU's market. A company with dominant position in two markets will have two businesses to the left of the 1.0 line. The number of SBUs to the left of the 1.0 line and especially to the left of the 1.5 line is a measure of the portfolio's strength. Notice that company X does not have any market leadership in its businesses, demonstrating a weak corporate portfolio. If we were able to further segment the lines of business into SBUs, it is possible that we would see strength in some market niches.

Market Growth: The Vertical Axis

The vertical y axis of the matrix represents market growth rates over a period of time, normally five years. If a five-year history is unavailable, a shorter period of time that is considered representative of the company's past can be used. Growth is shown in real terms to avoid distortion from inflation. We can calculate real growth by one of two methods: (1) unit sales, or (2) deflated dollar sales.

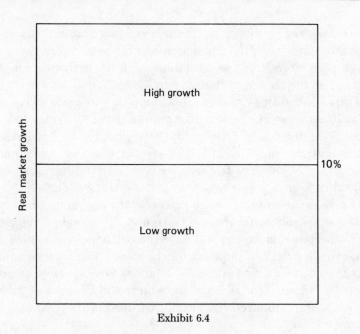

Exhibit 6.4

Remember that the measure of market growth is different for each SBU in the portfolio because *market* relates to the individual business, not the overall corporation. Company *X,* with four separate LOBs according to our definition, operates in at least three distinct markets: textbooks, trade books, and medical books. The college and elhi text LOBs must be shown against the growth rate in the textbook market, the general books LOB against the growth rate in the trade book market, and the professional/medical books LOB against the growth rate in the medical books market. The growth–share matrix does *not* show the growth of the SBU/LOB itself; it shows the growth of the market in which the business operates.

We must distinguish between high- and low-growth markets on the growth–share matrix. It is traditional to use a 10% real (deflated) growth as the dividing point, but the choice of 10% is not cast in stone. We will show the 10% convention here and draw a horizontal line on the matrix that intersects the *y* axis halfway up (Exhibit 6.4).

Sales growth may be calculated by the financial annuity method or by a more accurate statistical method using linear regression. We will cover the simpler financial method here and save the statistical method for Appendix 6B.

CALCULATING THE COMPOUND ANNUAL GROWTH RATE

The compound annual growth rate (CAGR) is conceptually the same as compounding interest on a bank account. You take a beginning amount and increase it each year by an interest rate. At the end of the first year, you have the amount you deposited plus interest. The new base for your account in the second year is the sum of the principal and interest, which in turn earns interest. Because you earn interest on the total amount in the account each year, you are compounding the growth of the account.

We can make the analogy to unit sales. Suppose you begin with 1,000 units and grow at 10% a year. The second year you will have 1,000 plus 10% of 1,000, or 1,100 units; the third year 1,210 units (1,100 plus 10% of 1,100); the fourth year 1,331 units (1,210 plus 10% of 1,210); and the fifth year 1,464 units (1,331 plus 10% of 1,331). Notice how the base we start with has increased each year because of the 10% growth producing the compounding effect.

We have given an example in which you know the beginning amount and the growth rate and are solving for the ending amount. To calculate market growth for the growth–share matrix, you will have the beginning and ending amounts but not the growth rate. You can solve for the growth rate with an annuity formula, but the easiest way is to utilize the financial function on your calculator. We will take you through the series of steps on the TI Business Analyst, an inexpensive calculator produced by Texas Instruments that handles business functions nicely.

Year	Units	Year	Units
1	1,000	4	1,331
2	1,100	5	1,464
3	1,210		

STEP 1. Put the calculator in financial mode if there is more than one register.

STEP 2. Enter year 1 units as the present value (PV).

1,000 PV

STEP 3. Enter year 5 units as the future value (FV).

1,464 FV

STEP 4. Enter the number of periods. This is the number of years for which you have data, minus 1 because we are not compounding the last year of data. In our example, there are 5 minus 1, or 4 periods.

4 *N* (number of periods)

STEP 5. Compute the percentage interest.
%*i*

The calculator displays the answer: 9.9981%, rounded to 10%.

There is a more accurate way to calculate the growth rate using all the years of data, not just the beginning and ending years. This second method is preferred when the growth has been uneven from year to year. We created an example with exactly 10% growth every year, but in reality growth rates do not fall on a straight line. Variable growth rates call for a linear regression technique for precision, detailed in Appendix 6B.

Let us calculate market growth rates for company X's businesses with real data.

STEP 1. Find the market size in units or dollars for each of the years in the historical period.

STEP 2. Deflate dollar size to convert from nominal to real dollars, using the formula

$$\text{Real dollars} = \frac{\text{Nominal dollars}}{\text{Deflator}} \times 100$$

STEP 3. Calculate the growth rate.

We would like to have market data for the same breakdowns as Company X's businesses but find ourselves up against some problems. Only the Census produces data at the seven-digit SIC level, which is the level that divides textbooks into college and elhi texts. The Annual Survey of Manufactures surveys the five-digit level, which does not distinguish among types of textbooks. Our choice is to estimate sales for other years from the census year, 1977, or to use actual data on textbooks for all five years. We have decided to take the second course and use the data on all textbooks.

Market Size in Millions of Dollars*

	1976	1977	1978	1979	1980
Textbooks					
Nominal dollars	1,309.4	1,408.7	1,566.7	1,699.5	1,932.8
Books deflator†	123.0	134.4	148.1	160.7	177.3
Real dollars	1,064.6	1,048.1	1,057.9	1,057.6	1,090.1
CAGR‡, 1976–80: 0.6%					
Trade Books					
Nominal dollars	1,495.0	1,895.6	2,025.2	2,101.5	2,274.7
Books deflator†	123.0	134.4	148.1	160.7	177.3
Real dollars	1,215.5	1,410.4	1,367.5	1,307.7	1,283.0
CAGR, 1976–80: 1.4%					

Market Size in Millions of Dollars (*Continued*)

	1976	1977	1978	1979	1980
Medical Books					
Nominal dollars	97.0	140.5	193.8	214.0	239.9
Books deflator†	123.0	134.4	148.1	160.7	177.3
Real dollars	78.9	104.5	130.9	133.2	135.3

CAGR, 1976–80: 14.4%

* Markets correspond to Company *X*'s LOBs.
† Special books and maps deflator from the Bureau of Economic Analysis.
‡ Compound annual growth rate.

Representing the LOB or SBU: Circles

Corporate planning slang sometimes refers to the growth–share matrix and other graphs as "bubble charts." The name derives from the fact that SBUs are represented on the graph as circles or bubbles. Each SBU's circle is drawn proportionate to current sales. The first task is to find a scale that allows us to represent all of the SBUs in the portfolio in good esthetic balance. Our graphic presentation will not be appealing if one circle dominates the entire chart or all circles appear as small dots. It is necessary to experiment with different sizes to achieve proper balance among large and small SBUs in a trial-and-error procedure that soon becomes second nature.

Suppose your matrix covers two-thirds of an 8½-by-11-inch page. A circle this size may best represent the largest SBU for a company. (See Exhibit 6.5.)

If the company is comprised of a number of units with roughly equivalent sales, a small circle size may be better. (See Exhibit 6.6.)

Use an index of sales to millimeters to determine circle sizes for a graph. The index may make the largest unit's sales equal to a number of millimeters or it may be an arbitrary index such as 50 mm = \$250 million. Once we have decided on an index, we apply this formula:

$$\text{Circle size} = \text{mm factor} \times \sqrt{\frac{\text{LOB/SBU sales}}{\text{Index}}}$$

In our case of 50 mm = \$250 million, the formula reads like this:

$$\text{Circle size} = 50 \times \sqrt{\frac{\text{LOB/SBU sales}}{\$250 \text{ million}}}$$

Square roots can be computed by most calculators. The procedure to simplify our formula is to (1) divide the numbers under the square root sign, (2) take the square root of the result, and (3) multiply by the factor. We will run through the calculations with Company *X* data.

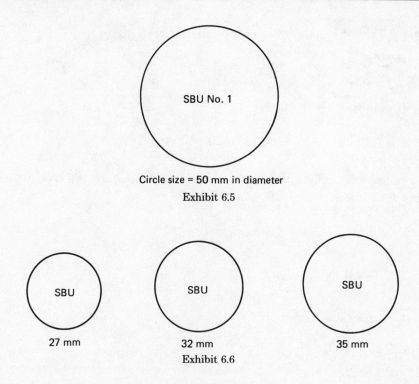

Circle size = 50 mm in diameter

Exhibit 6.5

27 mm   32 mm   35 mm

Exhibit 6.6

Our index will be 50 = the largest LOB sales, \$64 million in fiscal 1981 for general (trade) books. It is not necessary to use deflated sales in the calculation because we are converting everything to a proportion.

STEP 1. Insert LOB sales into the formula:

$$\text{Circle size} = \text{mm factor} \times \sqrt{\frac{\text{LOB/SBU sales}}{\text{Index}}}$$

College text sales = 33 million

$$\text{Circle size} = 50 \times \sqrt{\frac{33}{64}}$$

STEP 2. Divide within the square root.

$$\frac{33}{64} = 0.5156$$

STEP 3. Take the square root of the number in step 2:

$$\sqrt{0.5156} = 0.7181$$

STEP 4. Multiply by the factor:

$$50 \times 0.7181 = 35.9$$

Our circle size for college texts is 36 mm in round numbers. We repeat this sequence for the elhi texts LOB.

STEP 1. Elhi text sales = $25 million

STEP 2. $\dfrac{25}{64} = 0.3906$

STEP 3. $\sqrt{0.3906} = 0.6250$

STEP 4. $50 \times 0.6256 = 31.3$

The circle size for elhi texts is 31 mm. Since we made trade books our index, we already know that its circle size is 50 mm. The last category is professional (medical) books with sales of $35,815. Applying the same formula, we find its circle size to be 37 mm.

The last thing we must do is devise a key to the scale that can be shown on the graph in the lower right-hand corner. We could simply state that circle size of 50 mm = $64 million in fiscal year 1981 sales, but most people cannot imagine a circle described in millimeters. It is far better to draw the circle on the graph and give its sales dollar equivalent so that a reader can look at the circle size and know what it means. Remember, the purpose of the growth–share matrix is to show numbers graphically. But, we certainly cannot show our large index circle of 50 mm in the lower right-hand corner of the graph. We must translate the index into a smaller scale that will fit into its allotted space. The translation is achieved with a simple proportional formula of circle size to sales:

$$\frac{\text{Index circle size}}{\text{Index sales}} = \frac{\text{Scale circle size}}{\text{Small sales dollars}}$$

You can either (1) decide on the size circle you wish to show as the scale, insert the number of millimeters in the formula, and solve for sales dollars, or (2) decide on a small, rounded sales dollar amount that will produce a small circle size and solve for circle size. We prefer the latter method because it provides neat, rounded sales dollars for the scale. Let us try to set a scale with Company X's numbers. Since we set the index as 50 mm = $64 million, we will choose $20 million as our small, rounded sales dollar amount and hope it gives us a small circle size to show as the scale.

$$\frac{50}{64} = \frac{X}{20}$$

Multiply diagonally across the equals sign:

$$50 \times 20 = 64X$$
$$1,000 = 64X$$
$$X = \frac{1,000}{64} = 15.6, \text{ or } 16$$

The number 16 means that a circle of 16 mm is equal to $20 million in sales, given our index of 50 mm = $64 million. Luckily, 16 mm is a small circle that will fit nicely, so we draw it on the graph and label the scale just developed.

$\bigcirc$ = $20 million in fiscal year 1981 sales

There is a bit of trial and error involved in finding the right small sales number to insert in the formula in order to achieve an esthetically proper circle size, but practice will make you an expert.

STEP 6.   Plot each LOB according to relative market share and market growth rates. Move along the x axis for relative market share (RMS) and up the y axis for market growth.

Putting It Together

We have learned the calculations for the three components of the growth–share matrix:

1.   Market growth rate
2.   Relative market share
3.   Circle size

All that remains is to utilize the data we have developed to plot the LOBs on the matrix. This becomes much simpler if you pull the data together in one place.

You will need three other items to draw the graph: special three-cycle log/linear paper, a metric circle template, and a ruler. The first two can be obtained in a good stationery or graphics supply store.

STEP 1. Combine all of the data needed for the graph into a table.

Company X Fiscal Year 1981
Growth Share Matrix Summary Table

	RMS	1976–80 Market Growth	Circle Size
College texts	0.28	0.6%	36
Elhi texts	0.14	0.6	31
Trade books	0.67	1.4	50
Medical books	0.90	14.4	37

STEP 2. Outline the graph on three-cycle log/linear paper. The relative market share x-axis scale is logarithmic and covers two full cycles and a portion of a third. Label the scale from the far right corner so that the first cycle goes from $0.1X$ to $1.0X$, the second from $1.0X$ to $10X$, and only the first block of the third cycle $20X$. The reason for using a log scale is so that equal percentage changes in RMS appear equal spatially. (See Appendix 9B on pages 143 and 144 for an explanation of logs.)

STEP 3. Market growth, the y axis, is a straight linear scale and should be labeled with percentages to represent market growth rates. Label percentages on the y axis from -10 to $+20$. Determine the percentage of real market growth that makes sense as a dividing point between high- and low-growth businesses and draw a horizontal line from that percentage on the y axis. We will use 5% real growth as our divider instead of 10% because Company X operates in the book publishing industry that had a real growth of only 2% over the time period. The choice of dividing point is a judgmental decision.

STEP 4. Label the graph with the company name, the time period covered, and the name of the graph. Our graph is labeled "Company X, Growth–Share Matrix, Fiscal Year 1981."

STEP 5. Draw and label the circle size key on the graph. Our key is 16 mm = $20 million in fiscal year 1981 sales.

STEP 6. Plot the circles by moving across the x axis according to RMS and up the y axis by market growth. Draw the circle with the proper circle size and label the LOB.

The matrix is drawn on log paper because logs change spatial relationships so that a given percentage difference always looks the same regardless of the numbers that went into the calculation. A 10% change may always equal ½″ whether the 10% came from the difference between 100 and 110 or between

1000 and 1100. For the purpose of the growth–share matrix, it is important only to know that a log scale better portrays the market share relationships. You will need semilog or log/linear paper that has a two-cycle log scale along the x axis for relative market share and a regular linear scale along the y axis. Chapter 17 tells you more about log paper—where to find it and what you need.

The completed growth–share matrix looks like Exhibit 6.7.

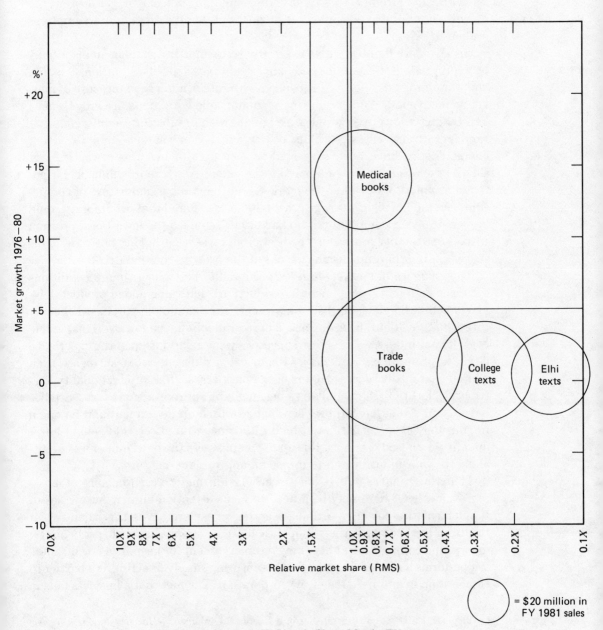

Exhibit 6.7 Company X, Growth–Share Matrix, FY 1981.

FURTHER THOUGHTS ON THE USE OF THE GROWTH–SHARE MATRIX

We spoke earlier about the value of the growth–share matrix when used intelligently. The growth–share matrix is a way to simplify a terribly complex business problem and allow managers to communicate with a common vocabulary. As with any attempt to simplify the complex, much can get lost if the growth–share matrix is applied as dogma and its objectives and assumptions are not understood.

Once you are familiar with the growth–share matrix and its meaning, it may be appropriate to make minor adjustments for your specific situation. Suppose you work for a conservative firm and growth rate is not a good measure of market attractiveness. Your firm is more comfortable with moderate growth markets that have lower risk profiles. You might wish to substitute a different criterion for attractiveness, such as degree of risk or market stability. Other characteristics have been suggested as measures of business attractiveness, such as the absolute size of a market, the extent to which it is difficult for potential competitors to enter the market, and the number and nature of competition. A study of eight *average* growth industries found that profitability could be significant for competitors who had either achieved the lowest cost position with a good quality product or the best product/service/quality position.* This suggests still other dimensions for use of the growth–share matrix.

The influence of market share on profitability is strongest under conditions such as a high labor component in production, high value-added products, significant entry barriers, markets where experience cannot be purchased cheaply through acquisitions, licensing or offshore production, and low overhead industries. If your industry's structure suggests a weak relationship of the experience curve to profitability, you may wish to use a different profit surrogate than market share. Key success factors of the business, such as product quality, distribution, location, sales, and servicing, might be appropriate measures. Studies have found a relationship between higher return on investment and having a fragmented set of customers instead of a concentrated set, and selling infrequently purchased products. It is up to you to assess the determinants of profitability in your industry and to devise an appropriate measure.

The growth–share matrix focuses on maximizing the cash balance of *existing* businesses. There may be a need to focus attention on new businesses to supplement the current portfolio. Another consideration is the balancing of risk from the economy, the sociopolitical arena, supply, technological change, unions, and competition. There may be an argument for keeping a dog business if it performs a needed function such as ensuring supply or acting as a barrier to competition in another area of the corporation. The fact that a business falls in

---

* William K. Hall, "Survival Strategies in a Hostile Environment," *Harvard Business Review* (September–October 1980), pp. 75–85.

a particular quadrant of the growth–share matrix does not mean the attendant strategy should be followed blindly. Use the matrix as a guideline and a starting point for discussion, not as the ultimate plan.

Let's say another few words about dog businesses. It has been conservatively estimated that half of all business units in the United States are low-growth, low-market share—dogs. The prevalence of these businesses in the American economy makes it worth taking a second look. A recent study did exactly that, using the PIMs data base, and discovered that "dogs are not all mangy cash losers."* The average dog business throws off more cash than is needed by the average question mark, suggesting that a dog may serve a useful function by funding several new ventures without having to relinquish market share in the process. The conclusion: "There are real prize-winning Dobermans as well as mangy mutts." Certain strategies were linked to high return on investment for dogs—liberal credit terms, high capacity utilization, employee efficiency, a narrow product line and few customers relative to competition, high product quality, and reasonable prices. We may conclude that dog businesses can serve an important function for the corporation if managed appropriately, and that labels are not everything.

A number of characteristics have been linked to businesses in each of the quadrants besides market share and growth rate. You may want to test your SBUs on these additional factors to confirm the diagnosis.

* Donald C. Hambrick and Ian C. Macmillan, *On the Product Portfolio and Man's Best Friend,* unpublished paper, January 1982.

	Star	Cow	?	Dog
1. What is the SBU's capacity utilization?	high	very high	low	high
2. What is the age of plant and equipment?	old	old	new	old
3. How high is R&D expense compared to the industry?	high	low	high	low
4. How high is marketing expense compared to the industry?	medium	low	high	medium
5. How broad is the product line?	broad	broad	narrow	narrow
6. What are sales per employee?	high	low	high	medium

	Star	Cow	?	Dog
7. What is the level of inventory per dollar of revenue?	high	low	high	medium
8. How much vertical integration is there?	high	high	low	low

The growth–share matrix is a starting point, the snapshot in time that profiles the corporation today. From here, we will now go on to other techniques for analysis.

APPENDIX 6A: DEFLATORS

Market data are frequently presented in dollars rather than units. To avoid being misled by inflation, we must convert actual or inflated dollars into real or constant dollars. Only by removing the effects of inflation can we tell how much the market has really grown. Suppose we were given the numbers in our last example as dollar sales for a five-year period. Beginning sales were $1,000 and ending sales were $1,464, a 10% compound annual growth rate over five years. Now, suppose inflation were 6% compounded over the same five-year period. Our real growth would be 4%—10% nominal growth minus 6% for inflation. It would be terribly misleading to say that the market had grown 10%.

How do we figure out what our real growth is if we have inflated sales numbers? The U.S. government has anticipated this need and publishes a series of indices for the inflation rate known as *deflators*. We can pick and choose to find the most appropriate index for our market, but a good general starting point is the deflator for gross national product (GNP). Deflators are published by the Department of Commerce's Bureau of Economic Analysis. They tell us the ratio of prices in any single year to the price level in 1972. The base year of 1972 has a deflator of 100.0 (the ratio of prices in 1972 to prices in 1972 equals 1 × a factor of 100 = 100.0). Years before 1972 had lower prices, so the ratio is less than 100; years after 1972 had higher prices, so the ratio is more than 100. The deflator in 1981 of 193.71 means that prices that year were 93.71% higher than in 1972. The inflation rate is the percentage change between deflators. Notice that the base 1972 is followed by 105.69 in 1973. The percentage change between deflators in 1973 and 1972 is 5.69%, the inflation rate for 1973.

We will use deflators to convert sales dollars from the nominal or inflated level to real deflated dollars. Since our deflators are based on 1972, the conversions will bring all of our numbers to constant 1972 dollars regardless of the sales year. This change will permit us to measure real growth of a market or of a company's sales without obscuring the truth with inflation. The procedure is

Implicit Price Deflators for GNP*

1971	96.01
1972	100.00
1973	105.69
1974	114.92
1975	125.56
1976	132.11
1977	139.83
1978	150.05
1979	162.77
1980	177.36
1981	193.11

* Source: Department of Commerce, Bureau of Economic Analysis.

simple: Divide actual sales dollars by that year's deflator, multiply by 100 to place the decimal point properly, and the result is real sales.

$$\frac{\text{Nominal sales year 1}}{\text{Deflator year 1}} \times 100 = \text{Real sales year 1}$$

Let us try the formula with some market data for the years 1975 and 1979. Assume sales were $1,000 in 1975 and $1,464 in 1979.

	Sales	Deflator
1975	$1,000	125.56
1979	$1,464	162.77

Divide sales by the year's deflator and multiply by 100.

$$1975 \quad \frac{1,000}{125.56} \times 100 = 796.4$$

This number means that 1975 real sales were $796 in constant 1972 dollars. Repeat the calculation for 1979 data.

$$1979 \quad \frac{1,464}{162.77} = 899.4$$

Real sales for 1979 were $899 in constant 1972 dollars. Now we can calculate a compound annual growth rate in real terms.

        1975   Year 1   PV   796
        1979   Year 2   FV   899

        4 periods
        CAGR = 3.09%, or 3%

A compound annual growth rate of 3% is quite different from the inflated growth rate of 10%. The 7% difference is inflation over the five-year period. We can check our answer by calculating the compound annual growth rate of the GNP deflator itself.

        1975   Year 1   PV   125.56
        1979   Year 2   FV   162.77

        4 periods
        CAGR = 6.7%, or 7%

There are other deflators besides the GNP deflator, such as the deflator for personal consumption expenditures, which is subdivided into durables, non-durables, and services. The definition of personal consumption expenditures (PCE) includes goods and services purchased by individuals, a better indicator of spending than the broad GNP for industry analysis. If you are measuring the market for eating out, you would be more precise with an index of personal consumption expenditures for services. If your market is refrigerators, you might wish to use the deflator for personal consumption expenditures of durable goods. If you are trying to measure cereals, personal consumption expenditures of nondurables is appropriate. If you want to be *really* precise, there are more than 100 further breakouts of the PCE that relate to specific products. Unfortunately, they are not published together in any one place, so you must call the National Income and Wealth Division of the Bureau of Economic Analysis (part of the Department of Commerce) in Washington to get the information. They will give you a limited amount of information over the telephone but will send you a detailed printout for a small charge.

The table for GNP and basic PCE deflators is shown in Exhibit 6.7.

APPENDIX 6B: GROWTH RATE CALCULATION WITH LINEAR REGRESSION

The compound annual growth rate calculation described in this chapter utilizes only the starting and ending years of data, ignoring all the fluctuation occurring in between. When a market is changing structurally or is impacted by an exogenous phenomenon such as recession that interrupts a clean upward trend, a point-to-point calculation becomes inaccurate. A more sophisticated method, used by statisticians, is *linear regression,* a procedure that utilizes all of the data to find the line that best fits the points, even if they are not all exactly *on* the line. We can plot our data and determine that while it looks somewhat like

EXHIBIT 6.7. Gross National Product in 1972 Dollars (billions of 1972 dollars; quarterly data at seasonally adjusted annual rates)

Period	Gross National Product	Personal Consumption Expenditures	Gross Private Domestic Investment			Net Exports	Exports of Goods and Services		Government Purchases of Goods and Services			Final Sales
			Non-residential Fixed	Residential Fixed	Change in Business Inventories		Exports	Imports	Total	Federal	State and Local	
1971	1,122.4	696.8	112.2	53.7	8.1	1.6	71.0	69.3	250.1	103.7	146.4	1,114.3
1972	1,185.9	737.1	121.0	63.8	10.2	.7	77.5	76.7	253.1	101.7	151.4	1,175.3
1973	1,255.0	768.5	138.1	62.3	17.2	15.5	97.3	81.8	253.5	95.9	157.6	1,237.7
1974	1,248.0	763.6	135.7	48.2	11.6	27.8	108.5	80.7	261.2	96.6	164.5	1,236.8
1975	1,233.9	780.2	119.3	42.2	−6.7	32.2	103.6	71.4	266.7	97.4	169.3	1,240.4
1976	1,300.4	823.7	125.6	51.2	7.8	25.4	110.1	84.7	266.8	96.8	170.0	1,292.6
1977	1,371.7	863.9	140.6	60.6	12.3	21.9	113.2	91.3	272.3	100.7	171.6	1,359.7
1978	1,436.9	904.8	153.4	62.4	14.0	24.6	127.5	103.0	277.8	99.8	178.0	1,422.9
1979	1,483.0	930.9	163.3	59.1	10.2	37.7	146.9	109.2	281.8	101.7	180.1	1,472.9
1980	1,480.7	935.1	158.4	48.1	−2.9	52.0	161.1	109.1	290.0	108.1	181.9	1,483.6
1981	1,510.3	958.9	162.4	45.2	7.1	44.9	160.4	115.5	291.7	111.5	180.2	1,503.2
1980: III	1,471.9	930.8	155.5	44.7	−5.0	57.6	160.5	102.8	288.2	106.9	181.3	1,476.9
IV	1,485.6	946.8	157.0	50.6	−7.2	48.5	157.4	108.9	289.8	107.4	182.4	1,492.7
1981: I	1,516.4	960.2	162.0	51.0	−1.4	50.9	162.5	111.6	293.6	111.2	182.5	1,517.8
II	1,510.4	955.1	161.1	47.8	10.8	46.2	161.5	115.4	289.5	108.7	180.7	1,499.6
III	1,515.8	962.8	163.9	42.7	14.9	43.2	160.1	116.9	288.3	109.6	178.8	1,500.9
IV	1,498.4	957.5	162.7	39.4	4.2	39.2	157.4	118.2	295.4	116.6	178.8	1,494.2
1982: I	1,482.2	964.4	162.4	38.9	−17.2	38.2	152.1	113.8	295.4	117.8	177.6	1,499.4

EXHIBIT 6.7 (Cont.)
Implicit Price Deflators for Gross National Product (1972 = 100; quarterly data are seasonally adjusted)

Period	Gross National Product	Personal Consumption Expenditures				Gross Private Domestic Investment		Exports and Imports of Goods and Services		Government Purchases of Goods and Services	
		Total	Durable Goods	Non-durable Goods	Services	Nonresidential Fixed	Residential Fixed	Exports	Imports	Federal	State and Local
1971	96.01	96.5	99.0	96.6	95.6	96.2	94.8	97.0	93.3	92.7	94.7
1972	100.00	100.0	100.0	100.0	100.0	100.0	100.0	100.0	100.0	100.0	100.0
1973	105.69	105.7	101.7	108.3	104.7	103.8	109.1	112.7	116.7	106.3	106.9
1974	114.92	116.3	108.2	123.1	113.0	115.4	120.3	134.7	164.6	114.9	117.4
1975	125.56	125.2	117.3	132.1	121.6	132.2	131.0	149.6	179.5	126.0	128.3
1976	132.11	131.6	123.9	137.0	129.6	138.6	140.7	155.2	185.5	133.5	137.0
1977	139.83	139.5	129.2	143.4	139.9	146.2	158.0	161.9	205.4	142.9	146.0
1978	150.05	149.1	136.2	153.2	150.1	157.7	178.3	172.4	214.0	153.7	156.9
1979	162.77	162.3	144.8	169.8	162.1	171.3	200.5	191.5	245.4	165.1	169.8
1980	177.36	178.9	156.0	188.6	178.1	186.8	218.6	211.0	290.1	183.9	184.7
1981	193.71	193.7	166.4	202.4	195.2	202.5	233.3	229.0	295.5	206.4	200.3
1980: III	179.18	180.7	157.5	190.0	180.3	189.1	221.9	213.4	289.7	182.4	186.7
IV	183.81	184.9	160.5	195.2	184.3	192.4	223.3	219.9	296.4	197.4	190.0
1981: I	188.14	188.5	162.3	199.2	188.4	195.0	228.7	226.1	303.1	199.4	194.5
II	191.06	191.5	165.4	200.4	192.2	201.4	231.8	228.0	301.2	201.9	198.0
III	195.61	195.7	168.3	203.7	197.6	204.5	235.4	229.8	289.8	206.6	202.8
IV	200.10	199.3	170.1	206.2	202.3	208.9	238.8	232.2	288.5	217.2	206.2
1982: I	201.84	201.7	171.5	207.2	206.3	207.7	240.2	234.4	288.0	215.6	209.7

Source: Department of Commerce, Bureau of Economic Analysis.

a straight line, actually drawing the line is difficult because some points lie outside it. Our problem is to find the best straight line, the one that minimizes the distance for the data points that do not lie exactly on the line. By minimizing the distance of the outlying points from the line, we will have reduced the error as much as possible. In statistical jargon, this is called the least squares method. Once the new line has been found, we can use any two points on it to calculate the growth rate.

Do not attempt a regression without a calculator or computer because the manual calculations are long and tedious. Most business calculators are equipped to do linear regressions. Here you will see how to perform the calculations on the TI Business Analyst, recognizing that the procedure will differ slightly with other brands.

Our sample data are shown below.

Year	Real Sales in Millions of Dollars
1975	$100
1976	150
1977	180
1978	165
1979	170

STEP 1.   Put the calculator into its statistical mode.

STEP 2.   Enter two pieces of data for each year: the year as the x variable and real sales as the y variable. Enter all five years of data in sequential pairs.

x	1975
y	100
x	1976
y	150
x	1977
y	180
x	1978
y	165
x	1979
y	170

The calculator computes a line from these points according to a linear regression formula.

STEP 3.   Check the fit of the line to the points by looking at the correlation coefficient. The closer the coefficient to 1.0, the better the fit. A very low coefficient means that the line and, therefore, the growth rate are not especially accurate. The degree of accuracy is information for you to use when you are interpreting the data. Our correlation in this example is reasonably good:

Correlation = 77.7%

STEP 4:   Find any two points on the new line to calculate a compound annual growth rate. Enter a year corresponding to the data you have already inputted, and the calculator will produce sales for that year from the new regression line.

Enter: 1975

Regression line sales: 122 (instead of 100 from the original data)

Enter: 1979

Regression line sales: 184 (instead of 170 in the original data)

STEP 5:   Switch to the financial mode and calculate a compound annual growth rate from the regression data.

PV	122
FV	184
N	4

CAGR = 10.8%

We used the sales data to calculate a compound annual growth rate without having drawn a regression line for comparison. The calculation ignores the high sales year of 1977, when sales reached 180, and the subsequent dip in 1978.

1975	PV	100
1979	FV	170

4 periods
CAGR = 14.2%

The compound annual growth rate of 14.2% is significantly different from the 10.8% we found through linear regression. Clearly, the calculation of a regression line first improves our accuracy greatly. The way to test for the improvement possible by doing linear regression is to plot the data on a graph. If the original points lie neatly on a straight line, there is no need to do the regression procedure. If there are a number of scattered points that do not fit exactly on the line, a regression will make a big difference in the accuracy of your results.

7

The Share–Momentum Graph

We have seen that the growth–share matrix is a snapshot view of a corporation's portfolio at one point in time, most probably today. It tells us the way things are but says nothing about changes from the past or those that might occur in the future. A second graph, the share–momentum graph, is used to provide this time perspective. *Momentum* refers to the movement of the business units over time, and *share* refers to market share. We will use this graph to observe the market share changes in our business units over time.

THE BASIC SHARE–MOMENTUM

The share–momentum graph contrasts two measures—market growth and company growth—over a historical time period. Both measures are in constant dollars to be consistent with the growth–share matrix. The horizontal x axis represents company growth, and the vertical y axis represents market growth. A 45-degree diagonal line intersects the two axes at the origin. The diagonal is called the "Line of Constant Market Share" (See Exhibit 7.1).

To the left of the Line of Constant Market Share, the market is growing faster than the company. This means that the business is losing market share to other competitors. To the right of the Line of Constant Market Share, the company is growing faster than the market and therefore gaining share at the

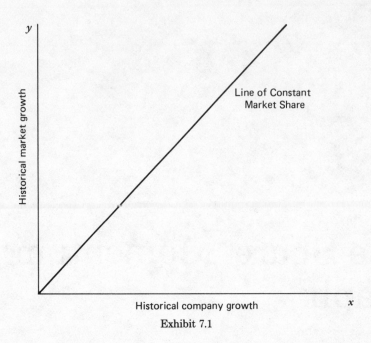

Exhibit 7.1

expense of other competitors. A business that falls on the Line of Constant Market Share is neither gaining nor losing share. Its share is constant, or stable (See Exhibit 7.2).

Each business in a competitor's portfolio is plotted on the share–momentum with its size proportionate to sales. Let us look at a hypothetical company's share–momentum to see what we can learn about its businesses (See Exhibit 7.3).

SBU *A* is a high-growth business that is holding its own in market share. Business *A* is in a faster-growing market and is growing at an equal rate to the market, neither gaining nor losing share. The size of the circle shows that *A* is the company's largest business. SBU *B* is a small, very high-growth business that is growing even faster than its high-growth market and is therefore gaining share. Business *C* is also growing fast, although not at the same rate as *B*. The difference is that it operates in a low-growth market. The fact that it is growing faster than its market means it is gaining share, shown by its position to the right of the diagonal. SBU *D* is holding share on the Line of Constant Market Share but is stuck in a shrinking market. Its sales are also shrinking but at the same rate as the market's decline; hence, it stays squarely on the diagonal. SBU *E* is a business that is losing share. Its market is growing moderately but the business is not growing at all. *E*'s position on the *y* axis indicates zero company growth. Business *F* is also losing share. It is growing slightly but operates in a very high-growth market. Since *F*'s growth is not keeping up with the market, we can see that it is losing market position.

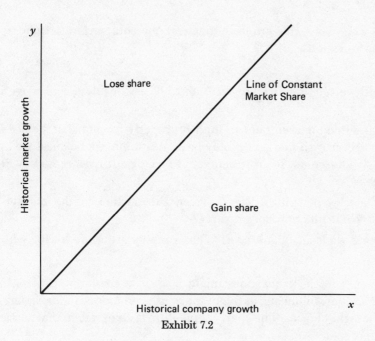

Historical market growth

Lose share

Line of Constant Market Share

Gain share

Historical company growth

Exhibit 7.2

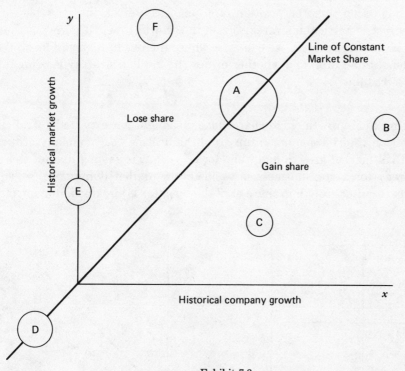

Historical market growth

F

Line of Constant Market Share

A

Lose share

B

Gain share

E

C

Historical company growth

D

Exhibit 7.3

If we were using this graph to diagnose the company's portfolio, we might ask a few questions:

Should we try to gain share in *A,* our biggest business, and move it to the right?

Was it a good decision not to fund *F* properly to gain share, since it is in a very high-growth market? *F* may be a question mark business we have consciously chosen not to grow in favor of placing our resources elsewhere. Was this wise?

Why are we keeping SBU *D,* given the decline in the market and its sales? What function does it serve?

Why are we losing share in *E?* What strategy are we following with it?

The answers to these questions might lead us to explore a different strategy than we are now following, or might make us even more confident that we have made the right choices. The share momentum is an excellent diagnostic tool for this purpose.

Another use of the share–momentum is as a check on the growth–share matrix. We have seen that the position of a business unit on the growth–share matrix suggests a particular strategy. From the growth rate and share positions on the growth–share matrix, we can infer where the business should be on the share–momentum graph and whether or not the implied strategy is being followed (See Exhibit 7.4).

Star. This high-growth, high-share business might be expected to fall in quadrant I on the share–momentum graph, indicating that company growth is faster than market growth and, therefore, the unit is gaining market share. The strategy for a star business is to maintain market dominance, so you would expect either growth in share or, if the business is already dominant, stable share.

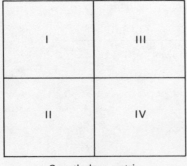

Growth share matrix

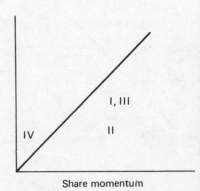

Share momentum

Exhibit 7.4

Cow.   Cash cows are dominant in their low-growth markets. They should appear in quadrant II on the share–momentum graph, where company growth is greater than or equal to market growth and market growth is low. Since the strategy is to maintain market share, cows must not fall on the left side of the diagonal where market share is lost.

Question Mark.   Question marks are high-growth, low-share businesses. They should appear in the high-growth, top right portion of the share–momentum graph, indicating a faster rate of growth for the company than the market. Question marks should be gaining share, but it is possible that they are growing fast because of a rapidly growing market at the same time as losing share to competitors. In this latter case, they would be positioned in the space above quadrant IV.

Dogs.   A dog business is both low in share and low in growth. It would appear in quadrant IV on the share–momentum graph, either on the diagonal showing stable share or losing share to competition to the left of the line.

The quadrant above IV to the left of the diagonal is no-man's-land. It indicates a high-growth market where you are losing share to the competition. Unless you are consciously harvesting this business, such as in the case of a question mark you have decided not to fund, you should not see any circles in this area. A business in a growth market should be gaining or at the very least maintaining share; a loss of share indicates strategic error.

The share–momentum graph dramatizes our market position over time and allows us to view the results of our strategy. We can see inconsistencies between intended and actual results and can make midcourse corrections. A comparison of our share–momentum graph with that of competition helps us see from whom we are gaining or losing market share and in what businesses various competitors are vulnerable. It may be easier to attack in an area where our competition is already entrenched than in one in which they have been adding share points in recent years.

Let us look at four possible patterns on the share momentum and identify their meaning.

Company A in Exhibit 7.5 is holding share in all of its business units, neither gaining nor losing. One interpretation is that holding onto established positions shows the company is well managed. A contrary view is that the company has failed to make any strategic decisions about the markets it really wants to win and those it is willing to trade off, so it stays dead center trying to hold onto everything but dominating nothing. Strategic planning argues against this middle-of-the-road philosophy and encourages companies to play to their strengths.

Company B in Exhibit 7.6 is missing on all fronts. It is losing share in its high-growth markets and gaining in low- or negative-growth markets. Its largest business, indicated by circle size, is beneath the horizontal x axis, meaning that the market is actually declining. This company should be doing the reverse of what its share–momentum graph shows—increasing share in the high-

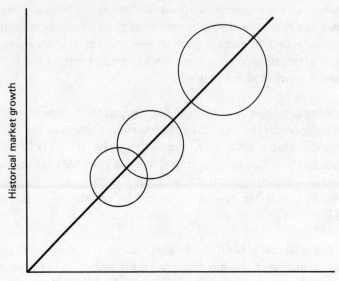

Exhibit 7.5 Company A.

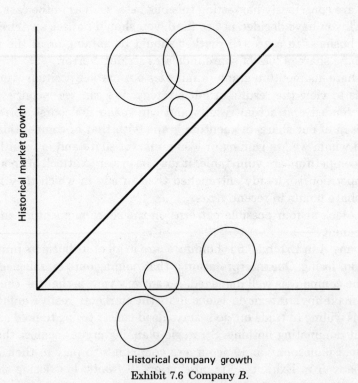

Exhibit 7.6 Company B.

growth businesses and decreasing share in the low-growth businesses. Its current strategy is both expensive and nonproductive for the long run. The portfolio will ultimately be dominated by low-growth products.

In Exhibit 7.7, Company C is growing all of its businesses at the same rate regardless of market growth, again showing the lack of strategic focus. Instead of choosing some businesses to grow rapidly, taking advantage of the high market growth rate and gaining share for a dominant position, Company C has chosen an arbitrary growth target across the board. The pattern indicates lack of strategic planning.

Company D, Exhibit 7.8, is a "focused competitor" managing its portfolio of businesses strategically. It is holding share in its low-growth businesses and gaining share in its high-growth businesses. We call it focused because the company is selectively growing its businesses according to their potential, rather than wasting resources in low-growth markets where it is more difficult to gain share.

There are other ways to use the share–momentum graph besides plotting company growth against market growth. The basic concept is to see what your momentum or direction and rate of change are in a business, to understand historical trends, and to help predict the future.

COMPETITIVE SHARE–MOMENTUMS

The share–momentum graph is a good tool for comparing your growth against competition. The competitive share momentum looks like Exhibit 7.9.

If you are growing faster than a competitor in a business, your business line will appear to the right of the diagonal in the "gain share" space. If your competitor's business is growing faster than yours, your business will be positioned to the left of the diagonal, showing your loss of share. If both of you are growing at equal rates, your business will appear on the Line of Constant Market Share.

This share momentum may be developed for one competitor against whose businesses you compare yours, or it may be a composite of your primary competitor in each business. Let us suppose you are in publishing, broadcasting, and video games. Your main competitors are Macmillan, CBS, and Atari, respectively. The composite competitor compares your growth rate with Macmillan for the publishing line, with CBS for the broadcasting line, and with Atari for the video games line. The three competitors would be represented on the same graph on the competitive growth axis; the circles would represent the size of your businesses (See Exhibit 7.10).

We would interpret the share momentum as follows:

You are gaining share against Macmillan in your publishing business.

You are growing at an equal rate to CBS in broadcasting so are holding share where you are.

You are losing share to Atari in video games, your smallest business.

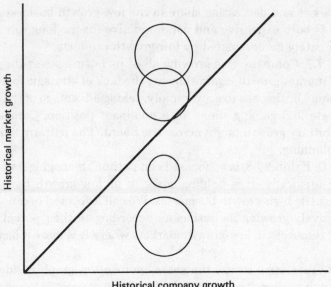

Exhibit 7.7 Company C.

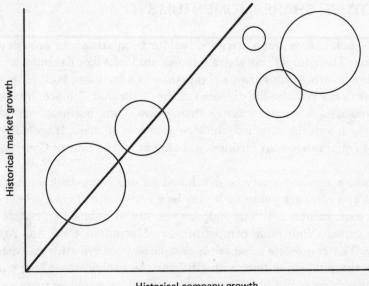

Exhibit 7.8 Company D.

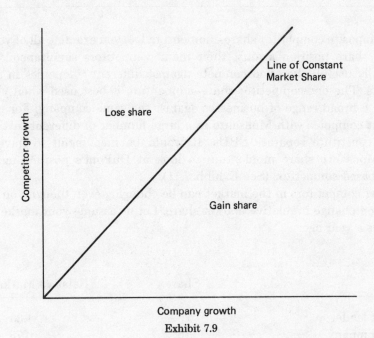

Exhibit 7.9

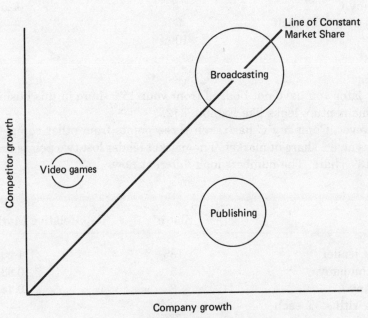

COMPOSITE COMPETITOR
Exhibit 7.10

The composite competitor share–momentum lets you examine all of your businesses' share position against their main competitors simultaneously. It is especially useful when you compete against different companies in different markets. The one-competitor share–momentum is best used when you compete in a broad range of businesses against the same company. For instance, DuPont competes with Monsanto in a large number of different textile types which constitute separate SBUs. It would be meaningful to have a Du-Pont–Monsanto share–momentum to look at DuPont's position against its broad-based competitor (See Exhibit 7.11).

Other competitors in the market can be changing even though you are not, causing a change in relative market share. Let us assume your market looked like this a year ago:

	Share	Relative Market Share
Market leader	20%	1.33
Your company	15	0.75
Company C	5	0.25
Others with <5% each	60	—
	100%	

A year later you have not budged from your 15% share in this business. Your share momentum looks like Exhibit 7.12.

However, Company C has taken three points from other competitors and now has an 8% share of market. The market leader lost two points and is down to an 18% share. The numbers look different now.

	Share	Relative Market Share
Market leader	18%	1.20
Your company	15	0.83
Company C	8	0.44
Others with <5% each	59	—
	100%	

Notice that your *relative* market share has changed even though your share has not, because the market leader lost two points. The relative market share dynamic would have been lost if we had just examined your share momentum and seen your business on the Line of Constant Market Share.

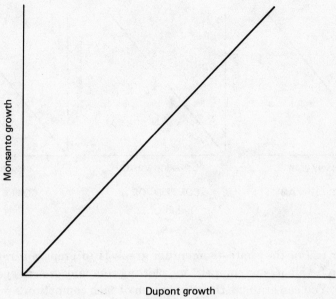

Dupont growth

Exhibit 7.11

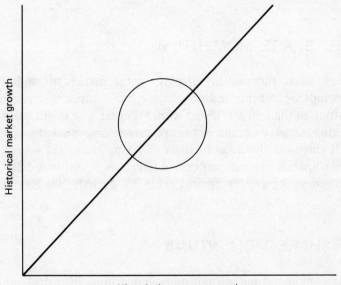

Historical company growth

Exhibit 7.12

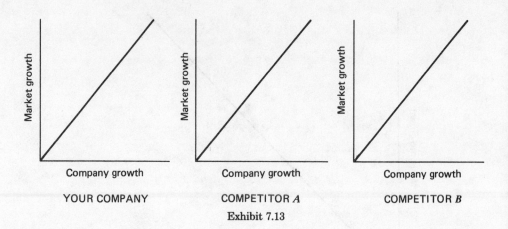

Exhibit 7.13

Another use of the share–momentum graph is to prepare a regular share momentum for all of your competitors, plotting company growth against industry growth. You can examine the momentum of each competitor's portfolio and use the findings (1) to make assumptions about their strategy, and (2) to compare to your own momentum (See Exhibit 7.13).

INDUSTRY SHARE–MOMENTUMS

An industry share–momentum displays total market or industry growth against a component of that industry to see if the component is gaining or losing its position in the market. If you were Polaroid, you might want to plot the picture-taking industry against instant picture taking to see if you were gaining business. If you were the manufacturer of 7-Up, you might want to plot soda consumption against the consumption of noncolas. If you were NBC, you might plot TV broadcasting growth against cable TV growth (See Exhibit 7.14).

FUTURE SHARE–MOMENTUMS

Future share–momentums are not as meaningful as historical share momentums, because data on the future is never very accurate while data on the past is factual. However, future share–momentums can be used in several ways for meaningful analysis.

STEP 1. Plot the basic share–momentum, market growth versus company growth, for the future. Compare it with the historical share momentum to see how differently you are viewing the future market from the past and whether your plans look realistic in that context (See Exhibit 7.15).

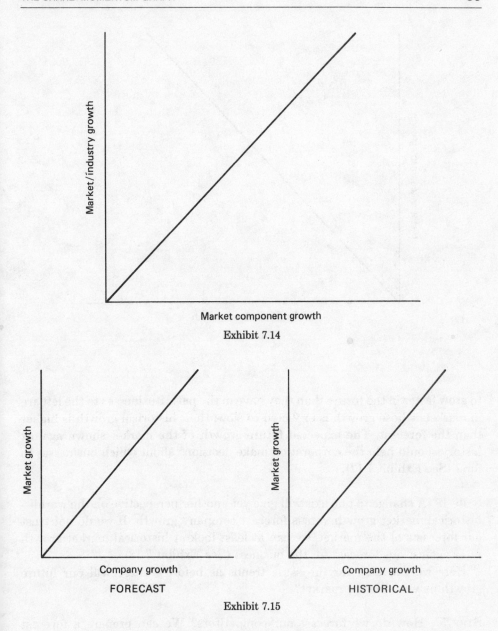

Exhibit 7.14

Exhibit 7.15

STEP 2.   Plot future company growth against historical company growth on one chart. This will highlight differences in growth rates between the two periods (See Exhibit 7.16).

When used in conjunction with resource allocation, the graph will point out some questions to be asked, such as, "Why are we funding this business aggressively when its market doesn't look very good over the next three years?"

STEP 3.   Plot businesses based on their market growth; past and future. Businesses on the right of the Line of Equal Growth are in markets that are forecast

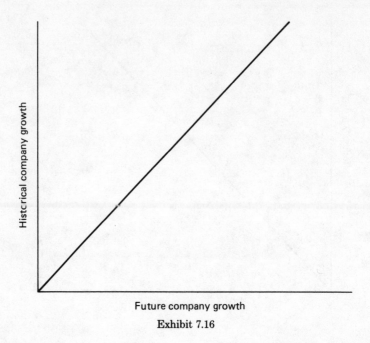

Exhibit 7.16

to grow faster in the future than they have in the past. Businesses to the left are in markets whose growth is expected to slow; their historical growth is higher than the forecast. The expected future growth of the market shown against history should help the corporation make decisions about which businesses to fund (See Exhibit 7.17).

STEP 4.   A change to one axis will give yet another perspective on the world—historical market growth versus forecast company growth. If we do not trust our forecasts of the market, we can at least look at historical market growth rates against our forecast for the business (See Exhibit 7.18).

Here we can look for the same trends as before—where will our future growth be vis-à-vis the market?

STEP 5.   How do we forecast our competitors? We can prepare a forecast share–momentum graph for us versus the competition if we feel we have good information about the competition's future plans (See Exhibit 7.19.).

The quality of the information is critical here. If we make a simple, straight-line assumption that our competition's businesses will continue on as before, we can graphically see how *our* planned changes will affect market shares. We can try different scenarios on our competitor: What if they grow LOB *A* but let LOB *B* decline? How will our shares be affected? These are questions that need to be asked during strategy development.

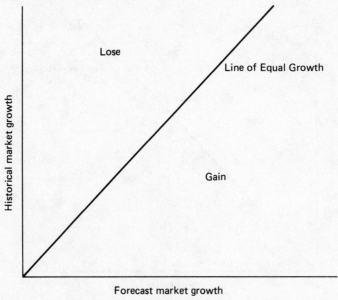

Exhibit 7.17

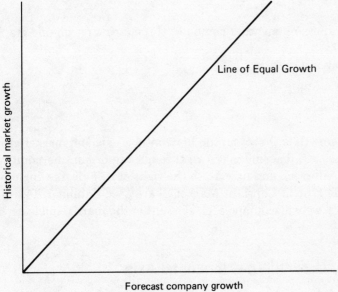

Exhibit 7.18

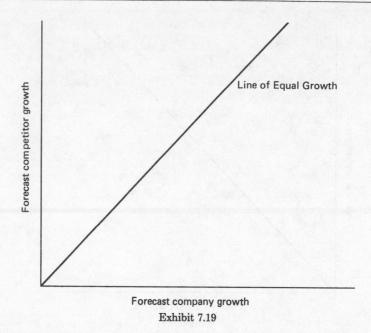

Exhibit 7.19

HOW TO DO IT

The basic share–momentum combines three measures on one graph:

1. Company growth
2. Market growth
3. LOB size

Company growth is shown on the horizontal x axis and market growth on the vertical y axis. A diagonal is drawn through the origin, the point where the x and y axes intersect, and upward to the right at a 45-degree angle. We will call this line the Line of Constant Market Share (See Exhibit 7.20).

As before, we will examine each element of the matrix and learn how to construct it.

Company Growth: The Horizontal Axis

The horizontal x axis represents our growth over the time period being shown on the graph. For a historical share momentum, the preferred time period is five years to allow us to view the long-term trend, although a shorter amount of history such as three years may be used if more data are unavailable.

Company growth should be calculated from the change in unit sales in each LOB over the period. We have learned how to calculate the compound annual growth rate (CAGR) or, better still, to draw a linear regression line and then calculate growth. Our procedure is to record sales for our company's LOBs for

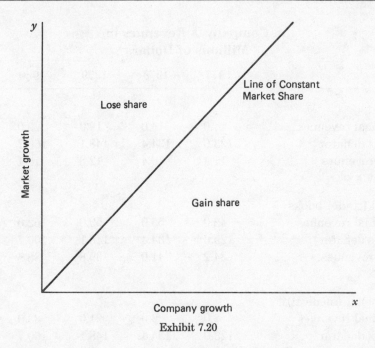

Company growth

Exhibit 7.20

each of the five years, deflate the numbers if they are in nominal (actual) dollars, and calculate the growth. We will use company X data and deflate sales with the special books deflator that is a subset of the deflator for personal consumption expenditures for durables.

STEP 1. Find the LOB size in units or dollars for each of the years in the historical period.

STEP 2. Deflate dollar size to convert from nominal to real dollars, using the formula

$$\text{Real dollars} = \frac{\text{Nominal dollars}}{\text{Deflator}} \times 100$$

STEP 3. Calculate the growth rate from real revenues.

Company X Revenues in Millions of Dollars

	1977	1978	1979	1980	1981
College texts					
Nominal revenues	25.0	30.0	30.0	32.0	3.0
Books deflator*	123.0	134.4	148.1	160.7	177.3
Real revenues	20.3	22.3	20.3	19.9	18.6
CAGR: (2.2%)					

Company X Revenues in Millions of Dollars

	1977	1978	1979	1980	1981
Elhi texts					
Nominal revenues	14.0	14.0	19.0	29.0	25.0
Books deflator*	123.0	134.4	148.1	160.7	177.3
Real revenues	11.4	10.4	12.8	18.1	13.8
CAGR: 5.5%					
General (trade) books					
Nominal revenues	42.0	55.0	59.0	62.0	64.0
Books deflator*	123.0	134.4	148.1	160.7	177.3
Real revenues	34.2	41.0	39.8	38.6	36.1
CAGR: 1.4%					
Professional (medical)†					
Nominal revenues	8.0	9.0	21.0	33.0	36.0
Books deflator*	123.0	134.4	148.1	160.7	177.3
Real revenues	6.5	6.7	14.2	20.5	20.3
CAGR: 32.9%					

* We use the deflator for the prior year because company X's fiscal year ends April 30. Fiscal year 1981 is really eight months of 1980 and four months of 1981.

† 1981 estimate from comment made by company; same proportion of sales in professional group taken in prior years. The big difference between fiscal years 1978 and 1979 is due to an acquisition.

Market Growth: The Vertical Axis

The vertical y axis of the graph represents market growth on the share momentum just as it did on the growth–share matrix. The procedure to calculate market growth is identical to the one we followed on the growth–share matrix.

STEP 1.   Find the market size in units or dollars for each of the years in the historical period.

STEP 2.   Deflate dollar size to convert from nominal to real dollars, using the formula

$$\text{Real dollars} = \frac{\text{Nominal dollars}}{\text{Deflator}} \times 100$$

STEP 3.   Calculate the growth rate.

Market growth is a composite name for growth in the market of *each* LOB. The educational text LOB must be compared against growth of the textbook market, the general books LOB against growth in the general (trade) books market, and the professional books LOB against growth in the professional books market. We will copy market data for company X's lines of business below. Our sources are the Census of Manufactures and Annual Survey of Manufactures.

Market Size

	1976	1977	1978	1979	1980
Textbooks					
Nominal dollars	1309.4	1408.7	1566.7	1699.5	1932.8
Books deflator	123.0	134.4	148.1	160.7	177.3
Real dollars	1064.6	1048.1	1057.9	1057.6	1090.1
CAGR, 1976–80: .6%					
Trade books					
Nominal dollars	1495.0	1895.6	2025.2	2101.5	2274.7
Books deflator	123.0	134.4	148.1	160.7	177.3
Real dollars	1215.5	1410.4	1367.5	1307.7	1283.0
CAGR, 1976–80: 1.4%					
Medical books					
Nominal dollars	97.0	140.5	193.8	214.0	239.9
Books deflator	123.0	134.4	148.1	160.7	177.3
Real dollars	78.9	104.5	130.9	133.2	135.3
CAGR, 1976–80: 14.4%					

Representing the LOB: Circle Size

Each LOB is represented as a circle on the graph, positioned along the x and y axes according to the company and market growth rates we just calculated. The circle is drawn proportionate to current sales, the last year in our historical period. Pick a scale that will allow you to show all the circles in good balance, as we did on the growth–share matrix, and apply the circle size formula.

$$\text{Circle size} = \text{factor} \sqrt{\frac{\text{LOB sales}}{\text{Index}}}$$

Index = largest LOB = 50 mm diameter circle

We have already calculated the circle sizes for Company X's lines of business in the previous chapter, but we'll repeat the formula here and run through one calculation. Remember that we use nominal sales for fiscal year 1981 in the formula.

$$\text{Circle size} = \text{factor} \sqrt{\frac{\text{LOB sales}}{\text{Index}}}$$

Index: 50 mm = \$64 million = General book sales

To determine the circle size for college texts:

$$
\begin{aligned}
\text{College text sales} &= 33 \text{ million} \\
\text{Circle size} \quad &= 50 \sqrt{\frac{33}{64}} \\
&= 50 \sqrt{0.5156} \\
&= 50 \times 0.7181 \\
&= 36 \text{ mm}
\end{aligned}
$$

We will not repeat the calculation for the other LOBs since we did them in the last chapter. The numbers we developed were:

Elhi texts   31
Medical   37

Putting It Together: Graphing

The share–momentum graph can be plotted on regular linear graph paper instead of the log/linear paper we used for the growth–share matrix.

STEP 1.   Combine all of the data in one place in a table.

	Company Growth FY 1977–81	Market Growth 1976–80	Circle Size
College texts	(2.2%)	0.6%	36
Elhi texts	5.5	0.6	31
Trade books	1.4	1.4	50
Medical	32.9	14.4	37

STEP 2.   Draw the axes on the graph and the 45-degree diagonal from the axis intersection. Label the diagonal "Line of Constant Market Share."

STEP 3.   Label each axis. The x axis should be labeled "Company Growth" and the y axis "Market Growth." Enter percentages to fit the data; a normal range might be from 0 to 30 on both axes.

STEP 4.   Label the graph with the company name, the time period covered and the name of the graph, "Share–Momentum."

STEP 5.   Label the key to the circle size scale in the lower right-hand corner as we did on the growth share matrix. Remember that the formula to find a usable scale is:

$$\frac{\text{Index circle size}}{\text{Index sales}} = \frac{\text{Scale circle size}}{\text{Small sales number}}$$

We found that the scale of 16 mm = $20 million in fiscal 1981 sales worked nicely for our purposes.

STEP 6.   Plot each LOB according to the company and market growth rates. Move along the x axis for company growth and up the y axis for market growth. Draw the circle with a template according to the circle size scale and label it with the LOB.

OTHER GRAPHS

We outlined a number of adaptations of the basic share–momentum, company versus market growth, earlier in the chapter. The calculations are similar to the basic calculations but the variables displayed are different.

There are eight other share momentums that may be useful in analysis. They are briefly summarized below, followed by an explanation of how to compose each.

Competitor

1.   One competitor: company growth versus one competitor growth.
2.   Composite competitor: company growth versus multiple competitors' growth.
3.   Basic share–momentum done for individual competitors.

Industry

4.   Submarket versus total industry.

Forecast

5.   Basic for forecast time period.
6.   Future company growth versus historical company growth.
7.   Future company growth versus historical market growth.
8.   Future company growth versus future competitor growth.

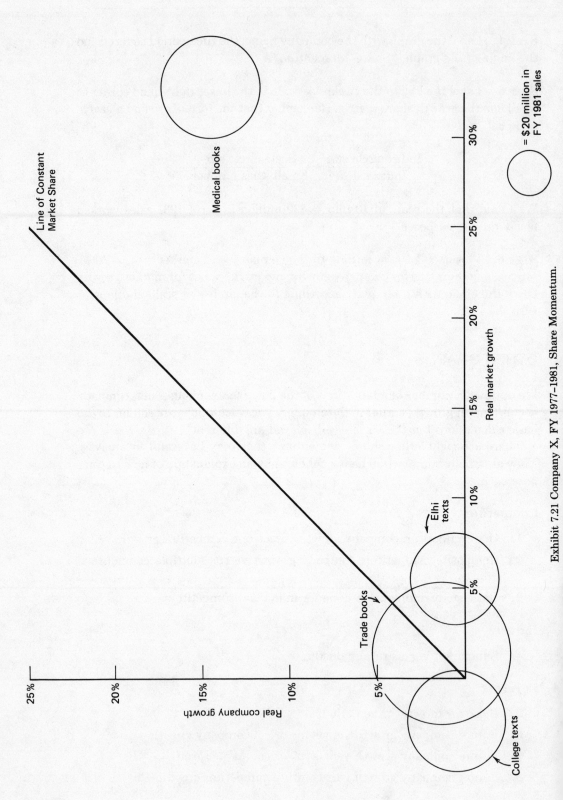

Exhibit 7.21 Company X, FY 1977–1981, Share Momentum.

Competitor Share–Momentums

1. One competitor. This graph shows company growth for a historical time period on the x axis and the growth of one competitor in your company's businesses on the y axis. If you participate in a business that this competitor does not, the business does not appear on the graph. Circles represent your SBUs, positioned according to your growth and your competitor's growth.

Data for the x axis are your company's sales in each LOB over a five-year historical time period. Put sales in real terms, either by using units or deflating nominal dollar sales, and calculate the growth rate for each SBU.

Data for the y axis are the one competitor's sales in each LOB over the same historical time period. Put sales in real terms and calculate the growth rate for each LOB. Ignore any LOBs that are not common between your company and the competitor. If you are a book publisher with a video games LOB, and your competitor is a book publisher with a cable TV LOB but not a video games LOB, you cannot plot the video games or cable TV LOBs on the graph.

Circles represent your company's SBUs. Your competitor's LOBs are not represented on the graph except through giving you the y-axis positioning. Your company's SBUs are sized according to sales. The Line of Equal Growth shows the points where you and your competitor's LOBs are growing at the same rate (See Exhibit 7.22).

2. Composite competitor. The one competitor graph is useful only when you and a competitor have several matched businesses. In the case where you

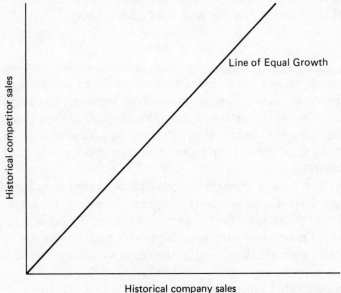

Exhibit 7.22

compete against different companies in different markets, a composite competitor is a better tool to view your momentum. The composite competitor lets you look at your position against the major competitor in each market.

The x axis is the growth rate of your company's historical sales in each SBU. As before, put sales in real terms and calculate the growth rate by SBU. The y axis is the growth rate of each major competitor, one per SBU. Put the competitor's sales in the business you have in common in real terms and calculate the growth rate. Do this for every SBU you have.

The circles represent your company's SBUs. The competitive LOBs are not shown on the graph except by giving you the y axis position for your SBUs. Because you can choose a competitor for each of your businesses, each one of your SBUs can be shown on the graph. Circle size is derived from your SBU sales. The Line of Equal Growth shows the points where you and your competitors' LOBs are growing at the same rate (See Exhibit 7.23).

3. Basic share–momentum for individual competitor. Here you are creating the basic share–momentum graph for one competitor, showing its company growth against market growth. Information about your company does not appear on this graph at all. You will use information about the competitor's LOBs and its market growth rates to develop the same graph as you did before for yourself. The purpose in doing this is to be able to look at the competitor's position and the momentum of its portfolio side by side with yours, and to use the interpretation to help figure out the competitor's strategy (See Exhibit 7.24).

The calculations are exactly the same as for your basic share–momentum except that we are now concerned with the competitor's sales in each SBU over a historical time period and the growth of its markets.

Industry Graphs

4. Segment versus total industry. This share–momentum graph displays total industry against a component of the industry. The horizontal x axis represents component growth and the vertical y axis is total industry growth. The diagonal Line of Constant Share defines the area where the component is growing at the same rate as the industry and neither gaining nor losing share (See Exhibit 7.25).

As in the basic share–momentum graph, data should be gathered for a historical time period of approximately five years. Component market data should be unit sales or dollar sales for the part of the market you want to examine. If dollar sales are used, they must be deflated so a real growth rate can be calculated. Industry data are developed in the same way as for the basic share momentum.

The circles plotted represent component markets, not SBUs. Circle size is proportional to the size of the component market. The scale may be based on the largest component market or some other index number.

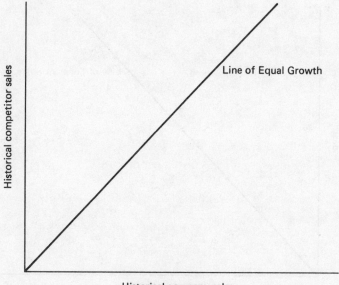

Line of Equal Growth

Historical competitor sales

Historical company sales

Exhibit 7.23

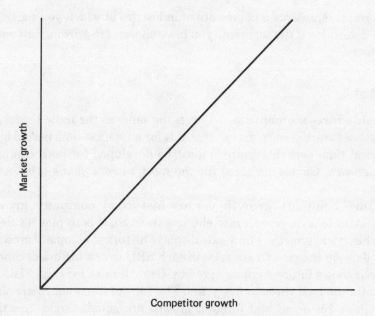

Market growth

Competitor growth

COMPETITOR SHARE MOMENTUM

Exhibit 7.24

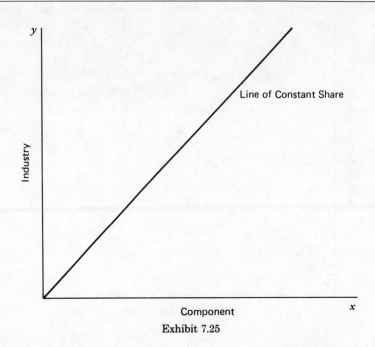

Exhibit 7.25

This graph represents a composite of industries in which you participate. It lets you determine if the segments you have chosen are growing fast relative to the industry.

Forecast

5. Basic share–momentum. This is the same as the basic share–momentum graph we started with, except that it is for a forecast time period instead of a historical time period. Forecasts must be developed for both company and market growth. Circles are sized for the most current year's sales, as before.

6. Future company growth versus historical company growth. A useful way to look at growth rate changes in an SBU is to plot future growth against historical growth. The x axis displays historical company growth. Data used to develop the growth are sales in each SBU over a historical time period. The y axis shows future company growth. Growth rates for each SBU must be forecast for the next three to five years. The Line of Constant Share shows the points where historical and forecast growth are equal. Circles are the company's SBUs and are sized according to the most current year's sales.

Circles plotted to the left of the Line of Constant Share are SBUs that are expected to grow faster in the future than they have in the past. Circles to the right will grow more slowly in the future than they have historically.

7. Future company growth versus historical market growth. This graph is a good check on forecasting because it compares the company's fore-

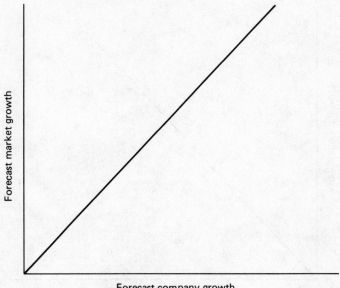

Forecast company growth

Exhibit 7.26

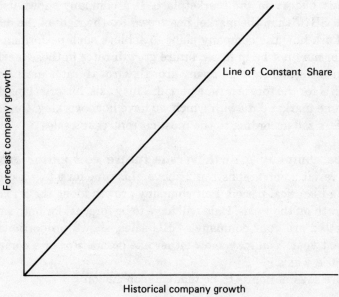

Historical company growth

Exhibit 7.27

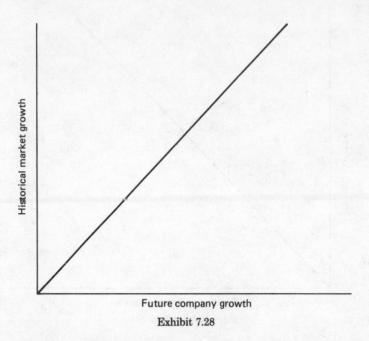

Exhibit 7.28

casts against history in the marketplace. If a company shows itself growing faster in all SBUs than the market has grown (to the right of the diagonal), we might well ask how the company plans to achieve such performance. The answer may or may not be in faster future growth rates in those markets.

The x axis shows future company growth. Growth rates must be estimated for each SBU for the forecast time period. The y axis, historical market growth, uses the same market data with which we have been working. Circles are company SBUs, sized according to the most current year's sales.

8. Future company growth versus future competitor growth. This graph is a variation on graphs 1 or 2 above, this time for a forecast time period instead of a historical period. Plot company growth along the x axis and competitor growth on the y axis. Data will have to be forecast for both sets of SBUs. Circles plotted are your company's SBU sales, shown proportionate to their most current year. You may show either one competitor or a composite competitor on the y axis.

There are several points to be made in conclusion.

You are limited only by your imagination in developing other types of share–momentum graphs. The idea is to contrast two variables relating to your businesses and to each other. The variables may include functions (sales versus advertising expenditures, profitability versus customer service expenditures), geography (northeast region sales versus western sales, Europe versus North America), or virtually anything else that seems to relate meaningfully.

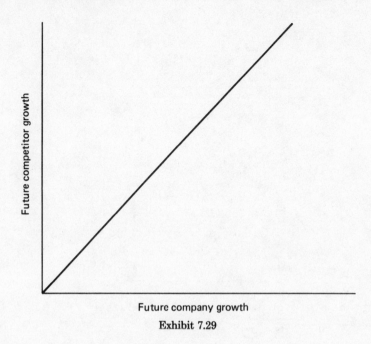

Exhibit 7.29

Don't be afraid to experiment. Theorize about the relationships that might exist and then try them out on the graph. Sometimes patterns pop up graphically that you would never have expected from looking at numbers on a table.

Label your graphs with care. It is easy to lose track of the data unless every element has been noted. Woe to the analyst who comes back a month later to an unlabeled graph and asks, "What scale did we use for circle size? What did we plot on the y axis?"

Figure out ways to get even more data out of the graphs. Shade circles to show other types of segmentation. Use dotted circles to indicate alternative scenarios.

8

The Competitive Picture: The Sector Graph

Until now, our analysis has been focused on one company's portfolio. The growth–share matrix displayed a corporate portfolio according to the relative market share of its SBUs and market growth rates. The share–momentum graph showed the company's growth in comparison with growth of the market. The *sector graph* is different from the first two because it shows a market segment instead of a company. It adds the perspective of the business line's standing within its market in comparison to all other competitors. The sector graph differs from the growth–share matrix because (1) it looks at the full range of competitors, not just the market leader, and (2) it shows one LOB or product/market at a time, not the entire portfolio.

WHAT IT IS

The horizontal x axis of the sector shows the relative market share for all competitors in the market in the most recent year. The vertical y axis shows the growth of each competitor over a historical time period. The other sides are filled in to make a rectangle. A second horizontal line is drawn to indicate aggregate market growth. Companies above the line are growing faster than the market; companies below the line are growing more slowly. (See Exhibit 8.1.)

The sector graph can be drawn at any level of detail—total market, component/segment, product line, or geographic area. Circles represent the various competitors' LOBs in that sector and are drawn proportionate to current year's sales. A percentage figure is shown within each circle to show the estimated

107

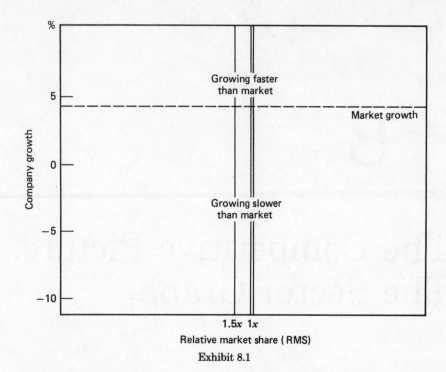

Exhibit 8.1

percentage of profits that comes from the LOB. The profit estimate is an important piece of information because it shows the value of that business to the parent company and indicates to what lengths the parent may go to protect the earnings flow. (See Exhibit 8.2.)

Let us look at some patterns shown by sector charts and discuss their implications.

Exhibit 8.3 shows a stable, consolidated sector. One competitor has established a clear leadership position that is unchallenged by the other participants. This picture is characteristic of a mature industry. The size and relative market share of the market leader suggest that the leader is way down its experience curve and probably enjoys a low cost position relative to competition. Because the market is not growing terribly fast, the leader probably will be able to maintain its position.

Exhibit 8.4 shows a sector in which there is a clear leader but enough competitive threats to suggest that a change in dominance might occur. The two high-growth competitors may catch up and take away market share over time. Because the market itself is low in growth, the high-growth circles may have found a new angle, through either market segmentation or superior technology, that is giving them their growth rates. If we saw this same pattern in a high-growth market, we might conclude that the leader took its profits too early when it should have been reinvesting them into the business.

A fractionated market that still lacks a clear leader is shown in Exhibit 8.5. Three competitors are close to the 1.0 line, but no one is on its left. Two sizable companies are growing so fast they are off the chart (this is shown by dashed-

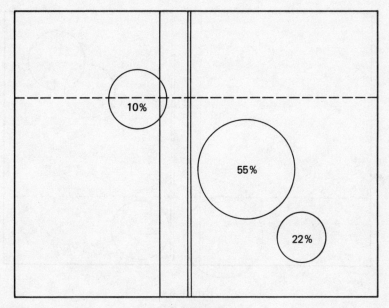

Exhibit 8.2

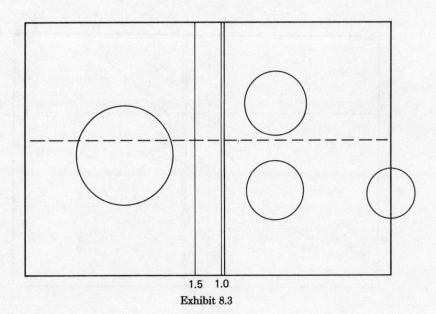

1.5   1.0

Exhibit 8.3

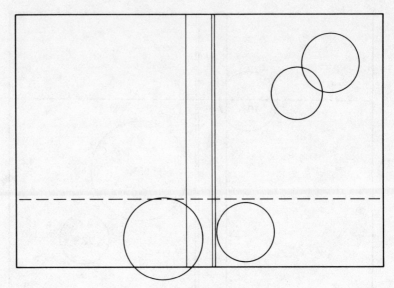

Exhibit 8.4

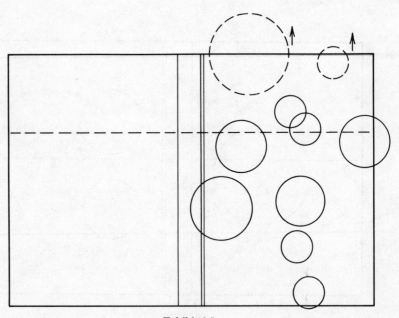

Exhibit 8.5

line circles and arrows pointing in the direction they are moving). Three years from now this sector may look completely different, more like Exhibit 8.3 and the game will have been won. This pattern indicates an emerging growth market where dominance has never been established, or it may show a market that recently underwent a severe transition and has not yet settled.

Sector graphs may be done for historical or forecast periods. It is useful to prepare one for each and make side-by-side comparisons. Like the share–momentum graph, the types of sectors you prepare are limited only by your imagination. Any product, market, or product/market intersection may provide the basis. You may look at imports and exports on a sector if they are important to your business. You may explode sales in one product and one geographic area to get a fine cut on competition. Think about what is meaningful to your business and then how you might display it on a sector graph.

HOW TO DO IT

The sector graph combines five measures on one graph:

1. Relative market share
2. Company growth
3. Market growth
4. Company size
5. Company profitability

We will discuss each of these in turn. (See Exhibit 8.6.)

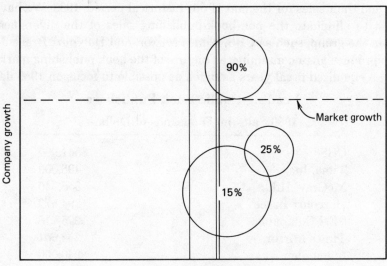

Relative market share (RMS)

Exhibit 8.6

Relative Market Share: The Horizontal Axis

The horizontal x axis represents relative market share for all competitors in the market. This is different from the relative market share we calculated in the growth–share matrix, which showed share versus the market *leader* in each market. Since the purpose of the sector is to portray the entire market or the segment of the market you have chosen to look at, relative market share is developed for each competitor in the market.

Relative market share is calculated by one of two formulas, depending on whether or not the competitor is the market leader.

$$\text{For the market leader:} \quad \frac{\text{Market leader sales}}{\text{Second-largest company's sales}}$$

$$\text{For all other companies:} \quad \frac{\text{Company sales}}{\text{Market leader sales}}$$

Relative market share can be developed by using sales in dollars, sales in units, or market share figures. Data should be for the most recent year available, the last year of the historical period, or the year before the first year of the forecast period. If our historical period is 1976–1980, relative market share should be calculated with 1980 numbers. If the forecast is for 1981–1985, relative market share should still be calculated using 1980 data. It is not necessary to deflate nominal sales dollars for the relative market share calculation because we are converting the data to scalar figures and are using only one year's sales in the computation.

We have been using company X as our example, a book publisher that participates in four different segments of the market. Suppose we now want to expand our knowledge of the total book publishing market by developing a sector graph for book publishers. Our first step is to list the major public book publishers and their sales for the end of our historical period, 1980. We have done our best to eliminate the non-book-publishing sales of the diversified companies in the group, such as CBS, Times Mirror, and Harcourt Brace Jovanovich, to produce an uncontaminated picture of the book publishing market. We have also equalized fiscal years as much as possible to focus on 1980 data.

Leading Public Book Publishers

1980 Sales in Thousands of Dollars

CBS	$541,900
Time, Inc.	498,000
McGraw-Hill	355,340
Harcourt Brace	294,673
SFN Companies	275,718
Times Mirror	263,601
Macmillan	240,000
Prentice-Hall	231,600
Company X	160,000

We can now calculate the relative market share for each book publisher using the second RMS formula. The market leader is CBS and the second largest publisher is Time, Inc.

$$\text{Relative market share} = \frac{\text{CBS sales}}{\text{Time, Inc. sales}}$$

$$= \frac{541{,}900}{498{,}000}$$

$$= 1.09$$

Our formula for all other companies except the market leader is

$$\text{Relative market share} = \frac{\text{Company sales}}{\text{Market leader (CBS) sales}}$$

For Time, Inc., we will use these numbers:

$$\text{Relative market share} = \frac{\text{Time, Inc., sales}}{\text{CBS sales}}$$

$$= \frac{498{,}000}{541{,}900}$$

$$= 0.92$$

We repeat this calculation for all other companies using CBS sales as the denominator. The final listing of relative market share (RMS) is

Leading Public Book Publishers
Relative Market Share

	1980 Sales in Thousands of Dollars	RMS
CBS	$541,900	1.09
Time, Inc.	498,000	0.92
McGraw-Hill	355,340	0.66
Harcourt Brace	294,673	0.54
SFN Companies	275,718	0.51
Times Mirror	263,601	0.49
Macmillan	240,000	0.44
Prentice-Hall	231,600	0.43
Company X	160,000	0.30

Remember that the matrix is divided along the relative market share dimension by two lines, a vertical line that cuts the x axis at 1.0 relative market share and another vertical line that cuts the axis at 1.5 relative market share. The circle to the left of 1.0 relative market share represents the market leader. If the circle is also to the left of 1.5 relative market share, chances are that the business is highly profitable. CBS, with a relative market share of 1.09, is the market leader but does not lead significantly over Time, Inc., at an RMS of 0.92. CBS is not to the left of the 1.5 line, suggesting that its leadership position may not carry exceptionally high profits with it.

There can be only one circle to the left of the 1.0 line on a sector graph, unlike the growth–share matrix where there may be many. The sector represents *one* market that, by definition, can have only *one* leader, while the growth–share matrix represents multiple markets, each of which has a leader.

Company Growth: The Vertical Axis

The vertical y axis of the graph displays the percentage growth rate of each competitor in the market over a historical time period, normally five years. As with the other graphs, a longer or shorter history may be used if deemed appropriate. Growth rates are calculated from a real sales measure to eliminate the impact of inflation. To derive real sales, we may use unit sales or we may deflate nominal dollar sales. Use CAGR or linear regression growth rate to calculate growth.

We will review these steps by using our book publishing example.

STEP 1.   List sales for each competitor for a five-year historical period.

Nominal Sales in Millions of Dollars

	1976	1977	1978	1979	1980
CBS	$224.1	$401.6	$442.3	$455.6	$541.9
Time, Inc.	227.6	258.2	360.9	425.0	498.0
McGraw-Hill	255.7	278.4	305.3	335.2	355.3
Harcourt Brace	201.5	218.5	248.0	272.6	294.7
SFN Companies*	181.9	194.2	229.7	259.2	275.7
Times Mirror	172.2	176.2	214.2	234.7	263.6
Macmillan	187.2	189.9	200.4	224.6	240.0
Prentice-Hall	154.9	169.9	189.0	208.0	231.6
Company X*	93.0	114.0	137.0	167.0	170.0

* Fiscal year ends April 30, so the next year's data were used.

STEP 2.   If sales are not unit sales, convert them into real terms by using the appropriate deflator. We are using the special books deflator, a subset of the Personal Consumption Expenditures Deflator.

$$\frac{\text{Nominal sales}}{\text{Deflator}} \times 100 = \text{Real sales}$$

Books Deflator*

1976	123.0
1977	134.4
1978	148.1
1979	160.7
1980	177.3

* Source: Bureau of Economic Analysis, Department of Commerce.

Repeat this for each competitor until all the nominal sales data in the table under step 1 have been converted into real sales.

Real Sales in Millions of Dollars

	1976	1977	1978	1979	1980
CBS	$182.2	$298.8	$298.6	$283.5	$305.6
Time, Inc.	185.0	192.1	243.7	264.5	280.9
McGraw-Hill	183.5	207.1	206.1	208.6	200.4
Harcourt Brace	163.8	150.0	167.5	169.6	166.2
SFN	147.9	144.5	155.1	161.2	155.5
Times Mirror	140.0	131.1	144.6	146.0	148.7
Macmillan	152.2	141.3	135.3	139.8	135.4
Prentice-Hall	125.9	126.4	127.6	129.4	130.6
Company X	75.0	85.0	93.0	104.0	96.0

STEP 3:   Calculate growth rates using real sales by CAGR or linear regression. We will use the simpler CAGR method without regression, but using regression is recommended so all five years of data are utilized to develop the result.

Five-Year Growth Rate 1976–80

CBS	13.8%
Time, Inc.	2.0
McGraw-Hill	2.2
Harcourt Brace	0.4
SFN Companies	1.3
Times Mirror	1.5
Macmillan	(2.9)
Prentice-Hall	0.9
Company X	6.4

This last step provides us with the data for our y-axis positioning.

Market Growth: The Dashed Horizontal Line

We wish to compare the growth of individual competitors in the market to the growth of the market as a whole to determine whether a company is gaining or losing share. The market growth line provides an important piece of information for the comparison. There are two ways to develop the market growth rate:

1. Use industry data on the overall market from a secondary source such as the Department of Census's Census of Manufactures, Annual Survey of Manufactures, or a trade association.
2. Define the industry yourself by aggregating the sales of major competitors.

Each of these approaches provides a different perspective on market growth. Use the first approach (1) when you can locate secondary data on the industry segment chosen for the sector, and (2) when you wish to compare competitors to the total market regardless of whether every company comprising the market is represented on the graph. The second approach should be used (1) if you cannot find secondary market size data matching the sector or (2) if the subgroup of competitors you have chosen to display is the meaningful referent, rather than the total market. The second case allows you to redefine the market for your purposes instead of using a generally accepted definition. An example of needing industry redefinition in book publishing would be if you were interested in scientific textbook publishers. The most disaggregated data available are for a category that groups together technical, scientific, and professional publishers. Let us assume that your knowledge of the industry allows you to identify and estimate the sales of publishers that operate only in the scientific sector. You can calculate company growth rates but do not have a proper market growth comparison from published data. In this case, you may choose to redefine the segment as scientific textbook publishers, add their sales together to develop a market estimate, and calculate the growth rate from your estimate.

The calculation for market growth is the same as for company growth:

1. Convert sales to real terms for the historical period that matches the company growth period.
2. Use the CAGR or linear regression method to find the growth rate.

Data for the book publishing industry appear below. We will accept the government's definition of the industry and use data from the Census of Manufactures in 1977 and the Annual Survey in other years. Our sales data are more specifically the value of shipments of the product class SIC 2731, book publishing.

Book Publishing Industry Sales*
in Millions of Dollars

	Nominal Sales	Books Deflator	Real Sales
1976	$4179.7	$123.0	$3398.1
1977	5007.7	134.4	3726.0
1978	5640.6	148.1	3808.6
1979	5711.3	160.7	3554.0
1980	6570.0	177.3	3705.6

CAGR 1976–80:   2.2%

* Source: Department of Commerce.

Representing Competitor Sales: Circles

Companies are represented on the graph as circles drawn proportionate to the current year's sales. We must find a scale that allows us to portray each company on the sector in an attractive graphic proportion.

Remember that the formula for circle size is

$$\text{Circle size} = \text{Factor} \sqrt{\frac{\text{Company sales}}{\text{Index}}}$$

The factor is the number of millimeters you choose to represent a sales level. You may take the market leader's sales as your index so it will be the largest circle or you may pick an arbitrary number. We have used 50 millimeters as the factor equal to company X's largest business line in previous chapters. Let us look at sales of the book publishers that will appear on the graph and visually determine which circle size to set as our factor.

Leading Public Book Publishers

	1980 Sales in Thousands of Dollars
CBS	$541,900
Time, Inc.	498,000
McGraw-Hill	355,340
Harcourt Brace	294,673
SFN Companies	275,718
Times Mirror	263,601
Macmillan	240,000
Prentice-Hall	231,600
Company X	160,000

We will arbitrarily choose a circle size of 50 millimeters to be equal to $600,000, a number slightly larger than CBS's sales. CBS will be displayed by a 48-mm circle, restricting the size of the remaining circles.

We can apply the formula with our index of 50 = $600,000 to each company's sales and calculate circle size. Remember to first divide under the square root sign, take the square root, and multiply the result by 50.

$$\text{Circle size} = \text{Factor} \sqrt{\frac{\text{Company sales}}{\text{Index}}}$$

$$\text{CBS} = 50 \sqrt{\frac{541,900}{600,000}} = 50 \sqrt{0.90} = 50 \,(0.95) = 48$$

$$\text{Time, Inc.} = 50 \sqrt{\frac{498,000}{600,000}} = 50 \sqrt{0.83} = 50 \,(0.91) = 46$$

The remainder of the calculations are done in the same manner and result in the following circle sizes for the market.

Circle Size Chart

	1980 Sales in Thousands of Dollars	Circle Size in Millimeters
CBS	$541,900	48
Time, Inc.	498,000	46
McGraw-Hill	355,340	38
Harcourt Brace	294,673	35
SFN Companies	275,718	34
Times Mirror	263,601	33
Macmillan	240,000	32
Prentice-Hall	231,600	31
Company X	160,000	26

Company Profitability: Inside the Circle

We are interested in knowing the profitability of a business to its parent company as input to our strategic decision making. If the lion's share of the parent's profits come from the business in question, we can assume the parent will go to great lengths to protect its position. If the business is minimally profitable or unprofitable, the parent may do little to protect it when it is threatened competitively.

The measure we use to indicate profitability is not important as long as we are consistent with all companies in our sector. If we have access to competitive data, we might choose operating income as the measure, before corporate allocations have been made to the business unit. It is more likely that we are making broad "guestimates" instead of working from real data. In this latter case, the level of accuracy is not great enough to try to refine the measure of profitability. The objective is to estimate how much profit the business contributes to the corporation's overall portfolio. Of course, a one-product/market company will derive 100% of its profit from that business.

The number we wish to develop is the percentage of total corporate profit derived from the business in question. Operating income is the level at which the numbers should be examined. Data from the most recent year of the historical period are appropriate, the same year as circle size data. The information can be found in the business segment or LOB part of the annual report.

Book Publishing Operating Income as a Percentage of Total

CBS	11.0%
Time, Inc.	15.6
McGraw-Hill	26.1
Harcourt Brace	64.6
SFN	100.0
Times Mirror	16.0
Macmillan	44.1
Prentice-Hall	62.3
Company X	100.0

Putting It Together: Graphing

STEP 1: Combine all the data elements in one place. We will use a table for this purpose.

Book Industry Sector Graph Summary Table

	RMS	1976–80 Company Growth	Circle Size	% O.I.
CBS	1.09	13.8%	48	11.0%
Time, Inc.	0.92	2.0	46	15.6
McGraw-Hill	0.66	2.2	38	26.1
Harcourt Brace	0.54	0.4	35	64.6
SFN	0.51	1.3	34	100.0
Times Mirror	0.49	1.5	33	16.0
Macmillan	0.44	(2.9)	32	44.1
Prentice-Hall	0.43	0.9	31	62.3
Company X	0.30	6.4	26	100.0

Market CAGR 1976–80:   2.2%

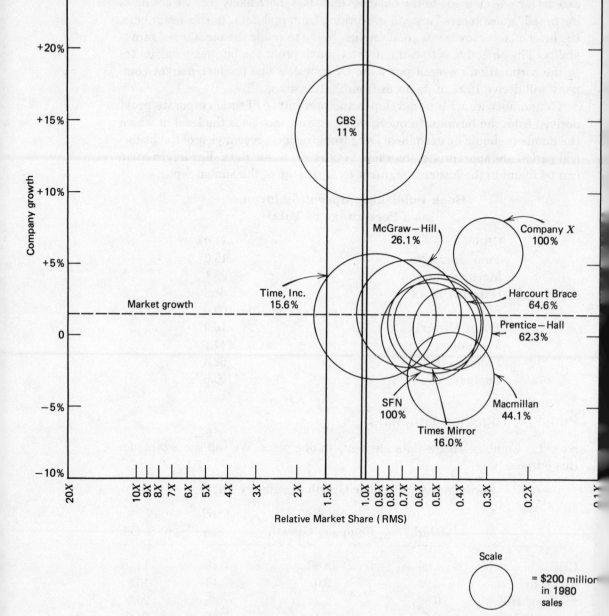

Market growth

+20%
+15%
+10%
+5%
0
−5%
−10%

Company growth

CBS
11%

McGraw—Hill
26.1%

Company *X*
100%

Time, Inc.
15.6%

Harcourt Brace
64.6%

Prentice—Hall
62.3%

SFN
100%

Macmillan
44.1%

Times Mirror
16.0%

20X 10X 9X 8X 7X 6X 5X 4X 3X 2X 1.5X 1.0X 0.9X 0.8X 0.7X 0.6X 0.5X 0.4X 0.3X 0.2X 0.1X

Relative Market Share (RMS)

Scale

= $200 million
in 1980
sales

Exhibit 8.7 Book Publishing Sector Graph, 1976–1980. (Percentages are percentages of operating income in book publishing.)

120

STEP 2:   Outline the graph on three-cycle log/linear paper. The relative market share x-axis scale is logarithmic and covers two full cycles and a portion of a third (see the appendix in Chapter 11 for a discussion of cycles). Label the scale from the far right corner so that the first cycle goes from $0.1X$ to $1.0X$, the second from $1.0X$ to $10X$, and only the first block of the third cycle $20X$. The reason for using a log scale is so that equal percentage changes in RMS appear equal spatially. Company growth, the y axis, is a straight linear scale and should be labeled with percentages to represent company growth rates. We will label our y-axis scale from -10% to $+20\%$. Market growth is indicated with a dashed horizontal line starting at the appropriate percentage on the y axis.

STEP 3:   Label the graph with the market being shown, the title "Sector Graph," and the time period covered.

STEP 4:   Go back to the chart and plot each company on the graph, starting with the relative market share on the x axis and moving up the y axis according to the growth rate. Draw the circle based on circle size. Fill in the profit estimate inside each circle and footnote its meaning on the bottom of the graph.

STEP 5:   Develop a circle size scale and show the key on the graph. The formula is:

$$\frac{\text{Index circle sizes}}{\text{Index sales}} = \frac{\text{Scale circle size}}{\text{Small sales number}}$$

Our index was 50 mm = \$600 million. We will solve for the circle size at \$200 million:

$$\frac{50}{600} = \frac{X}{200}$$

$$600X = 10,000$$

$$X = 16.7, \text{ rounded up to 17 mm}$$

Our key to the scale is 17 mm = \$200 million in 1980 sales.
   The completed sector graph for book publishers looks like Exhibit 8.7.

9

Analyzing Competitors' Cost Position: The Experience Curve

The *experience curve* was "discovered" by the Boston Consulting Group (BCG) in the mid-1960s in the course of their work on cost and pricing. It derives from an older idea, the learning curve, which says that as experience with a product increases through more and more production, direct labor costs per unit decline. The learning curve was observed first in 1925 at Wright Patterson Air Force Base when the commander saw that the number of hours it took to assemble a plane dropped as more planes were made. BCG took this a big step further by claiming that not only did labor costs drop with increased production, but so did other product costs from the manufacturing process to marketing. After developing its theory with a study of semiconductors in 1966, BCG tested it on a variety of other products, from Japanese beer to automobiles, and always found the same effect.

Experience curve theory says: *Costs of value added decline approximately 20%–30% in real terms each time accumulated experience is doubled.**

* Bruce Henderson, "BCG Perspectives, Experience Curve Reviewed" (BCG, 1974).

Let us examine that statement in its component parts:

Costs of value added means costs relating to functions performed by the firm, such as production from raw materials, marketing, and distribution. It excludes the cost of materials purchased from outside for input into the production process.

Real terms means controlling for the effect of inflation on costs.

Accumulated experience means volume since the start of production. If a firm began to manufacture a product in 1953, accumulated experience means the sum of all units produced from 1953 to the present.

WHY IT HAPPENS

Why does this decline in costs occur? BCG gives four reasons:

1. *The old learning curve effect:* Workers become more productive as they learn a task through repetition.

2. *Specialization:* Workers who specialize in one task instead of performing all tasks gain more skill in the task as they practice it more. Specialization, which results from an increase in scale, compounds the learning effect.

3. *Investment:* Firms that invest to increase capacity and reduce costs will move down the curve faster.

4. *Scale:* Capital costs per incremental unit capacity decline as scale increases. In other words, each added unit of capacity becomes a smaller percentage of the total cost.

Certain conditions contribute to producing experience curve effects:

1. The more operations that are paced by workers rather than machines, the greater the amount of learning that can occur. A firm with a high labor-to-capital production ratio will show more cost decline than a similar firm with highly automated processes.

2. A stable labor force is essential, otherwise, the cost of training new workers will outpace learning effects. Similarly, low-quality workers will not achieve learning to reduce costs.

3. Process or material innovation/substitution can benefit firms, especially those that are not labor-intensive.

4. Product redesign can save money through saving material, substituting less expensive processes and greater efficiency in manufacturing.

5. Active participation by management and workers in managing costs is required. The experience curve effect rarely just happens; it results when direct efforts are made to obtain cost reduction.

There are situations in which the experience curve effect may not be felt. They include the converse of our list above, and also cases where:

1. The orientation is short term. It may take years for the true pattern to emerge with short-term deviations from the trend.

2. A large percentage of costs is not the result of free market trade, such as where a monopoly is in effect, supply is limited, or government regulation sets the supply.

3. There is a rapid change in technology or design. Changes mean there is no opportunity to benefit from experience with one product but may be necessary to stay ahead competitively.

4. The company has a high return-on-investment hurdle rate for new capacity and capital equipment, so investment is not made.

Another idea is important in understanding the workings of experience curves—shared experience. Suppose you make several different products, such as watches, calculators, and home computers, and produce the semiconductors used in their manufacture. If you examine the separate experience curves for each product individually, you ignore the tremendous volume of semiconductor manufacture accumulated for all three. This "shared experience" in making semiconductors among the three products can lead to cost declines far greater than for watches, calculators, or computers alone.

IMPORTANCE IN PLANNING

Why is the experience curve important in strategic planning? The answer comes from two basic concepts: market share and profits. We have seen that the more volume produced, the lower the manufacturer's costs. Let us apply this knowledge to the idea of market share. The producer with the greatest current volume will have the highest market share. Because of experience curve effects, that producer will also have the lowest costs. It has the ability to price as a market leader and, assuming other participants follow its lead, it will realize the greatest profits from its preferred cost position. Competitors may try to overtake its market leadership by underpricing to gain share, but the leader can reduce its prices further and longer without getting hurt because of its superior cost position. If a competitor cannot gain share to increase accumulated experience and move down its cost curve faster, it will never be in a favorable cost position in relation to the leader, and status quo will perpetuate itself.

Some interesting evidence for the importance of cost in gaining competitive position comes from a 1980 study of companies operating in mature, lower-growth industries.* The study found that leading competitors actually placed in the top 20% of the Fortune 1000 in return on equity. Marginal competitors, on the other hand, were distinguished by being high-cost producers in their segments, among other problems. Some of the problem companies were low-cost producers in their early days but made strategic errors in reinvesting their profits and lost their leadership. International Harvester was an example of the latter, having lost its 1965 leadership of the heavy-duty truck manufacturing industry by failing to reduce costs as fast as Ford and General Motors in the 1970s, and finding itself with high costs, low margin, and low share.

Pricing can follow several patterns. It can decline in parallel with costs so that the more volume produced, the lower the cost. It can be set below cost in the introductory period to encourage people to buy the product, held for a while as volume grows, and finally dropped close to cost to discourage competitors from entering the market. Another approach is to price relative to expected costs after the product matures; this is called "experience curve pricing." (See Exhibit 9.1.)

Pricing and costs determine profitability. The market leader who has lowest costs and prices will be the most profitable. The relationship between market share and profitability has been established empirically by the PIMS project, which found that 10 percentage points in market share translated into 5 percentage points in pretax return on investment. The experience curve relationship is a partial explanation for this phenomenon.

The experience curve tells us the importance of gaining market share in a growth market. It can help us determine how long it will take for a competitor to reach cost equivalence with the market leader or how long it can take for a new entrant to catch up.

THE OTHER SIDE

The experience curve has been the subject of some debate. It can be taken too literally, without applying judgment to the context and the meaning. Here are some of the arguments against the curve and response to those arguments:

1. *The experience curve effect vanishes over time.* This is not so. The effect is based on volume, not time, although the two are interrelated. In the later stages of product maturity, it takes a lot longer to double accu-

* William K. Hall, "Survival Strategies in a Hostile Environment," *Harvard Business Review,* September–October 1980, pp. 75–85.

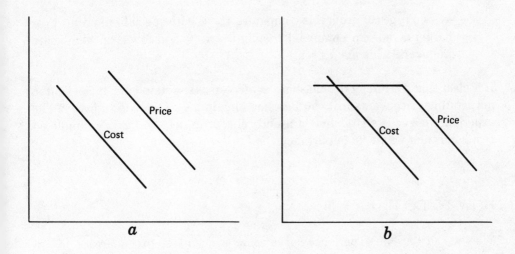

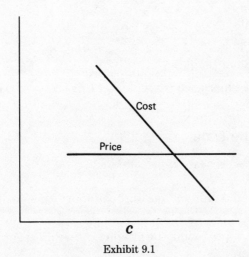

Exhibit 9.1

mulated volume than in the early, high-growth phase, so it may look as if cost declines are not occurring when they really are.

2. *Price cuts to gain share don't work.* Plenty of evidence says that they don't. This is a mistake in strategy and execution, not in the experience curve itself. The sad case of DuPont cutting nylon prices to gain share, raising them after achieving dominance, and finding consumers substituting other products can be attributed to new products and consumer behavior, not to faulty use of the experience curve.

3. *Some products are exceptions.* This is probably so. Mercedes-Benz is profitable despite its small market share. Another theory says that there

are two types of profitable companies, those with specialized products or markets who can command premium prices, and low-cost, high-share producers. This makes sense.

It is clear that a strategy to gain share at all costs is too simplistic. It can lead to devastating price wars, or it can take too long in a slow-growth industry. The experience curve is a guideline, a useful concept to help you gain a handle on costs and their strategic importance.

HOW TO DO IT

We will calculate an experience curve using a seven-step procedure:

1. Collect the data.
2. Convert to logs.
3. Plot the data.
4. Connect points.
5. Read off end-points.
6. Find the slope of the line.
7. Calculate the experience curve.

Step 1. Collect the Data

The experience curve uses two types of data:

1. The accumulated unit volume of the product since its first day of manufacture
2. The unit cost of producing the product at two different points in time, in constant dollars

The x axis is accumulated volume in units, and the y axis is the unit cost in constant dollars. The curve is plotted from those two pieces of information, with each point on the curve equal to unit cost at a particular accumulated volume. See Exhibit 9.2.

The theory says that as more of an item is produced, unit cost will drop because of productivity gains from experience in making the item. Thus, the curve starts out high on the cost axis at low volumes and declines as the cost of production drops with accumulated experience at greater volumes.

Accumulated volume of the product may be found in company records for an individual company's product, or through published sources for an industry.

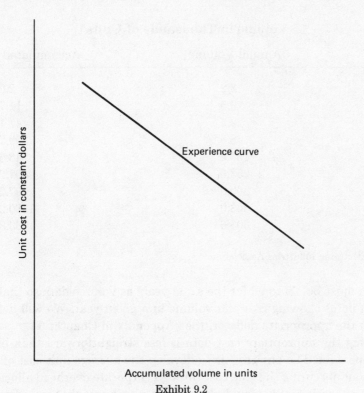

Exhibit 9.2

Sometimes neither source can produce a history back to the beginning of time, so it becomes necessary to estimate. An estimate can be made with three pieces of data:

1.   Unit volume sold during the last year
2.   The number of years the product has been sold
3.   Unit growth rate over the period

Ideally, we would like to have volume data for every year, since the product was first made and up to the present. We will settle for a minimum of two data points spread out over as much time as possible. Of course, the more data points we have, the more accurate the final curve. Be certain that the data you obtain are *unit* volumes, not *dollar* volumes, and that you calculate accumulated volume over the time period, adding the years together as you go along. Our example will use data on integrated circuits collected by the Electronic Industries Association, which show the beginning of circuit manufacture in 1964 up until 1972.

Volume in Thousands of Units*

	Annual Volume	Accumulated Volume
1964	2.2	2.2
1965	9.5	11.7
1966	29.4	41.1
1967	68.6	109.7
1968	133.9	243.6
1969	253.6	497.2
1970	300.0	797.2
1971	363.0	1160.2
1972	603.6	1763.8

* Source: Electronic Industries Association.

Cost data must be obtained for the same years as volume data so that we can plot each point showing cost and volume in a given year. We will deflate the data with the appropriate deflator. (See Appendix in Chapter 6.)

Choosing the appropriate cost data is less straightforward than obtaining the volume data. The objective is to develop the average unit cost of production without obscuring the true cost through corporate overhead allocations or joint cost allocations. We would like to have a unit cost that includes:

Manufacturing labor and overhead

Marketing, advertising, and promotion

Distribution

Here are some practical tips on collecting costs:

1. Use value-added costs, total costs minus raw materials. "Value-added" refers to the amount of value a manufacturer adds to the raw materials purchased in making its product. The reason for using value-added costs is that when raw materials are purchased from the outside rather than being made, they should not be subject to the experience curve effect.

2. Use standard accounting costs rather than actual costs.

3. Take the average annual cost for the product to correct for short-term fluctuations.

4. Check to see that the accounting system has not been changed from year to year over your historical period. If it has, adjust the data to compensate or you will be measuring the effects of the accounting system, not real experience effects.

5. Look at costs over a minimum of five to seven years because the experience effect is a long-term phenomenon.

You must apply judgment to the specific costs included since they will vary by business. The idea is to collect costs that can be affected by learning, scale of production, and investment. These should be controllable and should relate to the value you add to the product. The costs named in the list above are a basis; you may want to add others depending on the type of business being analyzed. In some businesses, the cost of engineering, applications support, and servicing are applicable and fit our definition of controllable, value-added costs.

Remember that you need these costs on a *unit* basis, although they may have been collected in a different manner, such as by department or allocated joint costs between products. It is necessary to spend time understanding the accounting methods used to prepare the costs in order to get your data in an appropriate form.

The unit you choose to analyze is a key factor in applying the experience curve. It is possible that one measure will not show the experience effect but a different unit for the same business will. For example, data on airplane manufacturing costs failed to demonstrate the experience curve but data on passenger seat miles did. If you do not see the effect the first time, think about a different way to cut the data.

If you are calculating an experience curve for an entire industry, weight the cost data for each company by the company's accumulated volume to develop industry cost. Industry accumulated volume is simply the sum of individual company accumulated volumes.

Sometimes it is impossible to locate cost data, especially if you are outside the subject company looking in or trying to calculate an experience curve for an industry rather than for one company. Price data may be used as surrogates when cost data are unavailable. Like any surrogate, they are less than perfect since costs and prices may not run exactly in parallel (remember our three pricing cases from before), but price will give you some indication of the trend in the industry.

We will use price data in our integrated circuit example because costs are not available.

	Nominal Dollars	Unit Price, Constant 1972 Dollars*
1964	$18.50	$25.41
1965	8.33	11.20
1966	5.05	6.57
1967	3.32	4.20
1968	2.33	2.82
1969	1.67	1.92
1970	1.49	1.63
1971	1.27	1.32
1972	1.03	1.03

* Source: Electronic Industries Association.

Step 2. Convert the Data to Logarithms

The experience curve calculation requires the use of logarithms (see Appendix 9B for an explanation). We will convert our data on accumulated volume and unit price to logs now and have them available for calculations later on. Conversion can be done with the log table in the back of the book or even more easily with a calculator that has a log function.

	Cumulative Volume	Log of Cumulative Volume	Unit Price, Constant 1972 Dollars	Log of Price
1964	2.2	.79	$25.41	3.24
1965	11.7	2.46	11.20	2.42
1966	41.1	3.72	6.57	1.88
1967	109.7	4.70	4.20	1.44
1968	243.6	5.50	2.82	1.04
1969	497.2	6.21	1.92	0.65
1970	797.2	6.68	1.63	0.49
1971	1,160.2	7.06	1.32	0.28
1972	1,763.8	7.48	1.03	0.30

Source: Electronic Industries Association.

Step 3. Plot the Data

We are now ready to plot the data on a graph. The above data points produce a curve when connected and drawn on linear paper; they produce a straight line when drawn on log paper. Exhibit 9.3 is done on a linear scale and therefore produces a curve.

We will plot the same data on log paper to convert the curve to a straight line, an important step for our analysis. Chapter 17 contains a discussion of log paper and its use.

The horizontal x axis represents the product's accumulated volume over time. The vertical y axis represents unit cost or price for each year in which we have a measure of accumulated volume. You use linear data to draw the graph but log paper to show the straight-line relationship.

Summarize the data to be graphed in one table.

	Cumulative Volume	Unit Price, Constant 1972 Dollars
1964	2.2	$25.41
1965	11.7	11.20
1966	41.1	6.57
1967	109.7	4.20

	Cumulative Volume	Unit Price, Constant 1972 Dollars
1968	243.6	2.82
1969	497.2	1.92
1970	797.2	1.63
1971	1,160.2	1.32
1972	1,763.8	1.03

Source: Electronic Industries Association.

Label the x axis "Accumulated volume in units" and the appropriate cycles to fit your data. Label the y axis "Real unit cost" or "Real unit price" and the scale in dollars and cents.

Start plotting points from the most distant time to the present. We will begin in 1964 by moving across the x axis to 2.2 million units and up the y axis to $25.41. Repeat this procedure for the other years of data, in our case to 1972. We now have nine data points plotted, lying more or less in a straight line. Contrast this with the same data plotted on a linear scale and notice how the points have straightened out because of the logs, lying almost in a line.

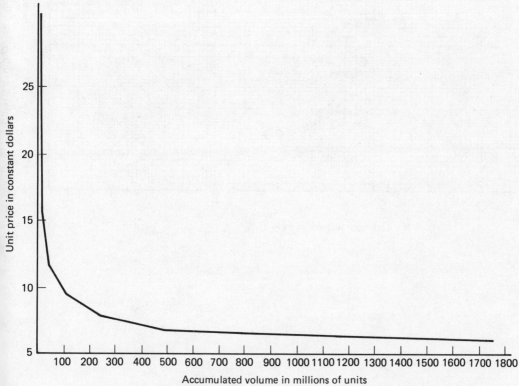

Exhibit 9.3 Integrated Circuits Experience Curve on Linear Scale, 1964–1972.

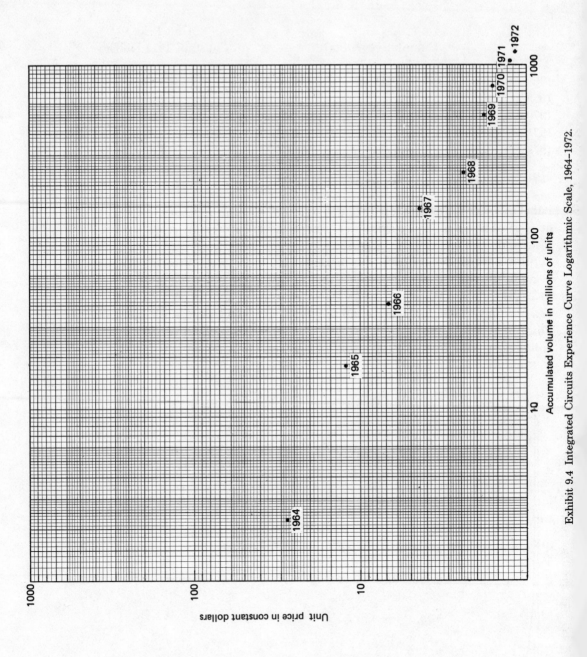

Exhibit 9.4 Integrated Circuits Experience Curve Logarithmic Scale, 1964-1972.

134

Step 4. Connect the Points

We can draw a straight line to connect the points of data and miss only a few points not directly in our path. This form of visual inspection is an easy but imprecise method. Data never lie exactly in a straight line, but we can "fit" a line by "eyeballing" a path that reduces the number of outlying points and their distance from the line. If you think this sounds like the lead in to a pitch for linear regression, you're right.

We must exercise some judgment to draw a good line visually, minimizing the number and distance of the points off the line. Everyone's estimate will differ slightly, so it is conceivable that a number of lines will represent these data.

By using linear regression, we can find the best straight line statistically. A linear regression for the experience curve must be done using logarithmic data. Since we have already converted our original linear data to logs, it is a simple matter to use logs in the regression. Appendix 9A takes you through a regression example with logs.

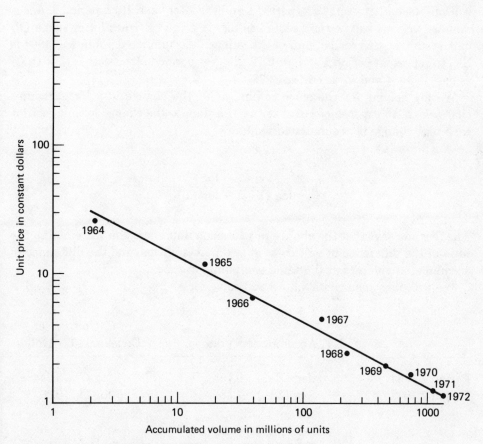

Exhibit 9.5 Possible Integrated Circuits Experience Curve on Logarithmic Scale, 1964–1972.

Step 5. Read Off End Points

Now that we have drawn a line, we can choose the two most distant points for use in our equation. The reason we want two *distant* points is to minimize the error. We may choose two years of actual data, such as 1964 and 1972 in our example, or we may extend the line past our real data and read off the x and y values even further out. To keep things simple, we will use 1964 and 1972 data.

	Accumulated Volume	Unit Price, Constant 1972 Dollars
1964	2.2	$25.41
1972	1,763.8	1.03

Step 6. Find the Slope of the Line

We will now introduce some mathematical notation for our values above. We will call the earlier year, 1964, period 1 and the later year, 1972, period 2. Accumulated volume will be represented as Sigma ΣV. The Greek letter sigma (Σ) means sum, so this reads "sum of the values." Accumulated volume in 1964 is ΣV_1 to represent period 1 and, in 1972, ΣV_2 for period 2. Unit cost is C, with C_1 as cost in 1964 and C_2 as cost in 1972.

We are solving for the slope (alpha, α) or the change in y for each unit change in x. In experience curve terms, the slope is the change in unit cost for each unit change in accumulated volume.

Our formula is

$$\alpha = \frac{\log C_2 - \log C_1}{\log (\Sigma V_2) - \log (\Sigma V_1)}$$

The formula says that the change in y for each unit change in x is equal to the ratio of the difference in unit costs at two points in time and the difference in accumulated volumes at the same two points in time.

We will plug in our data values and solve for α.

	ΣV, Accumulated Volume		C, Unit Price, Constant 1972 Dollars	
Period 1 1964	$\log (\Sigma V_1)$	0.79	$\log C_1$	3.24
Period 2 1972	$\log (\Sigma V_2)$	7.48	$\log C_2$	0.30

$$\alpha = \frac{\log C_2 - \log C_1}{\log (\Sigma V_2) - \log (\Sigma V_1)}$$

$$\alpha = \frac{0.30 - 3.24}{7.48 - 0.79}$$

$$= \frac{-2.94}{6.69}$$

$$= -0.4395$$

Notice that our C_2 value is smaller than C_1, as we would expect because the theory says costs drop as volume increases. This gives us a negative number in our answer, which tells us the slope goes downward from left to right, again consistent with the fact that our costs drop as volume increases. (See Exhibit 9.6.)

Step 7. Calculate the Experience Curve

The experience curve is a special case of the formula we have just used because it is defined as the relationship between cost and volume when accumulated volume has doubled. The slope we just calculated does not assume any volume relationships over time. There is a mathematical proof that shows that when you make volume in period 2 equal to 2 times the volume in period 1, the ratio of cost in the two time periods equals 2^α. Rather than taking you through the math to get to this conclusion, you only need to remember one fact: *The slope of an experience curve when accumulated volume has doubled equals 2^α.*

Since we have already calculated α, we need only to raise the base 2 to the exponent α.

In our example, α is -0.4395. Therefore, $2^\alpha = 2^{-0.4395}$, or 0.7374. This is rounded to 0.74 and is known as a 74% experience curve.

What does this number mean? It says that each time accumulated volume of the product doubles, costs drop by 26%—100% minus the experience curve percentage. Note that the lower the experience curve designation, the greater the

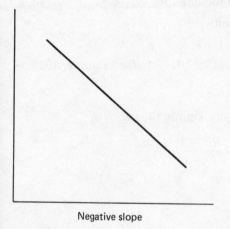

Negative slope

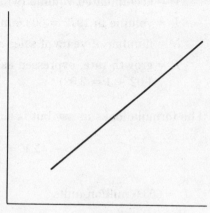

Positive slope

Exhibit 9.6

drop in costs. A 70% experience curve means cost has dropped 30%, while an 80% curve means cost has only dropped 20%.

Suppose you have worked through the calculations this far and fail to see the expected drop in costs. Why might this happen? The explanation could be that you have not defined the unit of experience properly (airplanes versus passenger seat miles in the earlier example), or that the company or industry has not taken the right steps to cause the cost decline to occur. Remember that the curve does not just happen; the effect must be managed. Some other causes of blips in the curve or a slower than expected decline are (1) changes in the product mix so that there is a different overall cost structure, (2) an improvement in product quality, (3) difference in capacity utilization over the period, or (4) shared experience in the manufacture of one component making it difficult to quantify costs properly.

ESTIMATING ACCUMULATED VOLUME

All too often, data on volume are not available back to the first year of production, so it becomes impossible to develop accumulated volume for use in the calculations. The best method to estimate accumulated volume is by applying the company's market share to historical industry data. If either of these numbers is unavailable, the second choice is to use a formula if we know (1) the volume sold in a particular year, (2) the number of years of sales that year represents, and (3) the average growth rate for all those years.

We will use the integrated circuit data so we can compare our estimate with the real answer. Sales in 1972, the ninth year of production, were 603.6 million units. The average growth rate over the nine years was 102%. We will assign some mathematical notation to our values.

ΣV = accumulated volume (what we're looking for)

L = volume in 1972 = 603.6 million units

N = number of years of sales = 9

R = growth rate, expressed as a percent of 100 + 1 (for example, 102% = 1.02 + 1 = 2.02)

The formula looks messy but is actually very simple to use.

$$\Sigma V = \frac{L}{R^{N-1}} \times \frac{R^N - 1}{R - 1}$$

L = 603.6 million units

N = 9 years

R = 2.02 growth

We are ready to plug the data into the formula. Substitute the numeric value for each letter on the right hand side.

$$\Sigma V = \frac{603.6}{2.02^{9-1}} \times \frac{2.02^9 - 1}{2.02 - 1}$$

Work on the second term of the equation:

1. Take 2.02 to the power of 9 on your calculator.

$$2.02^9 = 560.0$$

2. Subtract one from the terms on the top and bottom.

$$\frac{560 - 1}{2.02 - 1} = \frac{559}{1.02}$$

3. Divide.

$$\frac{559}{1.02} = 548$$

We have simplified the formula to this:

$$\Sigma V = \frac{603.6 \times 548}{2.02^{9-1}}$$

4. Now go to the first term. Take 2.02 to the power of $9 - 1$, or 8, on your calculator.

$$2.02^8 = 277.2$$

5. Divide the term.

$$\frac{603.6}{277.2} = 2.18$$

6. Multiply by the second term, 548.

$$2.18 \times 548 = 1194.6$$

Our answer is 1,195 million units of accumulated volume since the first year of sales nine years ago. This estimate will be as good as our estimate of the growth rate over the last nine years. Since we used real data, we can compare 1,195 to the actual accumulated volume in 1972, 1,763.8, and notice the sizable difference in results. This occurred because our 6% CAGR was not especially accurate, pointing to one of the hazards of the estimation method. Had we calculated a growth rate by drawing a linear regression line first, we would have come closer to the mark.

THE PRICE EXPERIENCE CURVE

Let us assume that you have obtained cost data for your company and are able to calculate the cost experience curve. It is useful to go a step further and plot the industry price experience curve so you can compare your costs to industry pricing. Industry prices also follow an experience curve pattern, generally with a 70% to 80% slope. By examining the spread between costs and prices, you can make some assumptions about the future of the business. If your costs are far beneath prices and there is a large profit margin, the industry will look attractive to outsiders and you may find a number of new entrants ruining the margins for everyone. This is the time to drop prices so that newcomers with higher costs will find it harder to participate. If there is a small spread between costs and prices, the industry will probably not look attractive to new competitors and you can assume status quo.

The price experience curve plots unit prices in constant dollars against industry accumulated experience. In contrast, the cost experience curve plots unit costs in constant dollars against company accumulated experience. Plot both curves on the same graph to see the relationship. It should take the form of one of the patterns we discussed before. (See Exhibit 9.7.)

USES OF THE EXPERIENCE CURVE

Now that you know how to calculate an experience curve, let us review the uses it has in strategic planning:

It can provide insight into competitors' market strategy. The low-cost producer will probably defend share far more vigorously than another competitor since it has more to lose and can afford to finance the war.

It can help you forecast prices and revenue and develop long-run pricing policies.

It can help evaluate the benefit of proposed capital expenditure in terms of cost reduction and competitive standing.

It can help you see how well you have managed costs and evaluate new cost-cutting proposals.

It can help you predict future market positions.

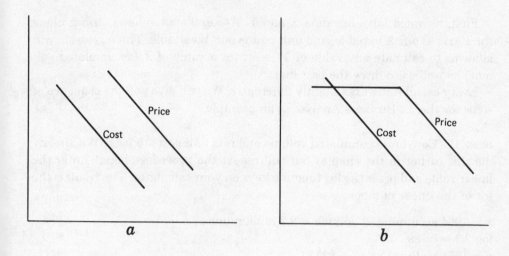

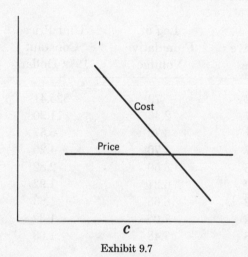

Exhibit 9.7

It can help you make more informed decisions about killing a product based on shared-experience effects.

It can help predict how fast suppliers' prices should drop.

APPENDIX 9A: LINEAR REGRESSION ON LOGARITHMIC DATA

There is really no difference between doing a linear regression on linear data and doing it on log data, except for the data themselves. The procedure is exactly the same as the one outlined in Chapter 6 except that we convert the data to logs.

First, we must label our data X and Y. Accumulated volume, drawn along the x axis, is our X variable, and unit cost is our Y variable. The regression will allow us to estimate any value of Y (cost) for a value of X (accumulated volume) as well as to draw the best line.

Every calculator works slightly differently. We will give you the sequence of steps for the TI Business Analyst as an example.

STEP 1: Convert accumulated volume and real unit costs to logs. (We already did this earlier in the chapter but will repeat the procedure here.) Enter the linear value and press the log function keys on your calculator. The result is the log of the linear number.

x = 1964 accumulated volume = 2.2 million units
log 2.2 = 0.789
y = 1964 real unit price = \$25.41
log 25.41 = 3.235

Repeat this procedure for all the data.

	Cumulative Volume	Log of Cumulative Volume	Unit Price, Constant 1972 Dollars	Log of Price
1964	2.2	.79	\$25.41	3.24
1965	11.7	2.46	11.20	2.42
1966	41.1	3.72	6.57	1.88
1967	109.7	4.70	4.20	1.44
1968	243.6	5.50	2.82	1.04
1969	497.2	6.21	1.92	0.65
1970	797.2	6.68	1.63	0.49
1971	1,160.2	7.06	1.32	0.28
1972	1,763.8	7.48	1.03	0.03

Source: Electronic Industries Association.

STEP 2: Set the calculator on the statistical mode.

STEP 3: Enter the first logarithmic X value and its corresponding logarithmic Y value and press a special function button after each.

$$x = 0.789, y = 3.235$$

Repeat for all values of X and Y in pairs, from 1964 to 1972.

STEP 4: Press two buttons to find the Y intercept of the regression line the calculator computed. The intercept is the point where the line crosses the y axis and $X = 0$. This will make it easy to draw the line correctly. Convert the y intercept back to a linear number. We are using linear values to plot on the graph, not to calculate the regression.

$$\log Y \text{ intercept} = 3.62$$
$$\text{linear } Y \text{ intercept} = 37.34$$

STEP 5: Enter a *linear X* value that is not in your original data, press a button, and its corresponding Y value appears.

$$X = 100 \text{ million units accumulated volume}$$
$$Y = \$4.37$$

STEP 6: You now have two new points that resulted from the regression, $x = 0$, $y = 37.34$, and $x = 100$, $y = 4.37$. Two points are all that are needed to draw a line. Plot these points on the graph and draw the regression line of best fit.

Notice how nicely you can use this line to predict cost at a future accumulated volume. Suppose you expect accumulated volume to reach 3,500 in five years and would like to know unit costs assuming the experience curve relationship holds. You can either extend your line to 3,500 units on the x axis and read off the Y value to get the cost per unit, or feed the value of 3,500 into the regression and have the calculator compute cost for you.

APPENDIX 9B: LOGARITHMS

Believe it or not, logarithms were introduced to simplify mathematical calculations back in 1614. Logs allow you to replace multiplication by addition, division by subtraction, find a power or exponent by simple multiplication, and find a root by division. Thus, it becomes relatively easy to solve a complex equation like this:

$$M = \sqrt{6{,}800^4 \times 0.041}$$

With logs, the equation becomes

$$\log M = \frac{4 \, (\log 6{,}800) + \log 0.041}{2}$$

You do not need to understand the rules and reasons why such a transformation can be done for our purposes: you should simply know that logs make calculations easier. The basic principle is that any number can be expressed as a power of 10 in our system. The powers (exponents) are the logs. For example, use your calculator to take 10 to the power of 0.301.

$$10^{.301} = 1.9999 = 2$$

The number 2 is the same as $10^{.301}$. Since we have said that the exponents of 10 are logs, 0.301 is the log of 2, written *log* 2.

A logarithmic table is a listing of all the exponents of 10 for each linear (regular) number. If you want to find the log for a linear number, go down the table for the linear number and read off the log across the horizontal line. This will be the exponent of 10 for that number. If you want to convert from log to linear, look for the log inside the table and read back to the marginal number, its linear equivalent. A logarithmic table is reproduced here. Most calculators do this work for you; consult your instruction book to see if yours will.

PART

The Financial Perspective

The next chapters add the other side of the picture, hard numbers that balance what we learned from market position. There are many clues to strategy in the financial health of a business. When added to market dynamics, they begin to draw us a clear picture.

10

How Financial Analysis Fits into Corporate Planning

The next few chapters of this book deal with the application of graphic techniques to financial analysis of the company. Up until now, we have focused on market characteristics—relative market share, growth rate, and competitive position. We are going to broaden our perspective to take into account financial characteristics of the firm. How does this all tie together?

Let's go back to the concepts we have already discussed. Research has found a high correlation between market share and return on investment. We have talked about how it is easier to gain market share when an industry is growing rapidly and there is room for all competitors. The strategy is to gain market share early so that you can accumulate experience faster than competition, come down the cost curve, and have more room to maneuver later on because of a superior cost structure.

Theory behind the growth–share matrix says that businesses with different market shares and growth rates need different amounts of cash to fund their growth. The higher the growth rate, the more cash is needed. Question marks are the biggest users of cash because they are high in growth but low in relative market share and therefore lack the cost advantages of a high-share business. Stars are the second-biggest cash users because of high growth, but their correspondingly high market share and lower costs act as a counterbalance so they do not need as much cash as a question mark. Cows are cash generators be-

147

* Cash used − − − Generated + + Net 0, −	**?** Cash used − − − Generated + + Net −
Cow Cash used − − − Generated + + + + + Net + +	**Dog** Cash used − Generated + + Net 0, +

Exhibit 10.1

cause they have high relative market share but are growing slowly and no longer have voracious cash appetites. Dogs may net out zero in cash used versus cash generated or may generate enough cash to fund some new ventures. A study of the PIMS data base found that cows have an average positive cash flow of 9% and question marks have a negative 3%, confirming the theory.*(See Exhibit 10.1.)

What determines the growth of a business? One variable is market demand and the company's ability to respond with products desired by the marketplace. The second variable is financial, the ability of the business to generate or obtain enough cash to satisfy the business's needs. We will talk about the financial variable in more depth.

FINANCIAL LEVERAGE: WHY WE LOOK AT DEBT TO EQUITY

Financial leverage refers to the idea of using borrowed money to make money for the owner's capital. As long as the business earns more than the after-tax cost of interest paid on borrowed money, shareholders will benefit from the use of debt. A profitable business that has no debt or a level far beneath the industry is not benefiting its shareholders by financing everything through equity.

We can define profit as the return on equity multiplied by the equity base employed. If there is no debt and all earnings are reinvested in the business, the rate of growth of the business will equal return on equity or the dollars the

* Bradley T. Gale and Ben Branch, "Cash Flow Analysis: More Important Than Ever," *Harvard Business Review*, July–August, 1981.

business produced. Here is the example of such a business with a return on equity of 20%. Note that return on equity equals return on assets because all assets were financed with equity.

Total assets	$1,000
Equity	100%
Return on assets and equity	20%
Profit	$ 200
Reinvest	200 = 20% = growth rate

Most financial managers would shun this capital structure as overly conservative. The addition of debt can lever both the return on equity and the growth rate. Let us assume that we finance our $1,000 of assets half by equity and half by debt. Our equity investment drops from $1,000 to $500, half the original amount. We must pay interest on the debt, reducing our profit, but the much lower equity investment means that return on equity will increase.

Total assets	$1,000
Equity	50%
Debt	50%
Profit	$ 200
Interest on debt (15%) = 500 × 0.15 =	$ 75
Profit after interest	$ 125

$$\text{Return on assets} \quad = \quad \frac{125}{1,000} \quad = \quad 12.5\%$$

$$\text{Return on equity} \quad = \quad \frac{125}{500} \quad = \quad 25.0\%$$

We reinvest our profit of $125 in the business, but since we have decided to finance by 50% debt we match the $125 in equity with $125 in debt. We have now reinvested $250 in the business, enough to sustain a 25% growth rate next year instead of 20% with an all-equity capital structure. The leverage we have gained with debt financing is significant because it gives our shareholders a better return on their money and lets us grow one and three-quarters times as fast as a competitor without debt. We pay a price in risk—the more interest we owe, the more return we must generate to be able to pay the obligation. Financial managers constantly balance the tradeoffs between risk and reward. The meaning of the use of leverage is important to comparing two different companies and understanding their rates of growth. For this reason, we always look at some form of a debt–equity ratio. A company that has a lot of debt may be able to accept a lower profit margin because return of equity will still be high enough to satisfy the shareholders. The company may be able to pay more for assets and gain capacity faster than competition or maintain a higher growth

rate than the industry. As long as the focus is return on equity rather than return on sales, the company will have more freedom to use its earnings for
growth purposes than unlevered competitors.

DIVIDENDS

Our example has not taken into account the payment of dividends to stockholders. We will see that a liberal dividend policy reduces the amount of earnings available for reinvestment and decreases the growth rate of the business.
Assume that the first company we looked at, the all-equity structure, decided
to pay half of its profit out in dividends.

Total assets	$1,000
Equity	100%
Profit	$ 200
Pay dividends at 50% of profit	100
Reinvest remainder	$ 100 = 10% of assets

The payment of 50% of profits in dividends took 50% of the reinvestment dollars away from the company. The company can now grow only at 10% a year
instead of 20% a year when it paid no dividends. A company that does not pay
dividends is at a competitive advantage over a company that does. When you
look at the use of debt leverage and dividend payments together, you can begin
to get a clearer picture of the rate of growth possible for a company. It may be
possible to grow rapidly with a high dividend payout, but the return on assets
or level of debt must be very high to compensate. We will look at dividend
payout rates for our financial analysis.

CALCULATING A COMPANY'S GROWTH RATE

Using these concepts, we can calculate the maximum rate of growth possible
for a firm if we have four pieces of information:

1. Debt-to-equity ratio
2. Return on assets
3. Interest rate paid on debt
4. Dividend payout (or percentage of earnings retained)

A company can grow in line with the amount of reinvestable profits it generates. This is the same as saying that the growth rate is equal to return on equity if no dividends are paid and after we have paid the interest on debt. If we

define profit as return on total assets minus interest on debt, we can, with substitution and algebraic manipulation, define the growth rate as:

Growth rate = Debt to equity × (Return on assets − Aftertax interest rate) ×
            Percentage of retained earnings + Return on assets × Percentage of retained earnings

This formula takes into account profits, debt, and dividend payout, all the factors that influence the growth of a company. It says that growth is a function of returns minus the amount spent on interest, which represents profit, times the percentage of these profits retained in the business and not paid out in dividends, times financial leverage, plus the profit kept in the business.

In symbolic form, the formula reads:

$$g = D/E \ (r - i)p + rp$$

where g = rate of growth
D = debt
E = equity
r = return on assets
i = interest rate
p = percentage of retained earnings

Company X's 1981 data may be substituted into the formula:

Debt-to-equity ratio (D/E) = 1.34
ROA (r) = 4.1%
Interest rate on debt (i) = 6.6% aftertax
   (derived by dividing $3.65 million interest into $27.031 in long-term debt, multiplied by 1 minus the corporate tax rate)
Percentage of earnings retained (p) = 62% (1 − payout ratio)

$$g = D/E \ (r - i)p + rp$$
$$g = 1.34 \ (0.041 - 0.066) \ 0.62 + (0.066) \ (0.62)$$
$$g = 0.021 + 0.041 = 0.020\%$$

Company X's maximum sustainable growth rate is 2.0%. The trouble lies in the first term, showing the company is paying more in interest than it is generating in returns. In order to turn the situation around, Company X needs to reduce its debt and/or increase its return. The existing financial structure says that the company can grow only 2% a year.

We can play with this formula to test some scenarios. Suppose we reduced dividend payout from 38% to 25%? What if our interest rate were cut in half?

Suppose we paid the same interest rate but had less debt, reducing our debt-to-equity ratio? By substituting our assumptions in the formula, we can test the results of each of these moves separately or in combination.

A company can select the means by which it will finance growth through manipulation of the mix of variables—rate of return on assets, leverage, and dividend payout. An empirical study has shown that some variables are more sensitive than others.* The greatest contributor to growth is return on assets, followed by dividend policy. The influence of dividend policy is an interesting finding because dividend payout is easily controllable by the firm, while the return is not so simple to change. Debt to equity and interest rates do not have as great an impact on growth as the first two variables, suggesting that small increases in debt or interest rates will not make a major difference.

What does this mean for financial analysis? Two conclusions can be drawn:

Returns and dividend payout are keys to analyzing the potential growth of a firm.

Debt is a factor, but a secondary one.

Keep these in mind as we look at the key financial ratios in later chapters.

Let us return to some of the implications of these relationships.

A company must generate at least enough funds to grow with the industry or else it will lose share. If an industry grows at 20% a year, our company must earn 20% in reinvestable profits just to stay even and to add enough capacity to meet the demand. *Reinvestable* profits means:

Aftertax

After interest payments (or no debt)

After dividend payments (or no dividends)

This is why we call high-growth businesses cash users. They cannot afford to contribute anything to the corporate coffers and probably have to rely on a cash infusion unless they have tremendously high margins (40% pretax for a 20% aftertax return). If you are trying to gain market share, you must invest in marketing and other expenses that rarely leave you flush with cash profits.

Financial strategy can be important to consolidating a high-share position in a growth industry. A firm that uses debt aggressively and withholds dividends may be able to cut price and finance higher growth, solidifying its position early in the product life cycle. Return on sales alone may be a poor indicator of the attractiveness of a business.

Some businesses may be successful early in the game but fail to reinvest their earnings or invest in poorly chosen assets. These mistakes cause trouble in later life and make the company unable to fulfill its dividend commitments

---

* Gary Sprakkman, *Effective Use of Financial Goals in Planning*, Managerial Planning, July/August 1980, p. 16.

to shareholders as the business matures. Retained earnings, or profits built up during the growth phase that were not reinvested, should be paid out to shareholders in dividends only when earnings and depreciation are greater reinvestment needs. As a business matures and growth slows down, a company may use more debt as its business risk declines and it may generate enough cash to pay dividends. The market leader needs the least debt because its margins are best through the cost experience curve. A marginal firm will still be highly leveraged and unable to pay dividends.

FINANCIAL MANAGEMENT OF A PORTFOLIO

A company with a portfolio of businesses has options that a single-line company does not. It can balance cash-generating businesses with cash-using businesses, for the greater good of the whole. One division can borrow from another without having to worry about going to the financial markets or generating enough cash itself to finance growth. A diversified company chooses which businesses to grow and how to finance that growth. Strategists must decide on the role each business is to play—cash generator or growth generator. The two are incompatible.

We go back to the growth–share matrix. Market share and growth position a business on the matrix, with each quadrant having associated cash characteristics. The movement of cash comes from our financial strategy, which is to use cash generators to fund cash users. Over time, we hope that the users become generators ready to fund the next generation of businesses.

$$+,0,- = \text{cash generation}$$
$$\text{Arrows} = \text{flow of cash}$$

Why do we care about the cash flow of a business? Companies can look terrific on paper but be on the verge of bankruptcy because they have run out of cash. Cash flow is a critical measure of financial health.

Strategy can help us control cash flow. We know from the research that businesses in fast-growth markets absorb cash and those in slow-growth markets throw off cash. Inflation is generally accompanied by decreased cash as rising costs offset rising prices, and it is necessary to tie up money in inventory and accounts receivable. When investment is increased relative to sales, we see a reduction in cash flow. By controlling the strategic variables of growth and investment intensity, it is possible to control cash even in inflationary times.

CAVEATS

Financial analysis is an invaluable tool in divining what a company is all about, yet it is not perfect. First, because it is numerical, it cannot cover the qualita-

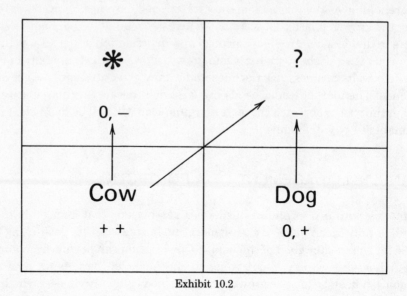

Exhibit 10.2

tive factors that influence a business. We can infer the qualitative from the quantitative. Second, differences in accounting practices from company to company make competitor analysis less accurate. Something as simple as a different depreciation or inventory valuation method can make one company look superior to another when in fact they are equal. Third, competitors are rarely in exactly the same businesses and we find ourselves comparing apples to oranges.

11

Where to Get Financial Data

Chapter 5 covered sources of information for market data on competition and industry growth rates that were needed to develop the market graphs. Financial data to prepare the financial graphs come from different sources:

1. Annual reports
2. 10Ks
3. Industry composite sources
4. Internal accounting data of your own company

Those of you who are financially proficient will probably want to skip ahead to the section on industry composite data. The rest of us will go for a review of the basic statements of a public company, the annual report and the 10K.

ANNUAL REPORTS

One of the best sources for information about a public company is its annual report, a document published once a year to inform shareholders and other interested parties about the company's performance. A report is typically divided into sections:

155

The chairman's letter to stockholders about the past year

Reports on operations, divided by group or division

Financial highlights for the past five or ten years

Financial statements for the past one to three years

The chairman's letter and reports on operations can be important for under-standing a company's thrust and gaining some insight into the financial results, but it should be remembered that the annual report is primarily a public rela-tions tool. The discussion of operations and results will contain the "party line" rather than being a balanced presentation of facts. We suggest using external sources to gain an understanding of the company's performance and using the annual report for its financial information.

Financial highlights for the past five or ten years are useful for looking at historical trends. The statement might include data from the balance sheet and income statement such as sales, operating income, net income, dividends per share, working capital, stockholder's equity, and long-term liabilities. There are two cautions:

1. Data abstracted in financial highlights vary from company to company so it can be difficult to do industry comparisons. There is no standard format for this section.

2. Only pieces of the whole are presented, so much information is excluded. The section is intended to show highlights and may leave out the detail you need. A solution to this problem is to use five years of annual reports for a company so all the income statement and balance sheet data are available historically.

The section headed "Financial Statements" generally includes four different items:

1. The income statement
2. The balance sheet
3. Statement of changes in financial position
4. Notes to the financial statements

Income Statement.   This is a presentation of sales or revenues for the year, the expenses incurred in generating those revenues, and the amount of income earned before and after taxes. (Sales − expenses = income − taxes = net in-come.) Net income is the figure most often used in determining a company's profitability, and it refers to aftertax income. This is the famous "bottom-line" number, so called because it sits on the bottom line of the Income Statement. The Income Statement covers performance over a 12-month period, ending on

EXHIBIT 11.1. Consolidated Statements of Income, Company *X*

For the years ended April 30th	1981	1980	1979
	All dollar amounts in thousands except per share data		
Net sales	$160,034	$159,449	$129,060
Other publishing income	5,915	5,352	6,795
Income from distribution services	4,283	2,314	1,233
Net operating revenues	170,232	167,115	137,088
Costs and expenses (Notes 1, 5 and 8):			
Cost of sales	80,672	79,895	65,719
Selling, editorial, general and administrative	74,290	72,974	62,110
	154,962	152,869	127,829
Income from operations	15,270	14,246	9,259
Other expenses	3,419	4,624	2,539
Income before income taxes	11,851	9,622	6,720
Provision for income taxes (Notes 1 and 6):			
Federal	4,781	4,171	2,905
State and local	1,276	1,035	725
	6,057	5,206	3,630
Net income	$ 5,794	$ 4,416	$ 3,090
Net income per share (Note 1)	$1.89	$1.44	$1.12

the last day of the company's fiscal year. Exhibit 11.1 shows company *X*'s Income Statement.

Balance Sheet. The Balance Sheet shows the company's financial position on one day only, the last day of the fiscal year. It shows company assets—what it owns—against company liabilities and shareholder equity—what it owes to other parties. One point of confusion may be why shareholder equity, the investment of the owners of the company (whether they are the founders or Aunt Nelly buying 10 shares on the NYSE), falls on the liability side of the Balance Sheet. Remember that liabilities are defined as claims against the company. A bank that lends money has a claim; similarly, an investor who buys equity in the firm by becoming a shareholder has a claim for the amount of stock he or she owns. It makes no difference whether the claim is debt, like a bank loan, or stock equity; the result is the same.

The Balance Sheet always must balance. This means the two sides are equal; total assets on the left-hand side must equal total liabilities and stockholders' investment on the right.

Think of the Balance Sheet as a record of everything the company owns and owes on the last day of the fiscal year. (Fiscal year is the 12-month period a company has chosen as its financial recordkeeping year; it may or may not be the same as the calendar year.) Assets—what is owned—must equal liabilities and shareholders' equity—what is owed. Company *X*'s balance sheet is shown in Exhibit 11.2.

EXHIBIT 11.2.   Consolidated Balance Sheets, Company X

Assets April 30th	1981	1980
	All dollar amounts in thousands	
Current Assets:		
Cash	$ 1,581	$ 3,224
Marketable securities, at cost which approximates market	29	635
Accounts and notes receivable, less allowances for doubtful accounts of $1,515 in 1981 and $2,830 in 1980 and estimated future returns of $6,116 in 1981 and $7,289 in 1980 (Note 1)	40,127	37,520
Inventories, at lower of cost (first-in, first-out) or market	35,608	39,764
Future tax benefits (Note 1)	4,589	7,880
Prepaid expenses	609	855
Total current assets	82,543	89,878
Property and Equipment, at cost (Notes 1, 5 and 6):		
Land and land improvements	1,174	1,118
Buildings	540	540
Machinery and equipment	8,602	8,013
Leaseholds and improvements	10,295	10,062
Less: accumulated depreciation and amortization	(9,033)	(8,147)
	11,578	11,586
Goodwill, less accumulated amortization of $1,276 in 1981 and $815 in 1980 (Notes 1, 2 and 3)	20,403	21,351
Royalty advances to authors	10,178	11,724
Plates, less accumulated amortization of $8,449 in 1981 and $7,302 in 1980	11,638	10,601
Other assets	849	1,515
	$137,189	$146,655

Liabilities and Stockholders' Investment April 30th	1981	1980
	All dollar amounts in thousands	
Current Liabilities:		
Notes payable and current portion of long-term debt (Note 3)	$ 2,840	$ 3,509
Accounts payable	16,362	14,827
Accrued royalties	7,225	7,499
Income taxes payable	3,509	6,379
Other accrued liabilities	9,695	12,277
Total current liabilities	39,631	44,491
Long-term Liabilities and Deferred Items:		
Long-term debt, less current portion (Note 3)	25,324	32,700
Unfunded vested pension liability of acquired company (Note 8)	1,971	2,198
Long-term royalties payable	1,299	2,043
Unearned subscription income	5,431	5,219
Deferred income taxes (Note 1)	1,010	1,073
	35,035	43,233

EXHIBIT 11.2. (cont.)

Stockholders' Investment (Notes 3 and 4):		
Common stock at par value of $.10 per share		
—authorized 5,000,000 shares		
—issued 3,197, 882 shares	320	320
Paid-in capital	22,933	22,933
Retained earnings	39,677	36,085
Less: treasury stock, at cost; 140,100 shares	(407)	(407)
Total stockholders' investment	62,523	58,931
	$137,189	$146,655

Statement of Changes in Financial Position. This statement used to be called "Sources and Uses of Funds," so if you are looking at old annual reports you may find that reference. It tells you from what sources the company got cash and working capital over the period of a year and to what uses it put the money. A company may have received funds from its operations and by selling off a division; it may have used money to expand its plant or pay down debt. The statement will tell you whether the company used more cash or working capital than it received in the year in an item called "Change in Working Capital (or Cash)." A company can present this statement in terms of working capital—the difference between current assets and current liabilities which gives its short-term liquidity position—or in cash terms. The theory behind showing working capital is that working capital represents the company's easily liquefiable position. Working capital items can be converted into cash within a year, so they are considered similar to cash. See Exhibit 11.3.

Notes to Financial Statements. These explain the company's accounting methods and will be of interest if you get into some of the more complicated types of analysis, need clarification on an accounting point, or want to equate several companies on a measure. Notes may include information on methods of depreciation, detail on the type and amount of long-term debt, type of stock issued, pension plans, and so on.

Business Segment Information. The information we have described up to now relates to the overall company's financial status. An important tool for analysis is information on individual business segments or lines of business within a company. We can look at company X's overall statements and still have no feel for how its textbooks are doing compared to general books or professional books. This is the information contained in business segment reporting, required of companies since the Financial Accounting Standards Board published statement FASB 14 in December 1976. FASB 14, to which all public companies must conform, instructs companies to select "significant" industry segments for special business line reporting. A significant segment is one which

EXHIBIT 11.3. Consolidated Statements of Changes in Financial Position, Company X

For the years ended April 30th	1981	1980	1979
	All dollar amounts in thousands		
Financial resources were provided by:			
Operations:			
Net income	$ 5,794	$ 4,416	$ 3,090
Expenses not affecting working capital:			
Depreciation and amortization	7,375	7,749	7,068
Amortization of goodwill	461	505	310
Deferred income taxes (decrease) increase	(63)	(334)	85
Working capital provided by operations	13,567	12,336	10,553
Other sources:			
Acquisition of Company Y (including working capital of $13,697 at the acquisition date), net	—	—	9,645
Decrease (Increase) in royalty advances to authors	1,546	1,126	(900)
Decrease (Increase) in other assets	666	(417)	(270)
Decrease in goodwill (Note 1)	487	1,330	—
Increase in unearned subscription income	212	287	1,366
Disposal of property, equipment and plates	103	1,763	217
	16,581	16,425	20,611
Financial resources were used for:			
Additions to property, equipment and plates	8,523	7,017	6,297
Decreases in long-term debt	7,376	2,981	2,048
Cash dividends paid	2,202	2,199	2,057
Decreases in long-term royalties payable	744	1,014	1,755
Other	211	(103)	(107)
	19,056	13,108	12,050
(Decrease) Increase in working capital	$(2,475)	$ 3,317	$ 8,561
(Decrease) Increase in components of working capital:			
Cash and marketable securities	$(2,249)	$ 676	$(4,748)
Accounts and notes receivable	2,607	(1,609)	15,302
Inventories	(4,156)	424	12,120
Future tax benefits	(3,291)	3,326	1,536
Prepaid expenses	(246)	(123)	431
Notes payable and current portion of long-term debt	669	(620)	161
Accounts payable	(1,535)	6,579	(9,235)
Accrued royalties	274	153	(2,334)
Income taxes payable	2,870	(5,376)	1,076
Other accrued liabilities	2,582	(113)	(5,748)
	$(2,475)	$ 3,317	$ 8,561

has either at least 10% of the total company revenues in it, 10% of operating profit of all segments that showed a profit or 10% of the loss of all segments that showed a loss, and/or 10% of the assets of the total company. Once identified as significant, the segment must report sales, operating profit or loss, assets, capital expenditures, and depreciation or amortization pertaining to it. The information can be shown in any one of three places: in the body of the financial statements, in the footnotes, or in a separate schedule of the statements. Information must be presented for three fiscal years.

Company X's business segment information is shown in Exhibit 11.4. It is a separate section presented after the financial statements and footnotes. Company X has chosen to divide its business into three groups: educational texts, general books, and professional books. As required by FASB 14, it shows data on revenues, operating profit, depreciation and amortization, assets, and capital expenditures (purchases of property, equipment, and plates).

10K

A second source of information that in many ways is more valuable than the annual report is the 10K, a document required of all public companies by the Securities and Exchange Commission under regulation S-K since December 1977. The purpose of the regulation is to standardize nonfinancial disclosures by companies. The 10K contains none of the glossy pictures and purple prose of the annual report. It is a straightforward black and white filing that is required to describe a company's business in detail and present financial statements. Few members of the general investing public ever see a 10K, which contains such interesting tidbits as the sources and availability of raw materials used in producing the company's products, importance of patents and trademarks to the business and when they expire, seasonality of sales, dependence on a small number of customers, dollar amount of firm backlog orders, how much of the business is in government contracts that can be terminated at will, competitive conditions and the basis of competition, the amount spent on R&D for new product development, number of employees, how much the directors make, and pending lawsuits. While this information is more complete than the annual report, it is still the party line, so don't let your senses become dulled by it. You must go to outside sources for a clear competitive picture.

Financial information about industry segments must cover a three-year period; selected financial data such as sales, income, assets, long-term obligations, and cash dividends per share must be presented for five years. Much of the financial information is the same as in the annual report but some of the schedules are more detailed. Company X presents information on its fixed assets in a more easily understandable and complete manner in the 10K than in the annual report. Compare Exhibits 11.5 and 11.6.

The treatment of competition is nonexistent in the annual report, but it is

EXHIBIT 11.4.   Business Segment Reporting

A summary of information about operations by segment for the fiscal years 1981, 1980 and 1979 follows:

	1981	1980	1979
	All dollar amounts in thousands		
Net operating revenues:			
Educational texts(1)	$ 60,379	$ 64,298	$ 50,929
General books(2)	68,786	65,516	61,832
Professional(3)	41,067	37,301	24,327
Total net operating revenues	$170,232	$167,115	$137,088
Operating profit:			
Educational texts(1)	$ 6,909	$ 9,220	$ 4,043
General books(2)	8,655	5,641	7,278
Professional(3)	3,599	2,787	792
Total operating profit	$ 19,163	$ 17,648	$ 12,113
General corporate expenses(4)	(4,354)	(3,906)	(3,164)
Interest expense	(3,654)	(4,518)	(2,677)
Other	696	398	448
Income before taxes	$ 11,851	$ 9,622	$ 6,720
Depreciation and amortization:			
Educational texts(1)	$ 3,278	$ 3,478	$ 3,421
General books(2)	2,474	2,739	2,491
Professional(3)	1,623	1,532	1,156
Total depreciation and amortization	$ 7,375	$ 7,749	$ 7,068
Purchases of property, equipment and plates:			
Educational texts(1)	$ 3,899	$ 2,622	$ 2,918
General books(2)	2,598	2,668	2,325
Professional(3)	2,026	1,727	1,054
Total purchases of property, equipment and plates	$ 8,523	$ 7,017	$ 6,297
Assets:			
Educational texts(1)	$ 35,174	$ 39,570	$ 42,569
General books(2)	49,637	50,742	54,306
Professional(3)	28,480	27,758	21,588
Corporate(5)	23,898	28,585	30,537
Total assets	$137,189	$146,655	$149,000

[1] Educational texts include primarily college and school product lines.
[2] General books include primarily trade, junior, religious and professional product lines.
[3] Professional includes primarily medical, criminal justice, and other professional product lines.
[4] General corporate expenses include compensation to corporate officers, legal and accounting fees, amortization of goodwill and other expenses not allocable to each segment.
[5] Corporate assets include cash, marketable securities, prepaid expenses, goodwill, a portion of future tax benefits applicable to purchase adjustments, and other.

EXHIBIT 11.5. Excerpt from Consolidated Balance Sheets, Company *X* (Annual Report)

Assets	April 30th	1981	1980
		All dollar amounts in thousands	
Current Assets:			
Cash		$1,581	$3,224
Marketable securities, at cost which approximates market		29	635
Accounts and notes receivable, less allowances for doubtful accounts of $1,515 in 1981 and $2,830 in 1980 and estimated future returns of $6,116 in 1981 and $7,289 in 1980 (Note 1)		40,127	37,520
Inventories, at lower of cost (first-in, first-out) or market		35,608	39,764
Future tax benefits (Note 1)		4,589	7,880
Prepaid expenses		609	855
Total current assets		82,543	89,878
Property and Equipment, at cost (Notes 1, 5 and 6):			
Land and land improvements		1,174	1,118
Buildings		540	540
Machinery and equipment		8,602	8,013
Leaseholds and improvements		10,295	10,062
Less: accumulated depreciation and amortization		(9,033)	(8,147)
		11,578	11,586
Goodwill, less accumulated amortization of $1,276 in 1981 and $815 in 1980 (Notes 1, 2 and 3)		20,403	21,351
Royalty advances to authors		10,178	11,724
Plates, less accumulated amortization of $8,449 in 1981 and $7,302 in 1980		11,638	10,601
Other assets		849	1,515
		$137,189	$146,655

handled in some detail in the 10K. Consider this statement from company *X*'s 10K:

The company competes directly with many other publishing firms, a substantial number of which have sales, assets, and resources in excess of those of the company. The company encounters substantial competition from more than 70 other publishers of elementary and high school textbooks, from approximately 60 other publishers of college textbooks, from approximately 250 other publishers of trade books, from approximately 150 other publishers of children's books, and from more than 200 other publishers of medical books and journals. . . . In general, the company believes that the quality of an individual product, the reputation of its author, the manner in which it is promoted, its price and other terms, and conditions relating to its sale are important competitive factors.

EXHIBIT 11.6. Company X, Accumulated Depreciation and Amortization of Plates and Property and Equipment (10K)

For the Year Ended April 30, 1981

Classification	Balance April 30, 1980	Additions Charged to Income	Retirements or Sales	Other Changes	Balance April 30, 1981
			Amounts in thousands		
Plates	$ 7,302*	$6,116	$5,013	$44	$ 8,449*
Property and Equipment:					
Owned—					
Land improvements	116	21	—	—	137
Buildings	145	17	—	—	162
Machinery and equipment	4,644	484	34	—	5,094
Leaseholds and improvements	629	121	—	—	750
Investment credit allowed for Federal income tax purposes	237	—	—	(28)	209
Leased—					
Buildings	1,306	143	—	—	1,449
Property under capital leases	1,070	473	311	—	1,232
	8,147	1,259	345	(28)	9,033
	$15,449	$7,375	$5,358	$16	$17,482

For the Year Ended April 30, 1980

Classification	Balance April 30, 1979	Additions Charged to Income	Retirements or Sales	Other Changes	Balance April 30, 1980
			Amounts in thousands		
Plates	$ 6,130*	$6,492	$5,369	$49	$ 7,302*
Property and Equipment:					
Owned—					
Land improvements	99	17	—	—	116
Buildings	127	18	—	—	145
Machinery and equipment	4,234	444	37	3	4,644
Leaseholds and improvements	565	89	25	—	629
Investment credit allowed for Federal income tax purposes	204	—	—	33	237
Leased—					
Buildings	1,178	151	—	(23)	1,306
Property under capital leases	885	538	376	23	1,070
	7,292	1,257	438	36	8,147
	$13,422	$7,749	$5,807	$85	$15,449

* Accumulated plate amortization plus applicable investment tax credits of $315 in 1981, $271 in 1980 and $225 in 1979, have been credited directly to the asset account in the consolidated balance sheets.

Remember, you are still reading the content that management wants you to read rather than an outsider's unbiased presentation. Even the 10K data must be taken with a grain of salt.

INDUSTRY COMPOSITE SOURCES

There are several widely used sources for comparative industry data. Dun & Bradstreet's *Key Business Ratios* is published annually and is based on a computerized financial statement file containing more than 800,000 public and private companies. D&B aggregates these data according to 800 lines of business listed by four-digit SIC code numbers. Manufacturing, retailing, wholesaling, mining, and construction industries are covered. The data are broken into four size ranges based on net worth as well as given in total.

A second source is Robert Morris Associates, a national association of bank loan and credit officers which publishes a volume called *Annual Statement Studies*. It is less well known in business circles than D&B, and in fact was designed for commercial bankers, but its data in some cases are better. It presents industry Balance Sheets and Income Statements as well as ratios. Organization is also by four-digit SIC code. Four years of history are given in addition to the present year's data. Both of these sources cost less than $50.

A third publication is based on IRS data. The *Almanac of Business and Industrial Financial Ratios* gives a more complete breakdown of statistics by company asset size (11 categories as opposed to four for the other two sources) but lacks currency. The 1983 Almanac is based on July 1978 through June 1979 statistics, "the most recent year for which authoritative figures derived from tax return data of the IRS are available." It may be a good source to compare with one or more of the others but is not timely enough to be used alone.

INTERNAL ACCOUNTING DATA

You should be able to obtain the best financial data from your own company because you have access to a great deal more detail and can work with the accountants to reformat the data for your needs. The ability to structure data close to the ideal will make analysis simpler than dealing with public data, someone else's idea of what you should know. Get to know an accountant in your finance department. Find out what data are available presently and how you might go back to a more disaggregated level to put together your own categories.

There is one axiom in analyzing a company's published statements: the information is never in the right form. Companies do not like to present greatly disaggregated data because it is too easy to reveal a serious problem area or a business with embarrassingly high profits that is funding mediocrity in the rest of the company. Instead, they package business units together, obscuring many of the individual dynamics. Internal reporting may provide the insight a planner needs but you can rarely obtain such numbers for any company besides your own. We used the example of Dart & Kraft earlier in discussing the wrong way to construct an SBU; now we can use it as an example of clever financial packaging. Dart's Tupperware, the seller of plastic housewares through the party plan, was incredibly profitable, the golden goose funding many of Dart's new ventures and dog businesses in the 1970s. In the late 1960s, the corporation acquired a direct sales cosmetics company, Vanda Beauty Counselors. Dart's plastics marketers knew nothing about the high-fashion cosmetics business and Vanda was a disaster from the beginning. Yet, financial reporting lumped the two companies, one highly profitable and the other a sea of red ink, into a "Direct Sales" group that showed a decent but unspectacular profit. Pity the analyst who tried to uncover Tupperware's or Vanda's true performance.

There are many ways to approximate the truth if the data do not appear in the needed form. We will cover some of these techniques in later sections and you will undoubtedly develop your own methodologies to augment these. You may wish to double check your approximation technique with a financial person to be certain you have not violated any major accounting principles. A general rule in manipulating data is to follow the accounting method outlined in the notes section of the annual report.

We have reviewed the primary data sources for gathering financial information on public companies and your own company. Before you begin the financial analysis graphs, you should have the following resources at your fingertips:

For all key competitors. Five years of financial statements from Annual Reports or 10Ks. Most recent 10K and Annual Report.

For your company (or focus company). Five years of income statement and balance sheet information; three to five years of LOB information.

Industry growth rate for relevant time period.

Don't cut any corners. You may think you can get away without the balance sheet for competitor *X* four years ago but you *will* need it. It will slow progress while you wait for the company to find the old annual report and send it out by slow boat.

We will begin our graphs with a focus on something dear to every businessperson: profitability.

12

Measuring a Business's Financial Standing: The Profitability Graphs

We will examine two graphs that focus on the profitability of individual lines of business within the corporation. These graphs should be developed for your company and competition so we can look for these relationships:

1. The profitability standing and financial characteristics of a particular competitive LOB within the overall corporate portfolio to assess the LOB's importance to the corporation.

2. A comparison between your company and competition on the profitability of a particular LOB.

Our discussion on the determinants of growth in Chapter 10 equated profitability with return on assets in a nonleveraged company or with return on equity in a leveraged company. We will use return on assets as the measure of profitability in these graphs.

Throughout these chapters on financial graphs, we will cover the relevant accounting concepts before getting into graphic execution because some of you may be a bit rusty on accounting lingo. Feel free to skip over this first section if you are a CPA graduated from the Wharton School or if you know accounting cold from some other exposure.

This reminds me of a story about Fred the Accountant.

A while ago I needed some accounting information to begin analysis for developing a Management Information System and I ended up in Fred's office. I stated my request in general terms and was met with disdain, "What do you know about accounting? Our system is very complicated and you can't just walk in and understand it. You'll never be able to understand the numbers and what they mean." In former days, I probably would have put my tail between my legs and backed out into the hallway, but this time I stood my ground and assured Fred that I knew enough. We began to trade information and my use of the lingo convinced him that I was worth talking to. Another point for buzz words! Financial analysis invariably involves accounting data, so you should be prepared to have a friendly conversation with the company accountant.

ACCOUNTING CONCEPTS

The accounting concepts we need to understand before we can work with the profitability graphs are:

Return on assets

Asset turnover

Operating income/margin

Return on Assets (ROA)

Assets are properties owned by a business that are of value and can be objectively measured at the time of acquisition. They can be divided into three categories: current assets, fixed assets, and other. *Current assets* are either presently in the form of cash or are able to be converted to cash within one year, such as marketable securities, accounts receivable, and inventories. *Fixed assets* are tangible properties of relatively long life that are used to produce goods and services in the business, rather than being held for resale. Examples are land, buildings, and equipment. *Other assets* do not fit into either of the first two categories and include items like long-term investments and goodwill, the amount paid above book value in acquiring a business.

Assets represent the investment in a business and are part of an important measure of return to the investor. Just as we wish to know the amount of interest our cash earns in a NOW account, we want to know how much money our investment in the assets of a business produced. Return on assets is the earnings of the business—net income—divided by the average asset base for the year. Because the balance sheet presents the amount counted on the last day of the year instead of a year's flow, we need to calculate the year's average level to make it compatible with the sales number that represents a full year's flows.

Take the balance sheet number for this year and last year, add them together, and divide by two to get the annual average.

$$\text{Return on assets} = \frac{\text{Net income}}{\text{Average total assets}}$$

It is possible to get distortions in ROA when comparing company to company or industry to industry. Imagine comparing a high-technology firm with a firm that makes capital machinery. The high-tech firm spends a lot of money on R&D to stay on top of the technology, while the equipment firm grinds out the same machine year after year, perhaps making minor improvements. Think about how much computers have changed in five years and how much tractors have changed in that period. The technology firm expenses its R&D—writes it off as an expense each year instead of considering it an asset like a machine—so its investment never shows on the balance sheet. Its true investment is greater than the balance sheet indicates because it has spent money on R&D. The equipment firm invests in building new plants and buying machines, items that go directly on the asset side of the balance sheet.

Now assume the two firms invest and earn equal amounts of money. The technology firm invests in non-balance-sheet items like R&D, and the equipment firm invests in assets that show on the balance sheet. Return on assets is higher for the high-technology firm since it is dividing the same profit by a lower asset base.

	High-Tech Firm	Capital Equipment Firm
Net income	$ 50 million	$ 50 million
R&D expense (nonasset)	65	15
Assets	335	385
Total investment	400	400
$\text{ROA} = \dfrac{\text{Net income}}{\text{Assets}}$	$\dfrac{50}{335} = 14.9\%$	$\dfrac{50}{385} = 13.0\%$

Asset Turnover

Asset turnover is a measure of the efficiency with which the firm is using its assets to generate sales. The purpose of investing in assets is to make the company a more efficient producer by increasing capacity or purchasing better equipment for manufacturing. Some firms invest poorly, selecting assets that become obsolete too quickly or otherwise fail to generate sales. The ratio is determined by dividing net sales for the period by average assets.

$$\text{Asset turnover} = \frac{\text{Net sales}}{\text{Average total assets}}$$

A high turnover ratio means the company is good at using its assets to generate sales. You can tell whether a ratio is high or low by comparing it with the ratio for the industry. Suppose asset turnover is 1.20, meaning that for every $1.00 invested in assets, $1.20 of product is sold. This number must be compared with the industry average to determine if it is high or low. If asset turnover is 0.85, every $1.00 investment in assets produced only $0.85 in sales. There can be no doubt that 0.85 is a poor turnover ratio because we are selling less than the amount invested.

What do you do if the asset turnover for two companies is widely different? There are a couple of possible explanations. Look at the age of the assets on the books. The older the assets, the lower their book value and the higher the asset turnover. Depreciation method can also make a difference. Companies using accelerated depreciation, a method of writing off more expense in the early years of owning an asset, will show a smaller asset base than companies using straight-line depreciation, a depreciation method where equal amounts are written off each year of the asset's life, and therefore will have higher asset turnover.

Operating Income/Margin

Operating income, sometimes called income from operations or operating profit, is the profit left after the expenses of operating the business have been deducted. It does not include income or expenses from nonoperating transactions such as the sale of an asset, income taxes, discontinued operations, extraordinary items, or changes brought about by a different method of accounting. Operating income does include sales of the business, the cost of goods sold to produce sales, the expense of the selling effort (marketing, advertising, sales force, shipping), and general and administrative expenses relating to the business including personnel, accountants, service people, planners, and other staff support.

Operating income will be shown for the corporation as a whole and for individual LOBs. The LOB level may include allocations for corporate overhead in addition to overhead within the business line. A company that has financial people and planners both in the business unit and at corporate would show two charges, one at each level. The purest measure of the profitability of an LOB excludes charges for corporate services and interest chargebacks for debt. The use of debt is a financial strategy that does not directly bear on the success of the business in producing income.

Operating margin is the ratio of operating income to net sales. We will use it as a measure of LOB profitability.

$$\text{Operating margin} = \frac{\text{Operating income}}{\text{Net sales}}$$

There is a relationship among the three measures we have just discussed: return on assets, asset turnover, and income. If we multiply the profit margin by asset turnover, we will have return on assets. Here is the formula we used before for return on assets:

$$\text{Return on assets} = \frac{\text{Income}}{\text{Average total assets}}$$

Let us see how we derived it from profit margin and asset turnover.

$$\text{Return on assets} = \text{Profit margin} \times \text{Asset turnover}$$

$$\text{Return on assets} = \frac{\text{Income}}{\text{Sales}} \times \frac{\text{Sales}}{\text{Average total assets}}$$

$$\text{Return on assets} = \frac{\text{Income}}{\text{Average total assets}}$$

Some companies, such as furniture stores, have high profit margins and low inventory turnover, while others, such as grocery stores, have high turnover and low profit margins on sales. Return on assets factors in both components and gives a more accurate picture of profitability than either measure alone.

THE GRAPHS

We have discussed the accounting concepts needed to create the profitability graphs and can move on to the first graph, using data from company X.

RETURN ON ASSETS

The return on assets graph shows the profitability of individual LOBs of a corporation or a number of different companies in the same industry. We will assume you are creating the graph at the LOB level first and will detail changes for a corporate-level graph at the end of the section. The graph uses the algebraic relationship between income and asset turnover to create return on assets. (See Exhibit 12.1.)

Asset Turnover: The Horizontal Axis

The horizontal x axis shows asset turnover for a historical time period. We have defined asset turnover as sales divided by two-year average total assets. Since we are working at the LOB level, sales and assets are business unit sales and assets rather than corporate totals. The business segment reporting section

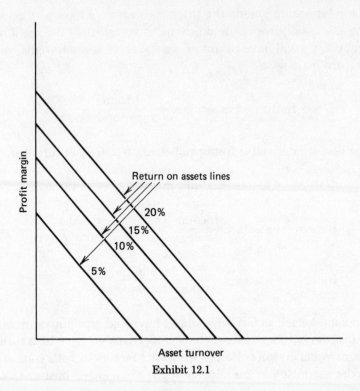

Exhibit 12.1

of the annual report contains data for individual LOBs as defined by the company. Company X's section is shown in Exhibit 12.2.

We will work with the three LOBs shown—educational texts, general books, and professional—rather than resegmenting as we did for the market graphs to get closer to true SBUs. The reason for this treatment is that there is no way to redefine the financial data into different segments.

STEP 1.   Go to the business segment reporting section of the subject company's annual report and copy (1) sales and (2) assets for each business line. We prefer to use at least a three-year average in all financial measures to avoid short-term distortions in the data, but we will perform our calculations on one year to keep the numbers simple. Remember that to determine average asset level for the year, we actually need two years of assets. We then take the two year-end numbers, add them, and divide for the year's average.

Company X FY 1981 in Thousands of Dollars

	Sales	Assets		
	1981	1980	1981	Average
Educational texts	$60,379	$39,570	$35,174	$37,372
General books	68,786	50,742	49,637	50,190
Professional	41,067	27,758	28,480	28,119

EXHIBIT 12.2.   Business Segment Reporting

A summary of information about operations by segment for the fiscal years 1981, 1980 and 1979 follows:

	1981	1980	1979
	All dollar amounts in thousands		
Net operating revenues:			
Educational texts(1)	$ 60,379	$ 64,298	$ 50,929
General books(2)	68,786	65,516	61,832
Professional(3)	41,067	37,301	24,327
Total net operating revenues	$170,232	$167,115	$137,088
Operating profit:			
Educational texts(1)	$ 6,909	$ 9,220	$ 4,043
General books(2)	8,655	5,641	7,278
Professional(3)	3,599	2,787	792
Total operating profit	$ 19,163	$ 17,648	$ 12,113
General corporate expenses(4)	(4,354)	(3,906)	(3,164)
Interest expense	(3,654)	(4,518)	(2,677)
Other	696	398	448
Income before taxes	$ 11,851	$ 9,622	$ 6,720
Depreciation and amortization:			
Educational texts(1)	$ 3,278	$ 3,478	$ 3,421
General books(2)	2,474	2,739	2,491
Professional(3)	1,623	1,532	1,156
Total depreciation and amortization	$ 7.375	$ 7,749	$ 7,068
Purchases of property, equipment and plates:			
Educational texts(1)	$ 3,899	$ 2,622	$ 2,918
General books(2)	2,598	2,668	2,325
Professional(3)	2,026	1,727	1,054
Total purchases of property, equipment and plates	$ 8,523	$ 7,017	$ 6,297
Assets:			
Educational texts(1)	$ 35,174	$ 39,570	$ 42,569
General books(2)	49,637	50,742	54,306
Professional(3)	28,480	27,758	21,588
Corporate(5)	23,898	28,585	30,537
Total assets	$137,189	$146,655	$149,000

[1] Educational texts include primarily college and school product lines.
[2] General books include primarily trade, junior, and religious product lines.
[3] Professional includes primarily medical, criminal justice, and other professional product lines.
[4] General corporate expenses include compensation to corporate officers, legal and accounting fees, amortization of goodwill and other expenses not allocable to each segment.
[5] Corporate assets include cash, marketable securities, prepaid expenses, goodwill, a portion of future tax benefits applicable to purchase adjustments, and other.

STEP 2.   Find asset turnover for each LOB by applying the formula:

$$\frac{\text{Sales}}{\text{Average assets}} = \text{Asset turnover}$$

Company X FY 1981 in Thousands of Dollars

	Sales	Average Assets	Asset Turnover
Educational texts	$60,379	$37,372	1.62
General books	68,786	50,190	1.37
Professional books	41,067	28,119	1.46

We can interpret asset turnover as saying that for each $1.00 of assets, educational texts produced $1.62 in sales, general books $1.37, and professional books $1.46. We know that a number less than $1.00 shows a poor use of assets because we are getting back less than the amount invested, but are the turnovers in company X's businesses "good" because they are over $1.00? The answer comes from a comparison with other companies and the industry overall.

Let us digress and look at an industry average to evaluate company X's turnover. Industry data on turnover are unavailable at the five- or seven-digit SIC level, so we must be content with the four-digit SIC that gives us the broad category "Book Publishing, Publishing and Printing." We would much prefer a finer breakdown that lets us look at textbooks, trade books (general books), and professional books separately, but such detail is unavailable from public data. An alternative is to develop an industry composite ourselves.

Robert Morris Associates' *Annual Statement Studies* for fiscal year June 1979 to March 1980 tells us that the publishing industry median for asset turnover was 1.8. Companies in the upper quartile had turnovers of 2.2, and companies in the lower quartile had turnovers of 1.4. Using these figures as a guide, company X's turnover is on the low end. However, we can wonder how applicable the industry numbers are to company X's specific businesses and should compare company X to some like competitors before making final judgment.

Operating Margin: The Vertical Axis

The vertical y axis measures the operating margin of the business. A multiyear average should be used to correspond to the asset turnover average and to correct for short-term fluctuations. We will stick with one year of data to keep the numbers simple here.

STEP 1.   Copy sales and operating profit for each LOB and divide to compute operating margin. Remember that operating margin is the best measure of business line profitability because it excludes charges out of the control of the business such as general corporate and interest expenses. Some analysts prefer to allocate corporate charges back to the business lines based on their percent of total profits, but this step does not add to the data's meaning since all units receive amounts in proportion to their profitability. We will stay with pure operating profit as our measure:

$$\text{Operating margin} = \frac{\text{Operating profit}}{\text{Sales}}$$

Company X FY 1981 in Thousands of Dollars

	Operating Profit	Sales	Operating Margin
Educational texts	$6,909	$60,379	11.4%
General books	8,655	68,786	12.6
Professional books	3,599	41,067	8.8

Representing the Business Line: Circle Size

Each line of business must be represented on the graph as a circle proportionate to the most current year's sales. The formula to determine circle size is:

$$\text{Circle size} = \text{Factor} \sqrt{\frac{\text{LOB sales}}{\text{Index sales}}}$$

STEP 1. Determine a sales index to represent a certain size circle. We will use sales of company X's largest business line, general books, as the index equal to a 50 mm circle. General books sales are $68,786.

STEP 2. Apply the formula to sales for other LOBs.

$$\text{Circle size} = 50 \sqrt{\frac{\text{LOB sales}}{68,786}}$$

Educational text sales = $60,379

$$\text{Circle size} = 50 \sqrt{\frac{60,379}{68,786}}$$

$$= 50 \sqrt{0.8778}$$

$$= 50 \times 0.9369$$

$$= 47$$

Professional books sales = \$41,067

$$\text{Circle size} = 50 \sqrt{\frac{41,067}{68,786}}$$

$$= 50 \sqrt{0.5970}$$

$$= 50 \times 0.7727$$

$$= 39$$

Our three LOB circle sizes are

Educational texts	47 mm
General books	50
Professional	39

Putting It Together: Graphing

STEP 1.   Gather the data to be graphed into one table.

Company X FY 1981 Summary Table

	Asset Turnover	Operating Margin	Circle Size
Educational texts	1.62X	11.4%	47 mm
General books	1.37	12.6	50
Professional books	1.46	8.8	39

STEP 2.   Outline the graph on 2×2 cycle log paper. The reason we use log paper is to straighten out the ROA line, which would plot as a curve on linear paper. Label the x axis "Asset turnover" with the years of data included. Label the intersection of the x and y axes 0.1, the end of the first-cycle 1X, and the end of the second-cycle 10X, filling in numbers in between. Label the y axis "Operating margin." The first cycle will go from 0% to 10% and the second cycle from 10% to 100%. Find a circle size that can serve as the scale representation.

$$\frac{\text{Index circle size}}{\text{Index sales}} = \frac{\text{Scale circle size}}{\text{Small sales number}}$$

$$\text{Index: } 50 \text{ mm} = \$68,786$$

$$\frac{50}{68,786} = \frac{X}{20,000}$$

$$68,786X = 1,000,000$$

$$X = 14.5, \text{ rounded up to } 15$$

Our scale will show a 15 mm circle equivalent to $20 million in sales.

STEP 3. Label the top of the graph with the company name, the period for which data are represented, and the name of the graph, "Return on Assets."

STEP 4. Draw ROA lines on the graph and label them. The meaning of the lines is that return on assets will equal the same amount any place along the line, at any combination of margin and asset turnover. A return on assets of 10% may be derived from a margin of 10% and $1X$ turnover, a margin of 1% and $10X$ turnover, or any combination in between. Remember the mathematic relationship between return on assets, margin, and asset turnover is

$$\text{Return on assets} = \text{Margin} \times \text{Asset turnover}$$

We will use this relationship to calculate the position of the ROA lines. Since our graph shows margin and turnover, we must be able to portray return on assets as the product of these two measures. We will provide you with a ready made shell graph with the return on assets lines already drawn. Read on if you are curious as to how we drew them; otherwise, skip to step 5.

Drawing ROA Lines

A line is determined by two points. We would like to draw lines for 5%, 10%, 15%, and 20% return on assets, so we will use these values in the formula. A margin value will be chosen arbitrarily (Y), and we will solve for asset turnover (X). We will begin with the 5% ROA line by plugging a 10% operating margin into the basic formula.

$$\text{Return on assets} = \text{Margin} \times \text{Asset turnover}$$

$$5\% \text{ ROA} = 10\% \text{ Margin } (Y) \times \text{Asset turnover } (X)$$

$$\text{Solve for asset turnover: } X = \frac{5\%}{10\%} = .5$$

The 5% ROA line has a point at $0.5X$ asset turnover and 10% operating margin. To find a second point, we arbitrarily plug a 5% margin into the formula.

$$\text{Return on assets} = \text{Margin} \times \text{Asset turnover}$$

$$5\% \text{ ROA} = 5\% \text{ Margin } (Y) \times \text{Asset turnover } (X)$$

$$\text{Solve for asset turnover: } X = \frac{5\%}{5\%} = .1$$

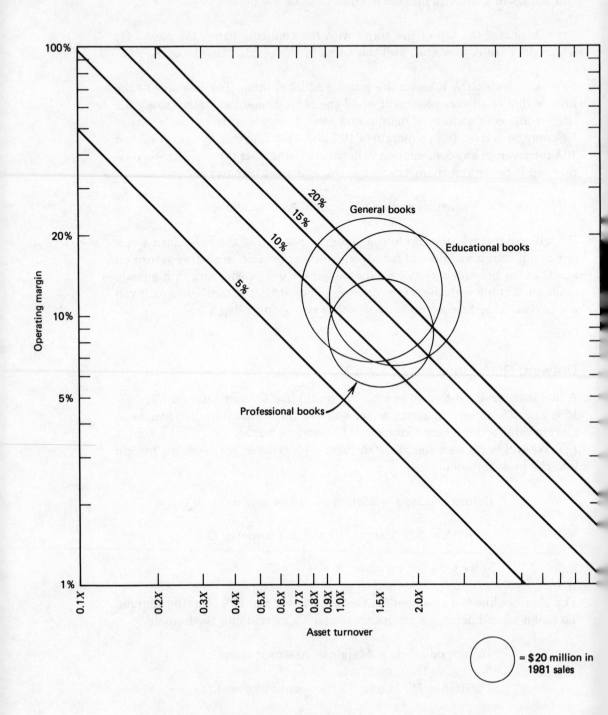

Exhibit 12.3 Company *X*, Return on Assets Graph, FY 1981.

The second point is located at $1X$ asset turnover and 5% operating margin. Since we have two points, we can now draw the line and label it "5% ROA."

This procedure is repeated for the other ROA levels we would like to represent on the graph.

	First Point		Second Point	
ROA	x	y	x	y
5%	0.5	10	1	5
10	0.5	20	1	10
15	0.5	30	1	15
20	0.5	40	1	20

STEP 5. Plot each business on the graph starting with asset turnover on the x axis and moving up the y axis according to operating margin. Draw the circle with your template to the correct circle size and label the line of business. Look at the midpoint of the circle for the ROA level. The circumference of the educational texts circle covers several ROA lines but actual return on assets is 18%, the place where the center of the circle is plotted.

You have now completed the ROA graph. Always keep track of the original data in case there is a need for a greater precision or manipulating the inputs. (See Exhibit 12.3.)

The graph tells us about the relative returns of company X's LOBs but also causes us to ask some questions:

What does a specific competitive profile look like?

How does company X stack up against all competitors in the industry?

How has company X's profile changed in recent years?

These questions can be answered by drawing other types of graphs.

Industry Level

We have addressed our procedures so far to producing an ROA graph for one corporation's LOBs. What happens when we want to show the same graph at the industry level? The graph is titled "Book Industry Return on Assets," and circles represent companies instead of business lines.

Two changes will have to be made in the data to properly represent the corporation.

Sales and assets must be for the total company's publishing operations, not for LOB sales.

Income used in the margin formula should be pretax but after all other corporate expenses.

We will compile the data for a book industry ROA graph showing the same nine competitors used in the sector graph. Sales and pretax income figures come from income statements and assets from balance sheets. A two-year asset average is taken as before. Watch for different companies' treatment of the fiscal year and do your best to get data relating to the same time period. You may recall that company X's fiscal year ends on April 30, so its 1981 report contains eight months of 1980 and four months of 1981. The period covered is more 1980 than 1981, so we will use 1980 data for the other competitors. Multiyear averages should be calculated, although we will stick with one year for simplicity as before.

Most of the companies in the industry are diversified into businesses besides book publishing, so we need to identify the financials relating specifically to their book publishing segments. This can be accomplished for sales and assets by reference to the business segment part of the annual report. Pretax income for a part of the business must be derived by determining the proportion of operating income accounted for by the line and applying that proportion to net income. For example, we know that CBS's Publishing Group had operating profits of $42.4 million in 1980. The $42.4 million represents 11.0% of total operating profit of $385.0 million. We multiply pretax income, found in the income statement or business segment section, of $347.7 million by 11.0% to determine the publishing group's part of the total and find the number to be $38.2 million.

Publishing group operating income	$ 42.4
Total corporate operating income	$385.0
Publishing group percentage of operating income	11.0
Corporate pretax income	$347.7
× Publishing group percentage of operating income	× .11
= Publishing group share of pretax income	$ 38.2

We have now developed the data needed to plug into the formulas. Book industry data are shown below.

Leading Public Book Publishers 1980, in Millions of Dollars

	Sales	Average Assets	Pretax Income
CBS	$541.9	$341.3	$38.3
Time, Inc.	498.0	393.8	34.7
McGraw-Hill	355.3	307.4	44.7

	Sales	Average Assets	Pretax Income
Harcourt Brace	$294.7	$201.8	$29.0
SFN Companies	275.7	226.7	68.9
Times Mirror	263.6	181.4	36.8
Macmillan	240.0	239.2	9.9
Prentice-Hall	231.6	188.5	35.5
Company X	160.0	142.0	11.9

We can apply the formulas used to create the graph.

$$\text{Asset turnover} = \frac{\text{Sales}}{\text{Assets}}$$

$$\text{Pretax margin} = \frac{\text{Pretax income}}{\text{Sales}}$$

We will not repeat the calculations but will show you the summary table. The scale for circle size is 50 mm = $600 million, established for the sector graph.

Book Publisher Summary Table

	Asset Turnover	Pretax Margin	Circle Size
CBS	1.59	7.1%	48 mm
Time, Inc.	1.26	7.0	46
McGraw-Hill	1.16	12.6	38
Harcourt Brace	1.46	9.8	35
SFN Companies	1.22	25.0	34
Times Mirror	1.45	14.0	33
Macmillan	1.00	4.1	32
Prentice-Hall	1.23	15.3	31
Company X	1.13	7.4	26

The industry level book publishers' ROA graph looks like Exhibit 12.4.

II. THE ASSETS VERSUS INCOME GRAPH

Another way to look at the efficiency of assets is to contrast assets directly with the income they produced. Our first graph addressed this issue by showing us the return on assets for the business line. The assets versus income graph highlights each business's income contribution to the corporation against the amount of assets the corporation has invested in the business. The display is in the form of a share momentum with a 45° diagonal line identifying the points

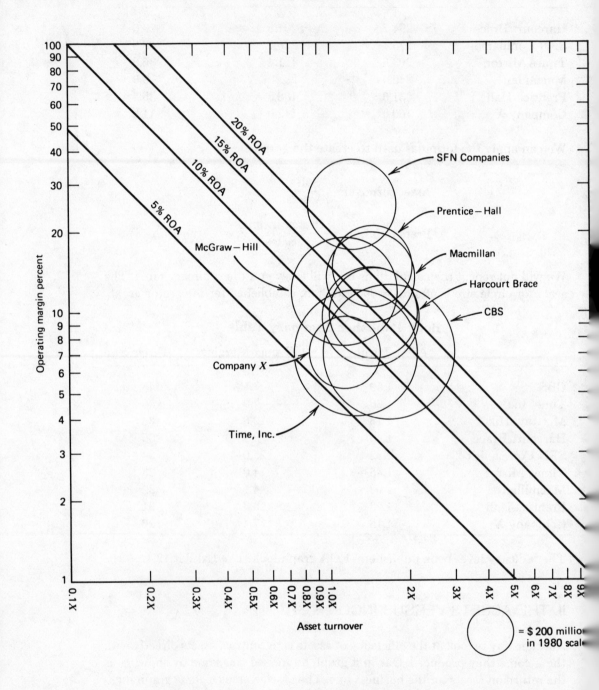

Asset turnover

Operating margin percent

20% ROA
15% ROA
10% ROA
5% ROA

SFN Companies
Prentice—Hall
Macmillan
Harcourt Brace
CBS
McGraw—Hill
Company *X*
Time, Inc.

= $ 200 million in 1980 scale

Exhibit 12.4 Book Publishing Industry, Return on Assets, 1980.

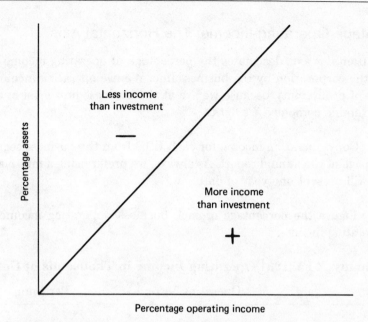

Exhibit 12.5 Company *X,* Assets versus Operating Income, FY 1981.

where asset investment and income throwoff are equal. A business located on the diagonal is returning proportionately the same income as the corporate assets invested in it. To the right of the line, the business is producing more income than its investment and to the left it is producing less. See Exhibit 12.5.

Several explanations are possible in the case where the percentage income exceeds the percentage of assets invested. The most favorable explanation is that of a mature business that has garnered a comfortable market share and is now providing a disproportionate amount of the profits. A second possibility is that the mature business is not really producing significant amounts of income but has a lower asset base because its assets have been depreciated over time. Third, we may have underinvested in the business and will begin to feel the effects of harvesting in the near future.

A business that shows a higher percentage assets than percentage income should have opposite characteristics. It may be an embryonic business that is receiving investment for the future, a question mark, or a star business that needs asset investment to continue its stellar performance. On the downside, it may be a poor performer that management cannot let go for emotional reasons. Investment continues to be made despite the lack of return.

The assets-versus-income analysis is meaningful only in comparing LOBs within a corporation. Ideally, we would like to have data at the SBU level. This may be possible only for our own company; for the remainder we will have to rely on the LOBs defined in business segment reporting.

Percentage Operating Income: The Horizontal Axis

The horizontal x axis designates the percentage of operating income contributed to the corporation by the business line. We use operating income as our measure of profitability because we are at the business unit level of analysis. Let us examine company X's data.

STEP 1.   Copy operating income for each LOB from the business segment reporting page of the annual report. As always, we prefer using a multiyear average but will present one year of data.

STEP 2.   Figure the percentage of each business's operating income against total operating income.

Company X FY 1981 Operating Income in Thousands of Dollars

	Operating Income	Percentage of Total
Educational texts	$ 6,909	36.1
General books	8,655	45.2
Professional books	3,599	18.8
	$19,163	100.0

Percentage Assets: The Vertical Axis

The vertical y axis represents the percentage of total corporate assets invested in the line of business. Business segment reporting contains this information but now we have to make a decision about the proper numbers to include. (See Exhibit 12.6.) Company X's annual report contains a category of assets designated as "Corporate" assets.

The footnote explains these to be unrelated to any LOB—cash, marketable securities, prepaid expenses, goodwill, tax benefits, and others that belong to the corporation as a whole. What to do with this number? We have two choices: ignore it or allocate it proportionately across the LOBs. We have decided to ignore the number because it does not affect the graph's meaning. If we allocated corporate assets across businesses proportionate to the assets already in the business, the only effect would be to make the asset base in each unit larger. The percentage of total assets in the LOB would not change. Since our only interest in the graph is in the percentage of assets, we do not gain anything by making the allocation.

The reason for so much detail on treating the corporate asset number is that it represents many instances you find in doing analysis. There is *always* a number that does not fit into the formula, or a missing number. You must think through what you are trying to achieve and develop a rational way to deal with the situation. There is often no right or wrong way; it is simply a matter of in-

EXHIBIT 12.6.   Business Segment Reporting

A summary of information about operations by segment for the fiscal years 1981, 1980 and 1979 follows:

	1981	1980	1979
	All dollar amounts in thousands		
Net operating revenues:			
Educational texts(1)	$ 60,379	$ 64,298	$ 50,929
General books(2)	68,786	65,516	61,832
Professional(3)	41,067	37,301	24,327
Total net operating revenues	$170,232	$167,115	$137,088
Operating profit:			
Educational texts(1)	$ 6,909	$ 9,220	$ 4,043
General books(2)	8,655	5,641	7,278
Professional(3)	3,599	2,787	792
Total operating profit	$ 19,163	$ 17,648	$ 12,113
General corporate expenses(4)	(4,354)	(3,906)	(3,164)
Interest expense	(3,654)	(4,518)	(2,677)
Other	696	398	448
Income before taxes	$ 11,851	$ 9,622	$ 6,720
Depreciation and amortization:			
Educational texts(1)	$ 3,278	$ 3,478	$ 3,421
General books(2)	2,474	2,739	2,491
Professional(3)	1,623	1,532	1,156
Total depreciation and amortization	$ 7,375	$ 7,749	$ 7,068
Purchases of property, equipment and plates:			
Educational texts(1)	$ 3,899	$ 2,622	$ 2,918
General books(2)	2,598	2,668	2,325
Professional(3)	2,026	1,727	1,054
Total purchases of property, equipment and plates	$ 8,523	$ 7,017	$ 6,297
Assets:			
Educational texts(1)	$ 35,174	$ 39,570	$ 42,569
General books(2)	49,637	50,742	54,306
Professional(3)	28,480	27,758	21,588
Corporate(5)	23,898	28,585	30,537
Total assets	$137,189	$146,655	$149,000

[1] Educational texts include primarily college and school product lines.
[2] General books include primarily trade, junior, religious product lines.
[3] Professional includes primarily medical, criminal justice, and other professional product lines.
[4] General corporate expenses include compensation to corporate officers, legal and accounting fees, amortization of goodwill and other expenses not allocable to each segment.
[5] Corporate assets include cash, marketable securities, prepaid expenses, goodwill, a portion of future tax benefits applicable to purchase adjustments, and other.

terpretation. The important issue is that you have a well-thought-out reason for proceeding in the chosen manner.

STEP 1. Copy the assets for each LOB. We have decided to leave out corporate assets, so total assets will equal the sum of the three business lines' assets.

STEP 2. Figure the percentage of each business's assets against total assets.

Company X FY 1981 Assets in Thousands of Dollars

	Assets	Percentage of Total
Educational texts	$ 35,176	31.1
General books	49,637	43.8
Professional books	28,480	25.1
	$113,291	100.0

Representing the Business Line: Circle Size

Each LOB is represented on the graph as a circle proportionate to sales. Even if you have used multiyear averages for other data, you must use the most current year's sales for the circle size calculation. We have calculated circle sizes so many times that we will just repeat the formula here.

$$\text{Circle size} = \text{Factor} \sqrt{\frac{\text{LOB's sales}}{\text{Index}}}$$

We have already found company X's circle sizes to be 47, 50, and 39, respectively, for educational texts, general books, and professional books using a factor of 50 mm = $68.786 million.

Putting It Together: Graphing

STEP 1. Gather the data to be graphed into one table.

Company X FY 1981 Summary Table

	Percentage O.I.	Percentage Assets	Circle Size
Educational texts	36.1	31.1	47
General books	45.2	43.8	50
Professional books	18.8	25.1	39

STEP 2. Outline the graph on linear graph paper. Label the x axis "Percentage Operating Income" and the years of data included. Label the y axis "Percent-

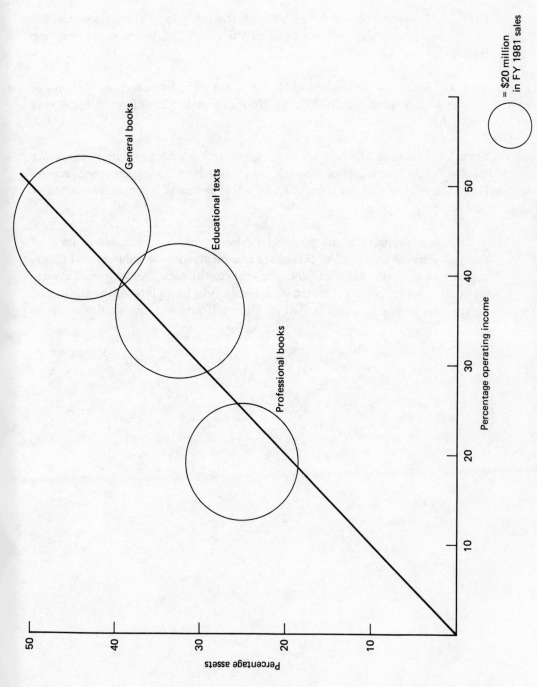

Exhibit 12.7   Company X, Assets versus Operating Income.

General books

Educational texts

Professional books

Percentage operating income

Percentage assets

= $20 million
in FY 1981 sales

age Assets" with the years of data. Draw a 45° diagonal line to show the points where income and assets invested are equal.

STEP 3.   Label the top of the graph with the company name, the period for which data are shown, and the name of the graph, "Assets versus Operating Income."

STEP 4.   Show the circle size scale in the lower right-hand corner. We will use the same scale as in the ROA graph, 15 mm equals $20 million in fiscal year 1981 sales.

STEP 5.   Plot each business on the graph starting with percentage operating income on the x axis and moving up the y axis according to percentage assets. Draw the circle with your template and label the line of business. (See Exhibit 12.7.)

The assets-versus-income graph could be applied at the industry level of analysis if we added up all of the assets and income in the industry and determined how each company was doing relative to the total industry asset investment and pretax income. The industry level could be an interesting additional perspective to aggregates provided by Dun & Bradstreet and similar services.

13

Clues to a Business's Strategic Importance: The Investment Tendency Graph

We have seen the importance of understanding how a firm invests its money because of the insight it gives us into business strategy. The profitability graphs focused on historical investment, the asset base that the company has developed over time. If we want to assess future strategy, it is important to know how the company is investing its money today. Capital expenditures can provide the current perspective.

By comparing investments in the historical and current time frames, we can infer the corporation's present thrust and strategy. A business unit accounting for a large proportion of past investment but very little current investment is being deemphasized, while a unit with a lot of current investment and a small asset base is being groomed for the future. Sometimes a company will state its strategy to be something different from what the numbers show, leading to one of two conclusions: (1) the company is not well managed, or (2) the stated strategy is not the real strategy.

ACCOUNTING CONCEPTS

In setting the stage for the profitability graphs, we have talked about the meaning of assets. Capital expenditures is the second concept we must understand before we can construct the investment tendency graph.

Virtually every business uses durable assets in its operations, including land, buildings, and equipment such as machinery, furniture, and tools. They are referred to as property, plant and equipment, plant assets, or fixed assets. Three characteristics are associated with such assets:

1. They are acquired for use in normal operations of the business.
2. They are supposed to last for a number of years and can be depreciated.
3. They are tangible, possessing physical substance.

Property, plant, and equipment represent one type of asset, fixed assets. A second category is current assets including cash, marketable securities, receivables, inventories, prepaid expenses, and intangible assets. We are excluding current assets from this analysis because of their short-term, nondurable character.

Capital expenditures is the amount spent to acquire property, plant, and equipment. Once the asset has been acquired, its cost shows on the balance sheet under "fixed assets" or "property, plant, and equipment." In succeeding years, the new asset will be depreciated and its value shown as a smaller and smaller amount.

The amount a company has spent on capital expenditures in the last year can be found on the "Statement of Changes in Financial Position," the third major statement in an annual report after the income statement and the balance sheet. The statement of changes presents a detailed summary of all the resources provided by the company during the period and the uses to which they were put. APB Opinion 19 in 1971 made it mandatory for companies to present this information on their financing and investing activities.

The statement of changes is divided into two major parts: one describes the *source* of financial resources and the other describes their *use*. We want to focus on the use section and specifically on the line that talks about additions to property, plant, and equipment. The amount of this item is the company's capital expenditures for the year. Business segment reporting is required to show capital expenditures by line of business. The total for all LOBs shown in business segment reporting will equal the amount we saw in the statement of changes.

Let us look at company X's statement of changes in Exhibit 13.1.

The highlighted section is titled "Financial resources were used for" [1]. Under the title, the category "Additions to property, equipment, and plates" [2] represents capital expenditures for the year, the only category in

EXHIBIT 13.1. Consolidated Statements of Changes in Financial Position, Company *X*

For the years ended April 30th		1981	1980	1979
		All dollar amounts in thousands		
Financial resources were provided by:				
Operations:				
Net income		$ 5,794	$ 4,416	$ 3,090
Expenses not affecting working capital:				
Depreciation and amortization		7,375	7,749	7,068
Amortization of goodwill		461	505	310
Deferred income taxes (decrease) increase		(63)	(334)	85
Working capital provided by operations		13,567	12,336	10,553
Other sources:				
Acquisition of Company *Y* (including working capital of $13,697 at the acquisition date), net		—	—	9,645
Decrease (Increase) in royalty advances to authors		1,546	1,126	(900)
Decrease (Increase) in other assets		666	(417)	(270)
Decrease in goodwill (Note 1)		487	1,330	—
Increase in unearned subscription income		212	287	1,366
Disposal of property, equipment and plates		103	1,763	217
		16,581	16,425	20,611
[1] Financial resources were used for:				
[2] Additions to property, equipment, and plates [Capital expenditures*]	**[3]**	**8,523**	7,017	6,297
Decreases in long-term debt		7,376	2,981	2,048
Cash dividends paid		2,202	2,199	2,057
Decreases in long-term royalties payable		744	1,014	1,755
Other		211	(103)	(107)
		19,056	13,108	12,050
(Decrease) Increase in working capital		$(2,475)	$ 3,317	$8,561
(Decrease) Increase in components of working capital:				
Cash and marketable securities		$(2,249)	$ 676	$(4,748)
Accounts and notes receivable		2,607	(1,609)	15,302
Inventories		(4,156)	424	12,120
Future tax benefits		(3,291)	3,326	1,536
Prepaid expenses		(246)	(123)	431
Notes payable and current portion of long-term debt		669	(620)	161
Accounts payable		(1,535)	6,579	(9,235)
Accrued royalties		274	153	(2,334)
Income taxes payable		2,870	(5,376)	1,076
Other accrued liabilities		2,582	(113)	(5,748)
		$(2,475)	$ 3,317	$ 8,561

* Author's clarification. Boldface type indicates emphasis added.

the use section referring to the acquisition of a fixed asset. The other items—decreases in debt, amount of dividends paid, and decreases in royalties payable—relate to liabilities and payment to shareholders.

Now let us compare the number for "Additions to property, equipment, and plates" (capital expenditures) of $8,523 in 1981 [3] with the business segment reporting figures. (See Exhibit 13.2.)

Here the category for capital expenditures is called "Purchases of property, equipment, and plates" [1]. Note the total in 1981 is $8,523 [2], the same number as in the statement of changes. The total is now broken down into amounts for each business unit—educational texts, general books, and professional books [3].

We have mentioned the need to compare historical investment with current investment. A good test of whether a company is funding its future is whether capital expenditures are keeping pace with depreciation. Is the company replacing its capital stock at the rate it is wearing out and staying even (although depreciation does not take inflation into account, so staying even is really falling behind), is it adding faster than depreciation and therefore growing, or is it adding less rapidly than depreciation, a danger sign? A simple ratio will give us the answer:

$$\frac{\text{Current year capital expenditure}}{\text{Current year depreciation}} = \text{Asset replacement ratio}$$

If the number is greater than 1, the company is growing. If it is less than 1, it is not replacing enough capital to maintain itself. A ratio of exactly 1 means the company is replacing at the rate capital stock is being worn out. Company X has an asset replacement ratio of more than 1, meaning that it is growing its asset base. We should compare it with the rest of the industry to see if ratio is average.

Company X FY 1981

$$\frac{\text{Capital expenditures}}{\text{Depreciation}} = \frac{8,523}{7,375} = 1.16$$

THE GRAPH

The investment tendencies graph contrasts assets invested in a line of business (the historical perspective) with capital expenditures invested (the current perspective). The graph displays investment in each business of a corporation. A 45° diagonal identifies all points where assets and capital expenditures are equal. To the right of the diagonal, capital expenditures exceed assets, meaning that a business is being more heavily funded now than in the past. To the left of the diagonal, asset investment is greater than capital expenditures, meaning the business is not receiving new funds. (See Exhibit 13.3.)

EXHIBIT 13.2.   Business Segment Reporting

A summary of information about operations by segment for the fiscal years 1981, 1980 and 1979 follows:

	1981	1980	1979
	All dollar amounts in thousands		
Net operating revenues:			
Educational texts(1)	$ 60,379	$ 64,298	$ 50,929
General books(2)	68,786	65,516	61,832
Professional(3)	41,067	37,301	24,327
Total net operating revenues	$170,232	$167,115	$137,088
Operating profit:			
Educational texts(1)	$ 6,909	$ 9,220	$ 4,043
General books(2)	8,655	5,641	7,278
Professional(3)	3,599	2,787	792
Total operating profit	$ 19,163	$ 17,648	$ 12,113
General corporate expenses(4)	(4,354)	(3,906)	(3,164)
Interest expense	(3,654)	(4,518)	(2,677)
Other	696	398	448
Income before taxes	$ 11,851	$ 9,622	$ 6,720
Depreciation and amortization:			
Educational texts(1)	$ 3,278	$ 3,478	$ 3,421
General books(2)	2,474	2,739	2,491
Professional(3)	1,623	1,532	1,156
Total depreciation and amortization	$ 7,375	$ 7,749	$ 7,068
[1] Purchases of property, equipment, and plates: [Capital expenditures*]			
Educational texts(1)	$ 3,899	$ 2,622	$ 2,918
General books(2)	2,598	2,668	2,325
Professional(3)	2,026	1,727	1,054
Total purchases of property, equipment and plates [2]	$ 8,523	$ 7,017	$ 6,297
Assets:			
Educational texts(1)	$ 35,174	$ 39,570	$ 42,569
General books(2)	49,637	50,742	54,306
Professional(3)	28,480	27,758	21,588
Corporate(5)	23,898	28,585	30,537
Total assets	$137,189	$146,655	$149,000

(The General books(2)/Professional(3) rows under Purchases of property are bracketed with **[3]**.)

[1] Educational texts include primarily college and school product lines.
[2] General books include primarily trade, junior, and religious product lines.
[3] Professional includes primarily medical, criminal justice, and other professional product lines.
[4] General corporate expenses include compensation to corporate officers, legal and accounting fees, amortization of goodwill and other expenses not allocable to each segment.
[5] Corporate assets include cash, marketable securities, prepaid expenses, goodwill, a portion of future tax benefits applicable to purchase adjustments, and other.
* Author's clarification. Boldface type indicates emphasis added.

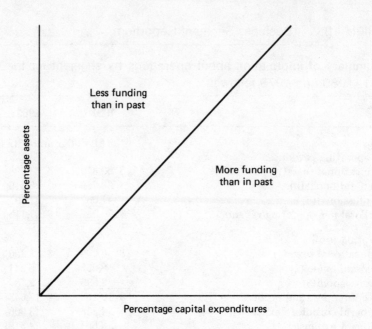

Exhibit 13.3

Percentage Capital Expenditures: The Horizontal Axis

The horizontal x axis shows the percentage of total capital expenditures made by the corporation that were allocated to the LOB. We will illustrate the calculations using one year of data, but a multiyear average is appropriate to eliminate short-term fluctuations.

STEP 1.   Copy capital expenditures for each LOB and total capital expenditures from the business segment reporting page of the annual report. Remember that capital expenditures are listed under "Purchases of property, equipment, and plates" in company X's reports.

STEP 2.   Figure the percentage of each business line's capital expenditures against total corporate capital expenditures.

Company X FY 1981 Capital Expenditures in Thousands of Dollars

	Capital Expenditures	Percentage of Total
Educational texts	$3,899	45.8
General books	2,598	30.5
Professional books	2,026	23.8
	$8,523	100.0

Percentage Assets: The Vertical Axis

The vertical y axis represents the percentage of total corporate assets invested in each LOB. These are the same numbers we used in the second profitability graph.

STEP 1.   Copy the assets for each LOB and total assets from business segment reporting.

STEP 2.   Figure the percentage of each business's assets against total assets.

Company X FY 1981 Assets in Thousands of Dollars

	Assets	Percentage of Total
Educational texts	$ 35,174	31.1
General books	49,637	43.8
Professional books	28,480	25.1
	$113,291	100.0

Representing the Business Line: Circle Size

Each line of business is represented on the graph proportionate to current year's sales. The formula to calculate circle size is:

$$\text{Circle size} = \text{Factor} \sqrt{\frac{\text{Business line's sales}}{\text{Index sales}}}$$

Company X's business lines have the following circle sizes, using a factor of 50 mm equal to the largest line's sales, $68.786 million.

Educational texts	47 mm
General books	50
Professional books	39

Putting It Together: Graphing

STEP 1.   Gather the data to be graphed into a table.

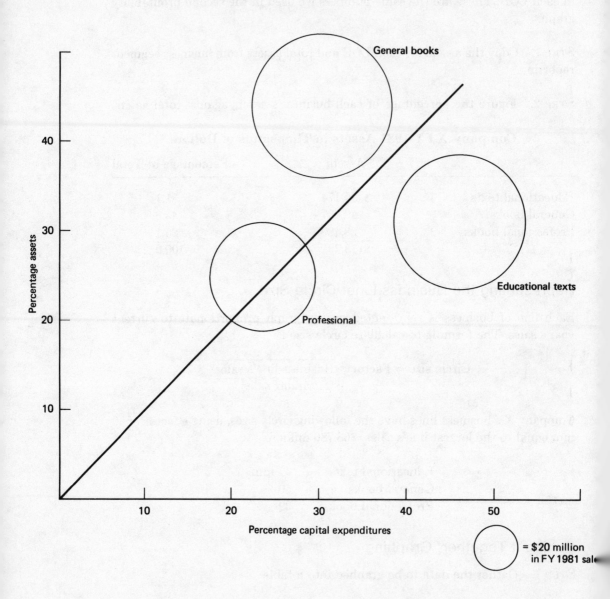

Exhibit 13.4 Company *X*, Investment Tendencies, 1981.

Company X FY 1981

	% Capital Expenditures	% Assets	Circle Size
Educational texts	45.8	31.1	47 mm
General books	30.5	43.8	50
Professional books	23.8	25.1	39
	100.0	100.0	

STEP 2.   Outline the graph on linear graph paper. Label the x axis "Percentage Capital Expenditures," and the y axis "Percentage Assets." Draw a 45° diagonal line to show the points where capital expenditures and assets are equal.

STEP 3.   Label the top of the graph with the company name, the period for which data are shown, and the name of the graph, "Investment Tendencies."

STEP 4.   Show the circle size scale in the lower right-hand corner with a 16 mm circle equal to $20 million in fiscal year 1981 sales.

STEP 5.   Plot each business on the graph, draw the circle, and label the business line. (See Exhibit 13.4.)

14

The Financial Health of a Business: The Cash Flow Graphs

We have seen the importance of cash flow to a business and its relationship to market position/growth on the growth–share matrix. Now we will create two graphs that allow us to look directly at a business's cash flow and make strategic observations. One of the graphs parallels the form of the growth–share matrix and provides an interesting financial overlay to the market characteristics.

The first graph breaks cash flow into its components—cash used and cash generated. It displays a company's investment in a business against the amount of cash provided by that business. The second graph adds the dimension of sales and contrasts cash flow with sales growth, the most direct analogy to the growth–share matrix. We can recreate the four quadrants of the growth–share matrix with this graph and relate cash flow to market share.

ACCOUNTING CONCEPTS

You will need to understand six accounting concepts to follow the discussion in this chapter:

1. Cash flow
2. Net income

3. Depreciation
4. Cash generated
5. Working capital
6. Cash used

1. Cash flow.   *Cash flow* is defined for our purposes as the difference between the amount of cash generated by a business and the amount of cash used. Cash flow is not really cash but is the total of income produced by operations after paying all expenses and taxes plus adding back charges against income that did not require a real expenditure, such as depreciation. Why do we want to know cash flow if we have income information? We have talked about the strategic use of cash flow; now we can add an accounting reason. Accrual accounting, the method of accounting for revenue and costs as they are incurred, not as they are paid, has too many noncash charges and credits, deferred taxes, amortization of intangibles, and so on, and has become removed from the real cash characteristics of the business. An income figure that includes all these accounting conventions but does not take inflation into account may not be a very good indicator of the company's earning power. The variations allowed in accounting for depreciation by different methods to speed up or slow down the expense in a given year can cause significant differences in income between two firms that will not be discovered without looking at cash flow.

While cash flow corrects for some problems, it adds others. One limitation of the data is found in interindustry comparisons, when we see that high-capital-expenditure industries have high cash flow and the converse for low-capital-expenditure industries.

2. Net income.   *Net income,* or aftertax income, is a profitability measure derived from the difference between revenues and expenses after all expenses have been paid. We used operating income in earlier graphs to show profit controllable by a business unit. Net income is the best measure of *corporate* profitability. Financial ratios focused on corporate profit use net income instead of operating income on the theory that all expenses are under the corporation's control, including taxes and the amount of interest paid on debt, and all are relevant in measuring performance. Company X shows two items between operating income and net income: other expenses and taxes. (See Exhibit 14.1.)

Extraordinary items, discontinued operations of a segment of business, the results of a change in accounting principle, material gains or losses not from operations such as foreign exchange or asset sales, and interest expenses are other items that might appear after operating income but before net income.

If you ever hear someone refer to the "bottom line," they're talking about net income, its name taken from the position on the very last line of the income statement.

EXHIBIT 14.1.   Consolidated Financial Statements: Consolidated Statements of Income, Company *X*

For the years ended April 30th	1981	1980	1979
	All dollar amounts in thousands except per share data		
Net sales	$160,034	$159,449	$129,060
Other publishing income	5,915	5,352	6,795
Income from distribution services	4,283	2,314	1,233
Net operating revenues	170,232	167,115	137,088
Costs and expenses (Notes 1, 5 and 8):			
Cost of sales	80,672	79,895	65,719
Selling, editorial, general, and administrative	74,290	72,974	62,110
	154,962	152,869	127,829
Income from operations*	15,270	14,246	9,259
Other expenses	3,419	4,624	2,539
Income before income taxes	11,851	9,622	6,720
Provision for income taxes (Notes 1 and 6):			
Federal	4,781	4,171	2,905
State and local	1,276	1,035	725
	6,057	5,206	3,630
Net income*	$ 5,794	$ 4,416	$ 3,090
Net income per share (Note 1)	$1.89	$1.44	$1.12

* Emphasis added.

3.   Depreciation.   *Depreciation* is the accounting writeoff of tangible fixed assets, or property, plant, and equipment, that shows an asset has a declining number of years of service left before it must be replaced. When an asset first is purchased, it is recorded on the asset side of the balance sheet at full cost.

The accountants then determine:

The number of years of "useful life" for the asset.

How much they think they can sell the asset for at the end of its "useful life."

The difference between original cost and what they can sell it for, the salvage value.

The method of depreciation—equal amounts each year or one of the special formulas that lets you take more depreciation in the early years and less later on.

The reason depreciation is important is that the annual writeoff of the asset is charged as an expense against income just like cost of goods sold or selling expense. It is as if we had taken the money out of our pocket and put it in a bank so we would have funds to buy a new asset when needed, but in fact we made no cash transaction. Depreciation is a *noncash* expense that reduces the amount of income on the income statement but does not use up any cash.

4.   Cash generated.   If we want to find out how much cash we have, we must add back noncash depreciation expense to cash generated from operations. The formula for *cash generated* becomes:

$$\text{Net income} + \text{Depreciation} = \text{Cash generated}$$

The concept may be clearer with an example. Let us assume the company buys a new machine for $100,000 that will be depreciated on a straight line, or equal amount each year, for 10 years—$10,000 per year—and will have zero value at the end of the period. The $100,000 of machine cost comes from a capital budget and decreases cash on our balance sheet, simultaneously increasing the fixed asset "Plant and equipment." Nothing happens on the income statement yet. After the first year of ownership, the company shows $10,000 depreciation as an operating expense and subtracts it from income even though we have not spent $10,000. This is the accounting entry for the noncash expense of depreciation. To calculate cash flow, we must add back the $10,000 to aftertax income because we have the money in our pocket.

5.   Working capital.   *Working capital* is the difference between current assets and current liabilities. Current assets are cash and other assets that can be converted into cash in one year such as amounts owed by customers, stock, and inventory. Current liabilities are amounts owed within the same time frame. Examples of current liabilities are amounts owed to suppliers, dividends, taxes, and bank notes due. If current assets increase and current liabilities stay the same, you have increased your working capital or the amount of liquid resources. Working capital comes from income from operations, sale of noncurrent assets, an increase in long-term debt, or the issuance of stock. An increase in current liabilities without a corresponding increase in current assets means there will be less working capital.

6.   Cash used.   *Cash used* is the amount of money that went into the purchase of assets, either short-term current assets such as stocks and inventory or long-term fixed assets such as plant and equipment.

THE CASH USED/CASH GENERATED GRAPH

The cash used/cash generated graph contrasts the amount of cash used by a business with the amount of cash it generates. A 45° diagonal identifies all points where cash used equals cash generated, where the business is neither contributing to nor borrowing from the corporation. To the right of the diagonal, the business is providing more cash than it is using, the sign of a star or a cash cow. Businesses to the left of the diagonal use more cash than they pro-

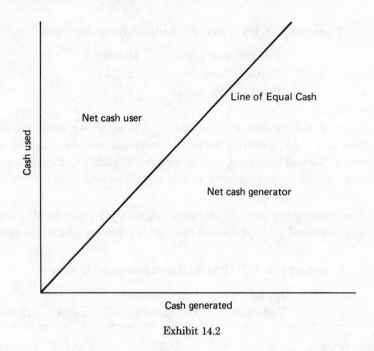

Exhibit 14.2

vide; they are cash drains. We are looking for a balanced portfolio containing some net users of cash and some generators. A corporation whose portfolio is entirely to the left of the diagonal is destined for financial trouble because it has an incessant appetite for cash and no providers. A portfolio entirely to the right of the line, all cash generators, may look fantastic on the surface but spells danger because the corporation is not investing enough for its future. There should be at least one or two businesses that use cash because of their growth and can ultimately become cash providers. (See Exhibit 14.2.)

The derivation of the cash used/cash generated formula is shown in appendix A. We will work with the basic formula derived there:

$$\text{Cash flow} = \text{Cash generated} - \text{Cash used}$$
$$\text{Cash flow} = \text{Net income} - \text{Change in total assets}$$

Cash Generated: The Horizontal Axis

The horizontal x axis shows the dollar amount of cash generated using the formula

$$\text{Cash generated} = \text{Net income}$$

STEP 1.   Go to the business segment reporting page of the annual report and copy operating income for each LOB.

Company X FY 1981 in Thousands of Dollars

Educational texts	$6,909
General books	8,655
Professional books	3,599

We are not given net income for the business lines so we must derive it by making adjustments to operating income. There are several ways to allocate other expenses. We will base ours on the amount of cash produced by the business unit, the sum of operating income and depreciation.

STEP 2.   Total operating income and depreciation for each LOB. Determine the percentage of total cash produced that each business unit represents.

Company X FY 1981 in Thousands of Dollars

	Operating Income	Depreciation/ Amortization	Total	Percentage
Educational texts	$6,909	$3,278	$10,187	38.4
General books	8,655	2,474	11,129	41.9
Professional books	3,599	1,623	5,222	19.7
			$26,538	100.0

The table above shows that educational texts produced 38.4% of the cash, general books 41.9%, and professional books 19.7%.

STEP 3.   Go to the income statement for the corporation and subtract net income from operating income. The difference is expenses to be allocated.

Company X FY 1981 in Thousands of Dollars

Operating income	$15,270
Net income	− 5,794
Expenses to be allocated	$ 9,476

STEP 4.   Multiply expenses to be allocated by the percentage of cash produced by the LOB found in step 2.

Company X FY 1981 in Thousands of Dollars

Educational texts	38.4% × $9,476 = $3,639
General books	41.9 × 9,476 = 3,970
Professional books	19.7 × 9,476 = 1,867
	$9,476

STEP 5. For each LOB, subtract allocated expenses found in step 4 from operating income to find LOB net income.

Company X FY 1981 in Thousands of Dollars

	Operating Income	Allocated Expenses	Net Income
Educational texts	$6,909	$3,639	$3,270
General books	8,655	3,970	4,685
Professional books	3,599	1,867	1,732

This net income figure is the cash-generated side of the equation.

There is a more complicated and precise method of allocating expenses between operating and net income that treats each item between operating and net income distinctly.

Corporate expenses are allocated according to the percentage of sales represented by each business unit on the theory that these expenses are in support of sales.

Interest expense is allocated according to the percentage of corporate assets in the business line on the theory that at least some of the assets are financed by debt.

Taxes are determined by applying the corporate tax rate to pretax profit after the first two allocations have been made.

Cash Used: The Vertical Axis

Cash used is the year-to-year change in assets, shown in business segment reporting for LOBs. Subtract the prior year's asset number from this year's to find the asset change. If this year's assets were lower than the year before, the reduction in asset base is reflected in a negative change.

Company X Cash Used in Thousands of Dollars

	1981	1980	Change in Assets
Educational texts	$35,174	$39,570	$(4,396)
General books	49,637	50,742	(1,105)
Professional books	28,480	27,758	722

A positive change in assets means that assets have increased and cash has been used. A negative change means total assets have decreased because more have been sold than purchased or assets are not being replaced at the same rate as depreciation, ultimately leading to liquidation. In company X's case, only professional books showed an increase in assets even though we know new assets were purchased for all three lines from the capital expenditure breakdown. It appears that company X is slowly liquidating its educational text and general books businesses.

The negative change in assets is shown as a special case when we graph the information. In fact, a negative change is not a *use* of cash but a *generator* of cash, although in a different sense from cash from operations. We will show the negative change in assets as a zero along the cash-used axis and a positive along the cash-generated axis.

Representing the Business Line: Circle Size

Each LOB is represented on the graph proportionate to the current year's sales. The circle size formula is:

$$\text{Circle size} = \text{Factor} \sqrt{\frac{\text{Business line's sales}}{\text{Largest business line's sales}}}$$

Company X's businesses have the following circle sizes using a factor of 50:

Company X FY 1981

Educational texts	47 mm
General books	50
Professional books	39

Putting It Together: Graphing

STEP 1. Gather the data to be graphed in one place.

Company X FY 1981 in Thousands of Dollars

	Cash Generated	Cash Used	Circle Size
Educational texts	$3,270	$(4,396)	47 mm
General books	4,685	(1,105)	50
Professional books	1,732	722	39

STEP 2. Outline the graph on linear graph paper. Label the x axis "Cash generated" and the y axis "Cash used." Draw a 45° diagonal line to show the points where cash generated and cash used are equal and label it "Line of Equal Cash."

STEP 3.   Label the graph with the company name, the period for which data are shown, and the name of the graph, "Cash Used versus Cash Generated."

STEP 4.   Show the circle size scale in the lower right-hand corner, 16 mm = $20 million in FY 1981 sales.

STEP 5.   Plot each business on the graph, draw the circle, and label the business line. Remember that a negative change in assets is plotted as a zero along the *y* axis for cash used and a plus along the *x* axis for cash generated, with a flag to show we are referring to a special liquidation situation. We will plot educational texts along the cash-generated axis at $7,666, the sum of cash generated of $3,270 and cash used of ($4,395). General books is plotted at $5,790 along the cash generated axis, the sum of $4,685 cash generated and ($1,105) cash used. (See Exhibit 14.3.)

The Corporate Level Graph

The cash flow graph is most typically used at the business unit level to examine the balance of cash flows within the corporation from a portfolio perspective. It may be useful to move the level of analysis up a notch and take a look at corporate competitors to understand their cash positions. Is the total corporation generating more cash than it is using? How strong is its cash position relative to competition?

There are two ways to approach the corporate level of analysis:

1.   Limiting our definition of cash receipts to those generated by the business.
2.   Expanding our definition to include other sources of cash such as debt financing.

The first approach utilizes the same formula as for the business unit except that now we do not have to derive the income numbers. Net income is read straight off the income statement and the change in assets from the balance sheet.

Cash flow = Net income + Change in total assets

The second approach uses a different statement for its information, the "Statement of Changes in Financial Position." The statement of changes registers the impact of operating leverage and financial leverage.

Two figures are relevant:

1.   The bottom line of the category "Financial resources were provided by" or "Sources of funds."

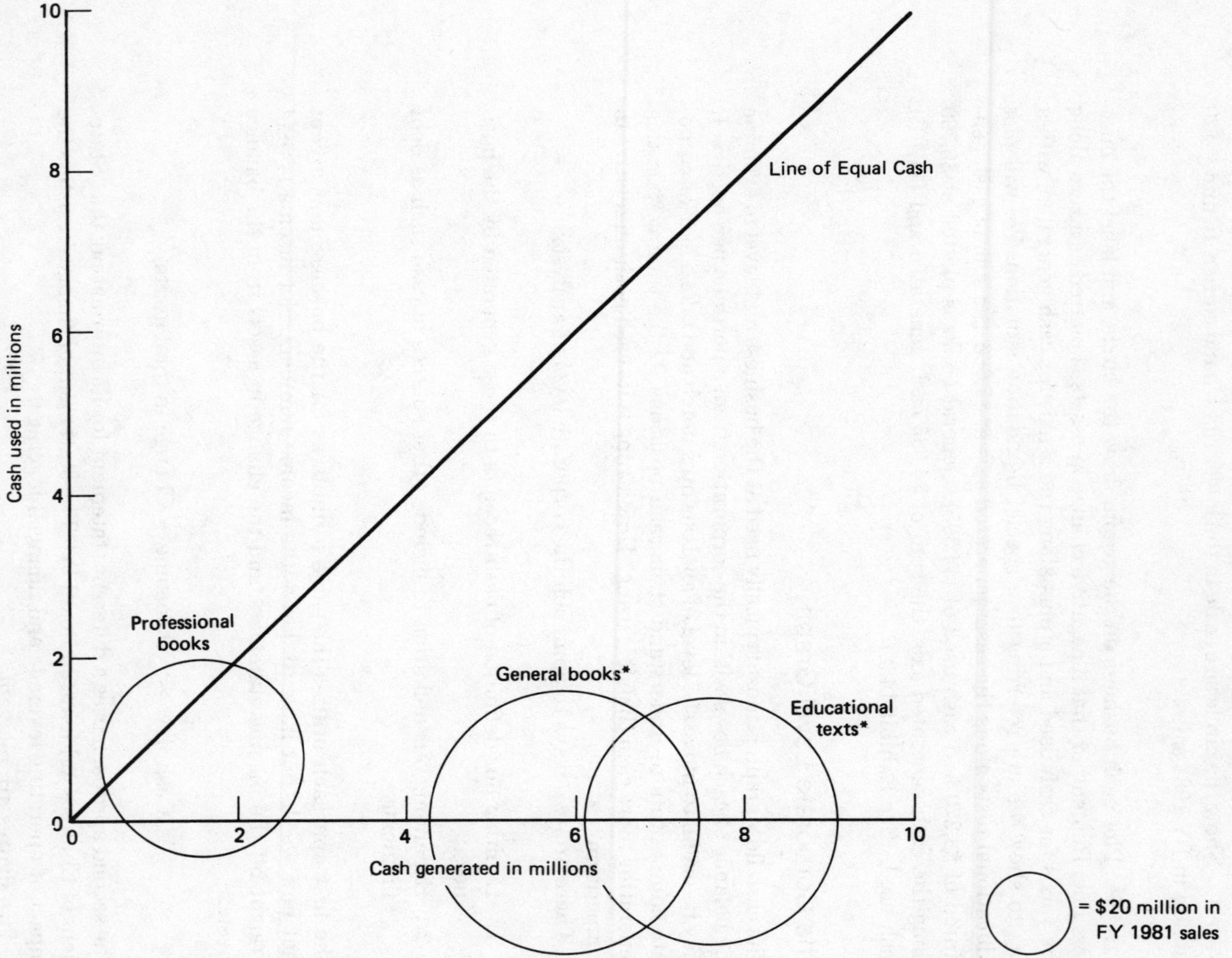

Exhibit 14.3 Company *X*, Cash Used versus Cash Generated, FY 1981, in Millions of Dollars.
positive cash generated.)

2. The bottom line of "Financial resources were used for" or "Uses of funds."

We may take the first as our cash-generated figure and the second as cash used. Note that the categories included in each figure include more than cash from the business. (See Exhibit 14.4.)

   We will use the first approach in our example for consistency in the assumptions about what is included in cash used and generated numbers. Let us look at company X and some of its competitors. We have eliminated the non-book-publishing activity of diversified competitors from our sales numbers.

STEP 1.   Copy net income and the change in assets for each competitor.

STEP 2.   Calculate circle size based on sales. We will use a scale of 50 = 600,000.

$$\text{Circle size} = \text{Factor} \sqrt{\frac{\text{Company sales}}{\text{Index sales}}}$$

$$\text{Circle size} = 50 \sqrt{\frac{\text{Company sales}}{600,000}}$$

STEP 3.   Summarize the data in one table.

1980 Book Publishers

	Cash Generated (Net Income)	Cash Used (Change in Assets)	Sales	Circle Size
Company X	$ 5,794	$ (9,466)	$160,034	26 mm
Macmillan	7,520	(22,400)	240,000	32
Harcourt Brace	15,767	15,615	294,673	35
Prentice-Hall	19,309	13,300	231,600	31
SFN Companies	36,091	21,448	275,718	34
CBS Publishing Group	21,255	91,900	541,900	48
Time, Inc.	22,064	36,400	498,000	46
Times Mirror	22,304	12,225	263,601	33

Circle size scale: 50 = $600,000

STEP 4.   Plot on the use/generation graph. Label the graph appropriately. The circle size scale is 17 mm = $200 million in 1980 sales.

The second approach gives a completely different view of the world. Using the Sources and Uses of Funds as our data, we see company X and two of its com-

EXHIBIT 14.4. Consolidated Statements of Changes in Financial Position, Company X

For the years ended April 30th	1981	1980	1979
	All dollar amounts in thousands		
Financial resources were provided by:			
Operations:			
Net income	$ 5,794	$ 4,416	$ 3,090
Expenses not affecting working capital:			
Depreciation and amortization	7,375	7,749	7,068
Amortization of goodwill	461	505	310
Deferred income taxes (decrease) increase	(63)	(334)	85
Working capital provided by operations	13,567	12,336	10,553
Other sources:			
Acquisition of Company Y (including working capital of $13,697 at the acquisition date), net	—	—	9,645
Decrease (Increase) in royalty advances to authors	1,546	1,126	(900)
Decrease (Increase) in other assets	666	(417)	(270)
Decrease in goodwill (Note 1)	487	1,330	—
Increase in unearned subscription income	212	287	1,366
Disposal of property, equipment, and plates	103	1,763	217
[CASH GENERATED*]	16,581	16,425	20,611
Financial resources were used for:			
Additions to property, equipment, and plates	8,523	7,017	6,297
Decreases in long-term debt	7,376	2,981	2,048
Cash dividends paid	2,202	2,199	2,057
Decreases in long-term royalties payable	744	1,014	1,755
Other	211	(103)	(107)
[CASH USED*]	19,056	13,108	12,050
(Decrease) Increase in working capital	$(2,475)	$ 3,317	$8,561
(Decrease) Increase in components of working capital:			
Cash and marketable securities	$(2,249)	$ 676	$(4,748)
Accounts and notes receivable	2,607	(1,609)	15,302
Inventories	(4,156)	424	12,120
Future tax benefits	(3,291)	3,326	1,536
Prepaid expenses	(246)	(123)	431
Notes payable and current portion of long-term debt	669	(620)	161
Accounts payable	(1,535)	6,579	(9,235)
Accrued royalties	274	153	(2,334)
Income taxes payable	2,870	(5,376)	1,076
Other accrued liabilities	2,582	(113)	(5,748)
	$(2,475)	$ 3,317	$ 8,561

* Author's clarification.

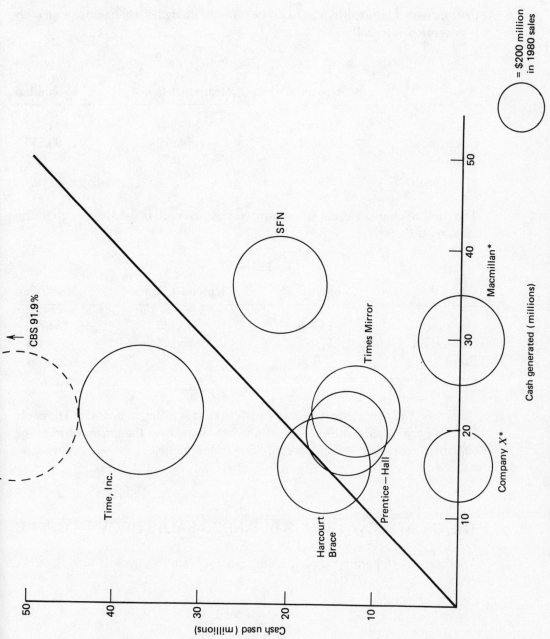

Exhibit 14.5 Book Industry Cash Used versus Cash Generated, 1980. (* Liquidation situation.)

petitors look a lot healthier than in the more limited view that assumes all cash is generated internally.

1980

	Company X^*	Harcourt Brace	Macmillan
Use	$19,056	$49,969	$44,797
Generation	16,581	70,919	35,355
Ratio	1.15	0.70	1.27

* Fiscal year 1981.

The picture changes again when a three-year average is used rather than the most recent year.

1978–80

	Company X^*	Harcourt Brace	Macmillan
Use	$14,738	$48,189	$39,823
Generation	17,872	58,104	26,421
Ratio	0.82	0.83	1.51

* Fiscal years 1979–81.

Company X is now generating more cash than it is using, in line with Harcourt Brace's position. Macmillan is in even worse shape over the longer term, using 50% more cash than it is producing. (See Exhibit 14.5.)

THE CASH FLOW VERSUS BUSINESS SALES GROWTH GRAPH

Another way to perform a cash used/cash generated analysis is to look at the ratio:

$$\frac{\text{Cash used}}{\text{Cash generated}}$$

We can easily restate our cash flow formula in the ratio form. Our formula gave us cash used equal to net income and cash generated equal to the change in assets. Expressed as a ratio:

$$\frac{\text{Change in assets}}{\text{Net income}} = \frac{\text{Cash used}}{\text{Cash generated}}$$

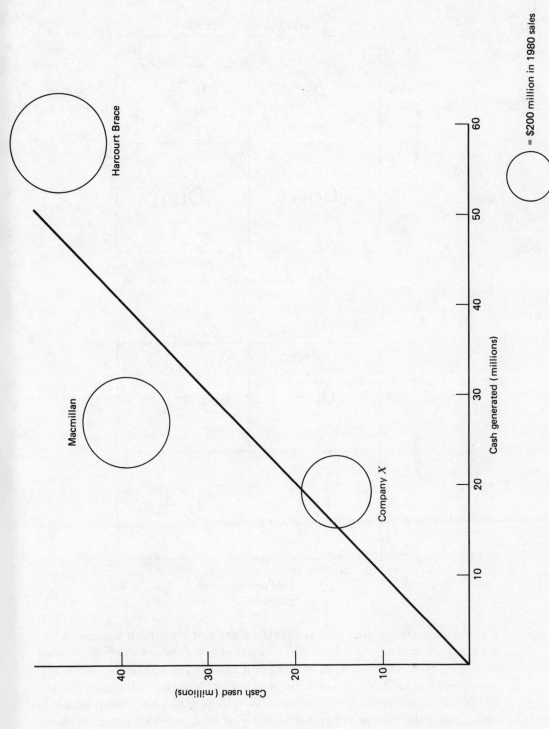

Exhibit 14.6 Selected Competitor Cash Used versus Cash Generated, 1978–1980 Averages.

◯ = $200 million in 1980 sales

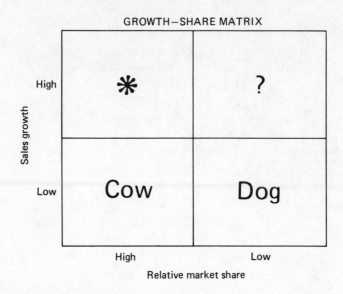

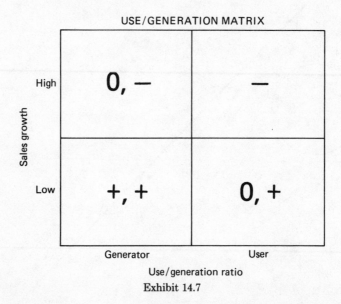

Use/generation ratio

Exhibit 14.7

When the used/generated ratio is equal to 1, use and generation are exactly the same as indicated on the 45° line on the prior graph. A ratio exceeding 1 means that more cash was used than generated; a ratio below 1 says more cash was generated than used. We can plot the ratio against historical sales growth to see how cash characteristics and business growth relate. This second graph is analogous to the growth–share matrix, showing cash rather than market share. Let us look at both graphs side by side. (See Exhibit 14.6.)

The growth–share matrix positions each business unit according to its relative market share and sales growth. The used/generated graph positions each business according to a cash flow ratio and sales growth. Theory says that a star business will be positioned in the upper left-hand quadrant of the used/generated graph and will either use cash or best case net out to zero, neither using nor contributing. The cash cow gained its name from its characteristic as a cash generator and should be positioned in the lower left-hand quadrant of the used/generated graph. The question mark is the most voracious user of cash, in the upper right-hand quadrant. The dog has traditionally been considered a zero on the graph, neither a user nor a generator, but recent research with the PIMS data base has shown that dogs can sometimes generate significant amounts of cash. For that reason, we show the lower right-hand quadrant as a zero and a plus. The importance of the used/generated graph comes from the strategic guideline that a business must either generate growth or cash to remain in a corporate portfolio. High-growth businesses will use more cash than low-growth businesses and the corporation must balance its financial resources among the buinesses in its portfolio. The financial overlay can help explain why a company keeps a seemingly losing business from a market perspective—a dog—or whether a market star is really a corporate earnings star. Incongruities between the two charts can provide some interesting grounds for strategy and understanding.

Cash Use/Generation Ratio: The Horizontal Axis

The horizontal x axis displays the ratio of cash used to cash generated, the same numbers that we calculated for the last graph. Recall that our definition of cash used is the change in total assets and cash generated is net income. The ratio is:

$$\frac{\text{Cash used}}{\text{Cash generated}} = \frac{\text{Change in total assets}}{\text{Net income}}$$

Copy the numbers for cash use and cash generation from the previous graph. Divide cash used by cash generated for the ratio.

Company X FY 1981 in Thousands of Dollars

	Cash Used	Cash Generated	Use/Generation Ratio
Educational texts	$(4,396)	$3,270	(1.34)
General books	(1,105)	4,685	(0.24)
Professional books	722	1,732	.42

As we have already commented, the negative numbers mean that educational and general book business units are retiring assets faster than they are replacing them. This trend has continued over the last three years and suggests that the company is disinvesting in those businesses. We will have to interpret this strategic signal in light of what we know about the market and company X.

Business Unit Growth: The Vertical Axis

The vertical y axis shows the real growth of the LOB over a historical time period. We would like to use the same amount of history as in the growth–share matrix so we can compare the two charts directly.

STEP 1: Copy business unit sales from business segment reporting for a historical time period.

STEP 2. Deflate sales to real terms.

STEP 3. Calculate the growth rate by the CAGR method or linear regression. We will use CAGR here.

Company X Sales in Thousands of Dollars

	1979	1980	1981
Educational texts			
Nominal revenues	$50,929	$64,298	$60,379
Books deflator	148.1	160.7	177.3
Real revenues	34,388	40,011	34,055
CAGR, 1979–81: (0.49%)			
General (trade) books			
Nominal revenues	58,700	61,800	63,800
Books deflator	148.1	160.7	177.3
Real revenues	39,635	38,457	35,984
CAGR, 1979–81: (4.7%)			
Professional (medical)			
Nominal revenues	21,342	32,870	35,815
Books deflator	148.1	160.7	177.3
Real revenues	14,411	20,454	20,200
CAGR, 1979–81: 18.4%			

Representing the Business Unit: Circle Size

Each LOB is represented on the graph proportionate to the current year's sales. The circle size formula is:

$$\text{Circle size} = \text{Factor} \sqrt{\frac{\text{Business line's sales}}{\text{Largest business line's sales}}}$$

Company X's businesses have the following circle sizes using the index we adopted earlier.

Index: 50 mm = $600,000 in fiscal year sales

Company X FY 1981

Educational texts	47 mm
General books	50
Professional books	39

Putting It Together: Graphing

STEP 1.   Gather the data to be graphed in one place.

Company X FY 1981

	Use/Generation Ratio	CAGR	Circle Size
Educational texts	(1.34)	(0.5)	47
General books	(0.24)	(4.7)	50
Professional books	.42	18.4	39

STEP 2.   Draw a matrix by outlining four sides of a rectangle on linear graph paper. Label the x axis "Use/Generation Ratio" and the y axis "Business Unit Real Sales Growth." Draw a vertical line to intersect the x axis at 1.0, the dividing point between businesses that are net users of cash (over 1.0) and net generators (under 1.0). Note that ratios less than 1, generators, are to the left of the divider and ratios over 1, users, are to the right, corresponding to the growth–share matrix. Draw a horizontal line to intersect the y axis at real sales growth of 10% or any number you think distinguishes between high and low growth in the industry. We will use 3% because the industry itself only grew 2% over the time period.

STEP 3.   Label the graph with the company name, the period for which data are shown, and the name of the graph, "Cash Flow versus Business Unit Sales Growth."

STEP 4.   Show the circle size scale in the lower right-hand corner, 16 mm = $20 million in FY 1981 sales.

STEP 5.   Plot each business on the graph, draw the circle and label the business line. Circles that fall off the chart are drawn with dotted lines, an arrow showing the direction of movement and the ungraphable number indicated next to the arrow. Footnote the negative use/generation ratios to draw attention to the special liquidation situation.

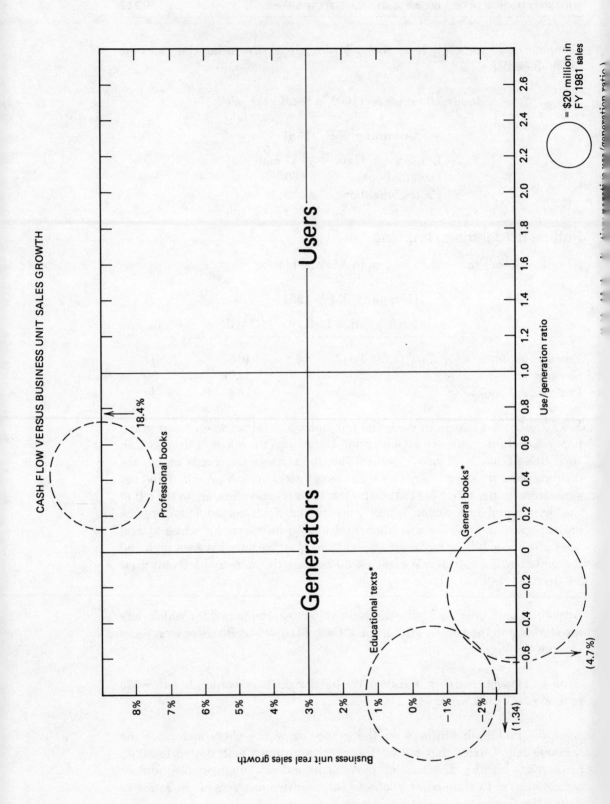

CASH FLOW VERSUS BUSINESS UNIT SALES GROWTH

Generators

Users

Professional books — 18.4%

Educational texts*

General books*

(4.7%)

(1.34)

Use/generation ratio

Business unit real sales growth

8%
7%
6%
5%
4%
3%
2%
1%
0%
−1%
−2%

−0.6 −0.4 −0.2 0 0.2 0.4 0.6 0.8 1.0 1.2 1.4 1.6 1.8 2.0 2.2 2.4 2.6

◯ = $20 million in FY 1981 sales

218

APPENDIX 14A: DERIVATION OF CASH FLOW FORMULA

The cash flow formula is

Cash flow = Net income − Change in total assets

We will derive the formula from the basic relationship

Cash flow = Cash generated − Cash used

This formula assumes (1) that the sum total of cash flows of the corporation is in balance, and (2) that the corporation is getting cash only from the business, not from outside sources. The statement of changes in financial position does not operate on this second assumption; the sources and uses of funds presented there includes external financing. Other assumptions made are that current liabilities are constant and taxes are a corporate function excluded from the analysis of a business unit.

Cash generated by the business includes income plus an addback for depreciation to correct for the noncash expense charge against actual cash. There is some debate as to the proper level of income to be shown in this business unit analysis. We have argued in our other graphs that operating income is the proper income level at which to assess business unit performance because the business unit has no control over financial policy decisions and the handling of tax liability (although some of its actions may have unique tax impacts such as the investment tax credit). For the sake of simplicity, we assume these items are the domain of the corporation and should only be taken into account at the corporate level of analysis. The other side of the argument says that a cash analysis differs from profitability analysis. We must look at all the changes that affect the amount of cash contributed to the corporation by the business unit, including the amount the business unit feeds into corporate for debt service and taxes. Both of these are valid arguments, and we leave the choice of income level to you, although we will use net income here. Unfortunately, there will be a major difference in the numbers depending on your choice, leading to a vastly different conclusion about the business unit's cash characteristics. As always, be consistent in your application of the formula, so that if you choose operating income, do the calculations at that level throughout analysis.

Cash generated = Net income + Depreciation

Cash used by the business is defined as

Capital expenditures + Change in current assets

Capital expenditures is the amount spent to purchase new fixed assets. It does not appear directly on the balance sheet but can be derived by looking at the change in fixed assets from year to year (it is also shown on the statement of changes in financial position as a separate line item). The amount of fixed assets owned this year minus the amount owned last year tells you the amount of money spent on new assets during the year. There is one problem: fixed assets shown on the balance sheet are net of depreciation. If we did not buy or sell anything during the year, there would be a drop in net fixed assets on the balance sheet because they were depreciated during the year. We must add back the year's depreciation to get to a zero starting point. We can then look at the change in net fixed assets on the balance sheet and conclude that the difference represents capital expenditures.

An example may make this explanation clearer. Suppose you bought $2 million of assets when you started a business four years ago. The $2 million went on the balance sheet initially; these were *gross,* or undepreciated, fixed assets. Each year you depreciate those assets by $200,000 because they have a ten-year life, zero salvage value, and you are using straight-line depreciation. After the first year, the fixed assets shown on the balance sheet were *net,* or depreciated, fixed assets. The balance sheet looked like this:

Year 1	
Fixed assets	$2,000,000
Less accumulated depreciation	0
Net fixed assets	2,000,000
Year 2	
Fixed assets	$2,000,000
Less accumulated depreciation	200,000
Net fixed assets	1,800,000
Year 3	
Fixed assets	$2,000,000
Less accumulated depreciation	400,000
Net fixed assets	1,600,000
Year 4	
Fixed assets	$2,000,000
Less accumulated depreciation	600,000
Net fixed assets	1,400,000

Suppose in year 5 we buy another $500,000 of assets. Our original assets are depreciated $200,000 during the year for a total of $800,000 depreciation, and we add $500,000 gross new assets to the base of $2 million for a new base of $2.5 million.

Year 5	
Fixed assets	$2,500,000
Less depreciation	800,000
Net fixed assets	1,700,000

If we looked at the change in net fixed assets from year 4 to year 5 without adjusting for depreciation, we would take the difference between $1.7 million and $1.4 million, or $300,000. Only by adding back the $200,000 in depreciation do we know the real capital expenditure number, $500,000.

This is a rather long-winded way of showing that

Capital expenditures = Change in net fixed (noncurrent) assets + Depreciation

The depreciation number is the same one that appears on the income statement for the year as a charge against income.

The second part of the cash-used equation is the change in current assets. We look at current assets rather than working capital because we want to focus on operational management, not financial management. Current assets includes cash, marketable securities, and inventory, with inventory the largest and most important category. A change in the inventory level has a significant impact on cash flow and reflects the operational efficiency of the business, the rapidity with which inventory is being converted into sales and accounts receivable. Other decisions on the use of cash, such as how fast to pay trade accounts and whether or not to obtain short-term loans, are financial judgments that we wish to exclude here and would be reflected in working capital.

We can now write the expanded equation

$$\text{Cash flow} = \text{Cash generated} - \text{Cash used}$$

$$\text{Cash flow} = (\text{NI} + \text{Depreciation}) - (\text{Change in NFA} + \text{Depreciation} + \text{Change in current assets})$$

Depreciation is the same number in both terms, so we can cancel it out. We are left with

$$\text{Cash flow} = \text{Net income} - (\text{Change in NFA} + \text{Change in current assets})$$

The right-hand term reduces to change in total assets. Our final equation is

$$\text{Cash flow} = \text{Net income} - \text{Change in total assets}$$

We can also state the equation as a ratio, using our derived definition of cash used as the change in total assets and cash generated as net income. By equating each cash element to its definition, we have a ratio that is useful in analysis:

$$\frac{\text{Cash used}}{\text{Cash generated}} = \frac{\text{Change in total assets}}{\text{Net income}}$$

Let us return to the concept. We are familiar with a change in assets that represents a use of cash. A company may use cash to purchase new fixed assets for a business such as plant and equipment. It may use cash to increase current assets such as the amount of inventory on hand so it can improve delivery time, to finance accounts receivable, to provide better terms for a customer, or to prepay expenses such as rent and insurance. All of these *uses* of cash have caused an increase in assets. What about changes in assets that *generate* cash? Suppose the business was to sell off an old plant after replacing it with a new building. The sales resulted in a cash receipt. When we talk about cash use, we are referring to the net increase in assets, including the purchase of new assets, the sale of old assets, and the increase in current assets. Suppose a business has sold more assets than it bought in a given year. The change in assets will be negative, reflecting a lower asset base. The negative number really says that no net cash was used and the sale of assets was a cash generator. We represent the generation of cash as a special case in our graphs.

15

Gaining Perspective on Today's Financials: The Long-Term Trend Graph

No financial analysis is complete without focusing on the long-term trend of the corporation, normally a period of five to ten years. Only by examining the long term can we get a feel for the company's financial strategy over time, recent changes, and likely future direction.

Competitor analysis is like detective work. You gather the clues and try to guess at their meaning. The long-term trend graph can help you answer questions such as:

How much is the company investing for future growth?

Is the company leveraged in line with the industry—is it more conservative, or is it more of a risk taker?

How well is the company being managed? How happy are the owners of the company (shareholders) with management?

Have there been any notable changes in financial policy in recent history? What does that indicate about strategy?

After we have calculated our chosen measures for the company or companies we are interested in, we will do the same for competitors and for the industry as a whole. Our analysis of the target company is meaningful only in the context of what the rest of the industry is doing. Some industries are characterized by high levels of debt, an important fact to know in looking at a financial leverage ratio. Others have a high return on sales but a low return on assets. The conclusions we make about our target company must be done within this context.

We will look at five ratios that measure different aspects of the financial picture:

1. Debt to equity for financial leverage
2. Return on equity for profitability
3. Return on sales for profitability
4. Dividend payout for investment and growth strategy
5. Market to book value for valuation

There are many other ratios that can be calculated to get into more depth on a given financial measure. We have chosen five of the most descriptive to cover the bases, but there is no reason to stop with these if you want to do further analysis. A good financial text always contains a chapter on financial ratios and can give you guidance on other measures you might develop.

DEBT TO EQUITY

The debt-to-equity ratio is a measure of financial leverage, an important concept in corporate financial management. Leverage refers to the funds supplied by owners or shareholders of the firm compared with financing provided by creditors, otherwise known as debt. A highly leveraged firm is one that is capitalized by a small amount of equity, funds provided by the shareholders, and a large amount of debt. There are several implications of high leverage:

Shareholders get a better return on their money than shareholders of an identical firm that does not use debt.

The business is riskier since it must pay interest on the debt and therefore must generate enough profits to cover interest expense along with the other expenses.

Shareholders can maintain control of the firm with a more limited investment.

A highly leveraged firm has more options in investing in new businesses or assets because it can provide an acceptable return to its shareholders even after using profits for investment purposes. It may also show a lower return on sales because it has paid interest expense. In an economic downturn, the leveraged firm is far riskier than the unleveraged firm because it must still generate enough profits to pay debt service even if sales are off. Other expenses vary with the level of sales; debt service does not.

The ratio of debt to equity measures the percentage of funds provided by creditors versus funds provided by owners. Debt includes both short-term debt, or obligations due within one year, and long-term debt such as bonds that may not be due for many years but are paid off in part each year. Equity gives us the amount of money invested by shareholders in the business. If the company makes a greater return on equity than it must pay in interest on borrowed funds, the shareholders will receive a higher return than if no debt had been used.

The debt-to-equity ratio is calculated from the right-hand or liability side of the balance sheet, the side that shows claims against the business. See Exhibit 15.1. Both owners and debtors have a claim against the assets of the business. Stockholders' equity, also called net worth or shareholders' investment, is the

EXHIBIT 15.1. Excerpt from Consolidated Balance Sheets, Company X (Annual Report)

April 30th	1981	1980
	All dollar amounts in thousands	
[1] Current Liabilities [Debt*]:		
Notes payable and current portion of long-term debt (Note 3)	$ 2,840	$ 3,509
Accounts payable	16,362	14,827
Accrued royalties	7,225	7,499
Income taxes payable	3,509	6,379
Other accrued liabilities	9,695	12,277
Total current liabilities	**39,631**	**44,491**
2] Long-term Liabilities and Deferred Items [Debt*]:		
Long-term debt, less current portion (Note 3)	25,324	32,700
Unfunded vested pension liability of acquired company (Note 8)	1,971	2,198
Long-term royalties payable	1,299	2,043
Unearned subscription income	5,431	5,219
Deferred income taxes (Note 1)	1,010	1,073
	35,035	**43,233**
3] Stockholders' Investment (Notes 3 and 4) **[Equity*]:**		
Common stock at par value of $.10 per share —authorized 5,000,000 shares —issued 3,197,882 shares	320	320
Paid-in capital	22,933	22,933
Retained earnings	39,677	36,085
Less: treasury stock, at cost; 140,100 shares	(407)	(407)
Total stockholders' investment [4]	**62,523**	**58,931**
	$137,189	$146,655

* Author's clarification. Boldface type indicates added emphasis.

third major category on the liability side [3]. Debt consists of the first two categories, current liabilities [1] and long-term liabilities [2].

We will calculate the debt-to-equity ratio for company X.

STEP 1.   Go to the balance sheet and add current liabilities and long-term liabilities together to arrive at total debt. Because we are dealing with balance sheet figures that show levels on one day, the end of the fiscal year, we must take a two-year average to find the average level during the year.

STEP 2.   Copy equity from the third category. Again, we must use a two-year average.

STEP 3.   Divide average debt by average equity.

Company X Debt-to-Equity Ratio in Thousands of Dollars

	1977	1978	1979	1980	1981
Current liabilities	$21,300	$25,497	$37,074	$44,803	$42,061
Long-term liabilities	16,627	18,936	32,773	45,229	39,134
Total debt	37,927	44,433	69,847	90,032	81,195
Equity	39,002	42,860	50,552	57,796	60,727
Debt to equity	0.97	1.04	1.38	1.56	1.34

Company X shows a clear trend toward higher leverage over the last five years, with its debt-to-equity ratio increasing from 0.97 in FY 1977 to 1.34 in FY 1981. The higher the ratio over 1, the less equity and more debt being used. A ratio of 1 means that debt and equity are in exactly the same proportions, and a ratio less than 1 means that there is more equity than debt. The 1.34 ratio tells us that company X has over half its capitalization in debt.

We still do not know if the amount of debt to equity is considered high or low for the industry. Dun & Bradstreet's 1980 *Key Business Ratios* tells us that in SIC code 2731, book publishing, for publishers with sales over $2 million, the median debt-to-equity ratio is 0.50. This is so different from company X that we double checked Dun & Bradstreet's definition of debt to equity, knowing that there are many ways to skin a cat. D&B's ratio is obtained by "dividing total current plus long-term debts by tangible net worth." *Tangible net worth,* defined as total assets minus total liabilities (which is also shareholder's equity), excludes intangible assets such as goodwill resulting from an acquisition, patents, trade names, franchises, and copyrights. We recall that Company X has acquired companies and indeed has goodwill on the asset side of thesheet. If we subtract that amount from net worth so we are left with only tangible net worth to meet D&B's definition, the debt-to-equity ratio looks far higher than before.

Company X FY 1981 Average

Debt	$81,195
Equity	39,850
Debt to equity	2.04

Comparisons to industry aggregate data can be tricky because definitions are rarely identical. Standard & Poor's publishes a debt-to-equity ratio that defines long-term debt as a percentage of invested capital, quite different from our definition of total debt as a percentage of equity. A comparison of the S&P ratios with the ratio we have developed would be inaccurate. Watch out for such traps. When in doubt as to how a measure was calculated, read all the footnotes and, if you still are confused, call the source directly and ask.

It is difficult to compare company X's debt-to-equity ratio to competition because company X is one of the few major book companies devoted entirely to books. If we look at the ratio of a diversified company such as CBS, we cannot segment our debt or equity associated with just the publishing group and will be misled in our conclusions. For this reason, we will limit our comparison to companies that have more than 50% of their sales in the book industry.

Company X	1.34
Harcourt Brace Jovanovich	1.37
Prentice-Hall	0.87
SFN Companies	0.37

There is a huge variation among companies in the industry in their approach to financial leverage. SFN, at one extreme, has taken a low-risk, low-leverage approach. Company X, along with Harcourt Brace, is at the high-leverage end of the spectrum. One consequence is seen in the amount of interest the company pays for the use of debt. SFN pays zero interest while Harcourt Brace paid $9.7 million in interest in 1980. Company X does not tell us the amount of its interest expense, but if we conservatively estimated 10% of its long-term debt of $25.3 million, we would calculate $2.5 million. At 15%, the number is $3.8 million in interest payments annually. This means that company X must generate $2.5 million to $3.8 million more in pretax income than SFN to simply break even on operations. Return on equity in the next section will tell us if the use of debt is worth the risk.

RETURN ON EQUITY

Return on equity is one of several ways to measure a firm's profitability, the ultimate indication of how well a firm is being managed. Other profitability ratios are return on sales and return on assets. Return on sales is an incomplete measure because it does not take the investment in the company into account. Two firms with the same margin may have vastly different amounts of dollars invested to achieve equal results. We might reach different conclusions about management if we knew the relative investments. Return on assets is a more inclusive measure of profitability because it looks at total investment. Yet, return on assets is not a perfect number because the asset base may differ from company to company or industry to industry, and because the age of the assets may affect the results. The older the assets, the lower their book value and the better the profit appears. Highly leveraged companies show a lower return on assets than companies without debt because interest payments reduce the earnings number in the numerator.

Return on equity is the broadest measure of profitability because it makes use of the company's financial structure as well as operating results in its calculation. It overcomes the objections to return on sales and return on assets stated above. Current fashion in financial analysis circles is to emphasize returns to shareholders for whom the business is being operated, and this is what return on equity measures.

The return on equity ratio is calculated by dividing aftertax profit by shareholders' equity. It tells us the profits realized on dollars invested in the company by its owners. Return on equity is always a larger number than return on assets because equity is smaller than assets and both are divided into net income.

STEP 1.   Copy net income from the income statement.

STEP 2.   Copy shareholders' equity from the right-hand side of the balance sheet. We must take the average of two years of equity to correspond to the income statement figure for the year.

STEP 3.   Divide.

$$\text{Return on equity} = \frac{\text{Net income}}{\text{Equity}}$$

Company X Return on Equity in Thousands of Dollars

	1977	1978	1979	1980	1981
Net income	$ 4,759	$ 4,940	$ 3,090	$ 4,416	$ 5,794
2-year avg. equity	39,002	42,656	50,552	57,796	60,727
Return on equity (%)	12.2	11.6	6.1	7.6	9.5

Company X shows an uneven trend in return on equity over the five-year period from fiscal 1977 through 1981. It dropped from a high in 1977 of 12.2%, to a low in 1979, and increased from there to 9.5% in fiscal 1981.

Compared to the book publishing industry, company X's return on equity is low. Dun & Bradstreet's *Key Business Ratios* places book publishers with more than $2 million in sales at an average 13.7% return on equity. When we compare return on equity to company X's competitors, our impression of company X's poor showing is confirmed. Recall that financial leverage, the use of debt, is supposed to have favorable impact on return on equity because it reduces the equity base in the denominator of the equation. Yet SFN with the smallest debt-to-equity ratio has the highest return on equity while company has the lowest. Harcourt Brace, similarly leveraged to company X, has a two-thirds greater return on equity.

1980 Return on Equity

Company X	9.5%
Harcourt Brace	16.0
Prentice-Hall	20.4
SFN Companies	21.9

RETURN ON SALES

Despite its limitations, return on sales is probably the most universally used return measure, and we would be remiss if we did not include it in our financial analysis. Return on sales measures the ability of the firm to operate its business profitably without taking into account the assets in support of the operation. A high return on sales means that the firm's prices are relatively high, its costs are low, or both.

It is much easier to show a respectable profit margin if we have a streamlined new plant that allows us to produce our product at low cost, even though the plant cost us many millions of dollars. The price of the plant is not reflected in the margin but shows up on the balance sheet. Another well-known example compares a supermarket and a telecommunications company. Margins in a supermarket are miserable—1% or so. In contrast, a telecommunications company may have a 12% ROS. Yet, the return on assets in a supermarket is far greater than the return on assets in telecommunications, which makes sense when we look at the amount of capital equipment it takes to run each operation. A supermarket has only real estate, food, inventory, and labor; a telecommunications company needs expensive high-technology equipment to operate. Because of this phenomenon, we always want to look at return on sales in combination with a return measure that takes investment into account.

Return on sales is defined as the ratio of net income to sales. The data come directly from the income statement and because of that we need only be concerned with data for one year in developing our numbers, not a two-year average as on balance sheet numbers. Company X's income statement shows two numbers representing volume, net sales, and net operating revenues. This distinction reflects the difference between sales of its primary products—books—and revenue from other sources that are not part of the main business such as copublishing ventures, syndication rights, and distributing books produced by other publishers. The net operating revenue figure best describes company X's total business so we will use it in our ratio.

STEP 1.   Turn to the section of the annual report, "Selected Financial Data," which gives a five-year history of some financial measures. (See Exhibit 15.2.)

STEP 2.   Copy the numbers for net income [1] and net operating revenues [2].

STEP 3.   Divide.

$$\text{Return on sales} = \frac{\text{Net income}}{\text{Sales (net operating revenues)}}$$

Company X Return on Sales in Thousands of Dollars

	1977	1978	1979	1980	1981
Net income	$ 4,759	$ 4,940	$ 3,090	$ 4,416	$ 5,794
Net operating revenues	93,192	114,424	137,088	167,115	170,232
Return on sales (%)	5.1	4.3	2.3	2.6	3.4

The long-term trend shows a decline from 1977's high of 5.1% to a low in 1979, and a slight recovery in 1981 to 3.4%. Industry data show us that the return on sales of book publishers with sales over $2 million was 5.2% at the median, placing company X below 50% of its competitors.

Return on sales is one measure that we can calculate for our full list of book competitors because we can segment book sales and income out of the diversified company total, thanks to business segment reporting. Recall that we developed pretax income for the books portion of each competitor's business in an earlier chapter. We must go one step further to convert pretax income associated with books to net income.

STEP 1.   Copy sales and pretax income for the books portion of the leading competitors' business. (See the earlier derivation of pretax income from operating income.)

STEP 2.   Find the overall corporate tax rate by going to the income statement and dividing income taxes by pretax income.

$$\frac{\text{Income taxes}}{\text{Pretax income}} = \text{Corporate tax rate}$$

EXHIBIT 15.2.   Company X, Selected Financial Data

For the years ended April 30th	1981	1980	1979	1978	1977
	All dollar amounts in thousands except per share data				
Consolidated Income Statement Data:					
[2] **Net operating revenues***	$170,232	$167,115	$137,088	$114,424	$93,192
Interest expense	3,654	4,518	2,677	1,133	594
[1] **Net income***	5,794	4,416	3,090	4,940	4,759
Per common share data:					
Net income	$ 1.89	$ 1.44	$ 1.12	$ 2.15	$ 2.10
Cash dividends declared	.72	.72	.72	.66	.52
Consolidated Balance Sheet Data:					
Current assets	$ 82,543	$ 89,878	$ 87,184	$ 62,543	$56,747
Current liabilities	39,631	44,491	45,114	29,034	25,230
Working capital	42,912	45,387	42,070	33,509	31,517
Current ratio	2.1	2.0	1.9	2.2	2.2
Total assets	137,189	146,655	149,000	91,797	86,195
Long-term debt, less current portion	25,324	32,700	35,681	14,131	16,281
Stockholder's investment	62,523	58,931	56,661	44,443	40,869
Number of common shares used in computing primary earnings per share (000)	3,065	3,060	2,753	2,297	2,261

* Emphasis added.

STEP 3.   Multiply the corporate tax rate by pretax income for the books portion of the business. The result is the amount of taxes to be paid on that income. Subtract taxes from pretax income, and you are left with net income attributable to books.

Leading Public Book Publishers 1980, in Millions of Dollars

	Sales	P/T Income	Tax Rate	Net Income
CBS	$541.9	$38.3	44.5%	$21.4
Time, Inc.	498.0	34.7	36.6	22.0
McGraw-Hill	355.3	44.7	49.2	27.2
Harcourt Brace	294.7	29.0	45.5	15.8
SFN Companies	275.7	68.9	47.8	36.1
Times Mirror	263.6	36.8	39.4	22.3
Macmillan	240.0	9.9	56.0	4.4
Prentice-Hall	231.6	35.5	46.0	19.2

The exact line of information to be used in trying to determine the corporate tax rate can be confusing if the company has had an extraordinary item, discontinued operations, or other special circumstances. Certain items can produce tax credits or otherwise be treated differently from normal operations. The company usually shows a line indicating taxes on continuing operations before it gets into the special case information, and this is the information we want.

We can now calculate return on sales for company X's competition, using the just-derived net income figure and sales for the book segment of each company.

Leading Public Book Publishers
Return on Sales 1980, in Millions of Dollars

	Sales	Net Income	ROS
CBS	$541.9	$21.4	4.0%
Time, Inc.	498.0	22.0	4.4
McGraw-Hill	355.3	27.2	7.7
Harcourt Brace	294.7	15.8	5.4
SFN Companies	275.7	36.1	13.1
Times Mirror	263.6	22.3	8.5
Macmillan	240.0	4.4	1.8
Prentice-Hall	231.6	19.2	8.3
Company X			3.4

Comparison with competitors further supports company X's weakness. Of the eight competitors listed, only one shows a lower ratio than company X: Prentice-Hall at 1.8%. The remainder range from 4.0% to 13.1%. This suggests that company X is not managing its costs of operation very well.

DIVIDEND PAYOUT RATIO

The dividend payout ratio tells us how much money the firm is conserving to fund its future growth. The more profits paid to shareholders in the form of dividends, the less money available for investment in the business. A firm with a low dividend payout is holding onto its profits for use in the future. It has been able to get acceptance for this strategy from its shareholders who are waiting for the business to mature to a cash cow so they can reap their just rewards.

The ratio is calculated by dividing dividends per share by earnings per share. Earnings per share is the total amount of profits available for shareholders; dividends per share is the amount actually paid out. The difference between dividends per share and earnings per share is the amount of earnings retained in the business.

Both dividends per share and earnings per share are presented in the "Selected Financial Data" section of company X's annual report, the five-year summary, and are required to be reported there by the SEC.

$$\text{Dividend payout} = \frac{\text{Dividends per share}}{\text{Earnings per share}}$$

STEP 1.   Copy cash dividends per share.

STEP 2.   Copy net income per share data.

STEP 3.   Divide.

Company X FY 1977–81

	1977	1978	1979	1980	1981
Dividends per share	$0.72	$0.72	$0.72	$0.66	$0.52
Earnings per share	1.89	1.44	1.12	2.15	2.10
Dividend payout ratio	0.38	0.50	0.64	0.31	0.25

Company X's long-term trend shows increasing conservatism in dividend policy. From a high of 64% in 1979, the company has dropped the payout ratio to less than half, 25% in 1981. This suggests that there is an increased emphasis on funding growth internally.

Our examination of competition shows us that company X is at the low end of the industry spectrum on dividend payout. The ratio ranges from company X's low of 0.25 to Macmillan's high of 0.99. Perhaps with its high leverage and an uncertain industry, the company has decided to conserve cash.

Leading Public Book Publishers
Dividend Payout Ratios 1980

	Dividends/ Common Share	Earnings/ Common Share	Ratio
CBS	$2.80	$4.63	0.60
Time, Inc.	1.77	5.02	0.35
McGraw-Hill	1.52	3.48	0.44
Harcourt Brace	1.56	5.56	0.28
SFN Companies	.92	3.09	0.30
Times Mirror	1.44	4.08	0.35
Macmillan	0.74	0.75	0.99
Prentice-Hall	1.50	3.11	0.48
Company X			0.25

Sometimes a company distinguishes between dividends declared and dividends paid. A difference may occur if the company is changing its dividend policy. If it is increasing dividend payout, the amount declared may be greater than the amount paid because of a time difference between the two events. We want to know the dividends actually paid if given a choice.

MARKET-TO-BOOK VALUE

The market-to-book-value ratio is a measure of the value attached to the firm by the marketplace. While we have heard many arguments against the market's valuation of a firm in the down stock market of recent years, the fact remains that market value reflects what the firm is worth today. The combined influence of risk and return are netted out in the market's assessment.

Book value, or the sum of the accounting values of a company's assets, tells us the historical cost of the physical assets of a company. If a company were to replace all those assets today, its book value would be far greater than the value of depreciated net fixed assets. The market value of the company is the value attached to management and organization of the going concern. A company with good management and well-organized operations should have a market value in excess of its book value.

The market-to-book ratio is calculated by dividing the book value per share of stock by the average market value per share for the year. Book value per share is the amount each share would receive if the company were liquidated, in other words, what the shareholders would receive if everything were sold off (retained earnings plus the initial cost of assets). This is the same as shareholders' equity. The number is calculated by dividing average shareholders' equity during the year by shares outstanding. Shares outstanding is normally found in a note to the financial statements, and shareholders' equity is on the balance sheet.

$$\text{Book value per share} = \frac{\text{Shareholders' equity}}{\text{Shares outstanding}}$$

Market value per share is the average stock price for the year. Companies are required by the SEC to report quarterly highs and lows in their annual reports, from which you can calculate an annual average. The average stock price goes into the numerator of the market-to-book ratio.

$$\text{Market to book} = \frac{\text{Average stock price}}{\text{Book value per share}}$$

Calculations for the market-to-book ratio can be accomplished in five steps.

STEP 1.   Go to the note in the annual report that describes the average number of shares outstanding for the year. Note that we specified an average number, not the year-end. If you cannot locate shares outstanding in the report, you can derive it by dividing net income by net income per share.

STEP 2.   Take the two-year average of shareholders' equity.

STEP 3.   Divide average shareholders' equity by average shares outstanding.

STEP 4.   Find the average share price for the year by adding low and high prices and dividing by 2. Since company X is traded over the counter, use the "Bid" column for the data, not the "Asked" column.

7½–12⅛ range, 10 average for the year

STEP 5.   Divide market value by book value.

Let us see how company X fared on this measure.

Company X Market to Book FY 1977–81

	1977	1978	1979	1980	1981
Average shareholders' equity (000)	$39,002	$42,656	$50,552	$57,796	$60,457
Shares outstanding	2,266	2,297	2,753	3,060	3,065
Shareholders' equity/shares outstanding (book value/share)	$17.21	$18.57	$18.36	$18.89	$19.72
Average share price (market value)	9.31	13.12	13.94	9.13	10.00
Market to book ratio	0.54	0.71	0.76	0.48	0.51

The long-term trend of market to book does not show improvement. In the last few years, the market has valued the company at around half its liquidation value, not much of a vote of confidence. Comparison with competitors having the majority of their sales in the book industry confirms our diagnosis. We see that SFN, which has consistently had the best financials in the industry, is recognized for its strength by the marketplace and is valued at almost two times book. Prentice-Hall and Harcourt Brace did not do as well as SFN but are far stronger than company X.

Book Competitor Market-to-Book Ratios, 1980

Harcourt Brace	0.93
Prentice-Hall	1.34
SFN Companies	1.88
Company X	0.51

We can consolidate all of the long-term trend measures on one graph to present a complete financial picture of a company over the five-year period studied.

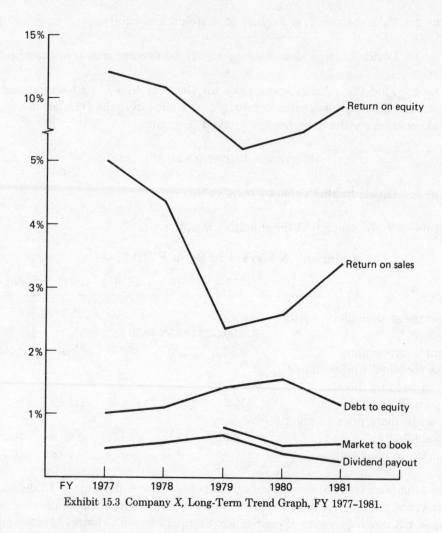

Exhibit 15.3 Company X, Long-Term Trend Graph, FY 1977–1981.

CLUES OF FINANCIAL ILLNESS

Suppose our tentative diagnosis of a company is that it has a slight fever, such as in the case of company X. How can we tell if the company is really sick and pinpoint the cause? We go back to the financial statements and look for more clues. Some of the signs used by accountants and financial analysts in confirming a diagnosis are:

High cost of borrowing.   Expensive borrowing can do a lot to erode profit margins. Look at the percentage of interest costs from year to year.

Solvency.   Take the ratio of current assets to current liabilities.

A continuing decline in net worth and reserve for bad debts.   If a company cuts back a large reserve, it may indicate the need to show profits.

Large dividends paid from subsidiary to parent.   This will make the parent look good to the detriment of the subsidiary.

Dividend policy.   If earnings are down, dividends should not be paid.

Cash flow problems.   A negative change in cash flow can mean a problem in solvency.

Ratios of major expense items to sales, such as cost of goods sold, general and administrative expenses, selling expense, and taxes.   Compare to prior years and industry averages to diagnose the high-cost areas.

Change in auditors or change in accounting methods.   This may mean there is something to cover up.

Look at the most current year and changes from year to year for insights. These measures can help you understand if a long-term trend has meaning.

Bringing It All Together

This is where we tie things together, showing you how the individual graphs build into a corporate picture. Following the analysis of our case company, we summarize all of the formulas and graphs for easy reference and talk about finding a consultant for those of you who do not want to go it alone.

16

Analysis: The Company X Case

We have purposely left you hanging after drawing each graph with company X case data, not telling you what it means because we wanted to do it all at once, the way a company would normally be analyzed. The graphs fit together like pieces of a puzzle, each one adding to our knowledge about a company and our hypotheses about its strategy. Analyzing one graph without being able to look at the others can bias our views and lead us to incorrect conclusions. Now we have a complete set of graphs with which to work, with the exception of the experience curve for which book industry data were unavailable.

The growth–share matrix (Chapter 6)

The share–momentum graph (Chapter 7)

Sector (Chapter 8)

Return on assets (Chapter 12)

Assets versus operating income (Chapter 12)

Investment tendencies (Chapter 13)

Cash used versus cash generated (Chapter 14)

Cash flow versus growth (Chapter 14)

Long-term trends (Chapter 15)

We will review these graphs one by one and, at the end, go back and put the pieces together.

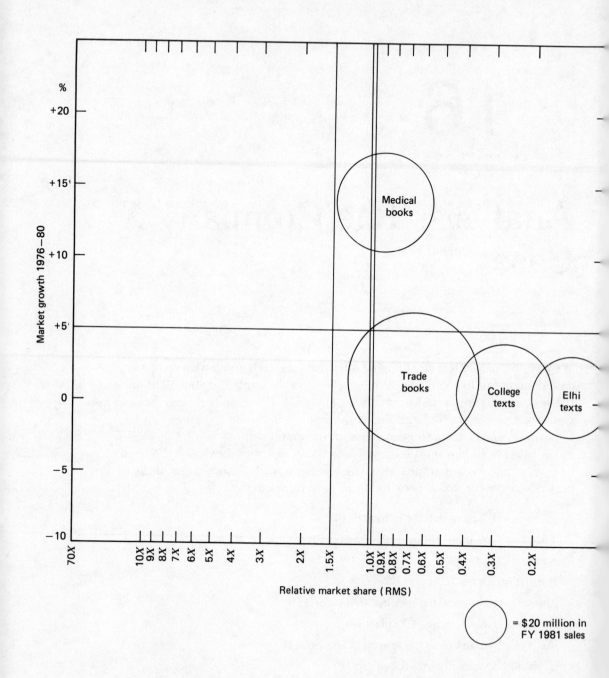

Exhibit 16.1 Company *X*, Growth Share Matrix, FY 1981.

243

GROWTH–SHARE MATRIX

The growth–share matrix shows us that company X is in a weak corporate position. Three of its four businesses are dogs, in the lower right-hand quadrant of the graph. Remember that a dog does not automatically mean that divestiture is indicated. The dog businesses may be throwing off cash, something we can check in our cash flow graphs. However, none of the three businesses has achieved market leadership and all are in low-growth markets offering little hope for change. Medical books is the only bright spot in the corporation, growing significantly faster than the market and in the number two competitive position. The fast market growth and strong competitive showing suggest there may be a chance to knock the leader off and take over the number one spot. The president of company X should be backing its medical books group fully since it is the only chance for glory in the corporate picture. (See Exhibit 16.1.)

SHARE MOMENTUM

The share–momentum graph confirms our diagnosis about hope for the future. Trade books, elhi, and college texts are stuck down at the origin of the graph with low company and market growth. Company X's elhi texts are growing faster than the market even though they are under 5%, meaning they are gaining market share. Medical books are once again the sterling performer, growing at an even faster rate than the rapid growth market. Company X is gaining market share in the medical arena, making our hypothesis that it could overtake the market leader from its already strong position even more credible. (See Exhibit 16.2.)

SECTOR

Now that we have some knowledge of our case company, we can see how it fits into the overall market. Is it a strong or weak competitor overall? The answer is that, relative to major book competitors, company X is smaller and weaker. Its relative market share is about 0.3, less than a third the size of the market leader. However, it has one unusual characteristic—a high growth rate relative to the market as a whole and most competitors. Only CBS, the leader, grew faster than company X over the five-year period, 1976–1980. In a market growing at just over 2% a year, company X has been able to sustain a 6% growth rate. Why is that? Our answer comes from the share-momentum graph that showed us how rapidly company X's medical books group has grown. Competitors may not be positioned in a high-growth market

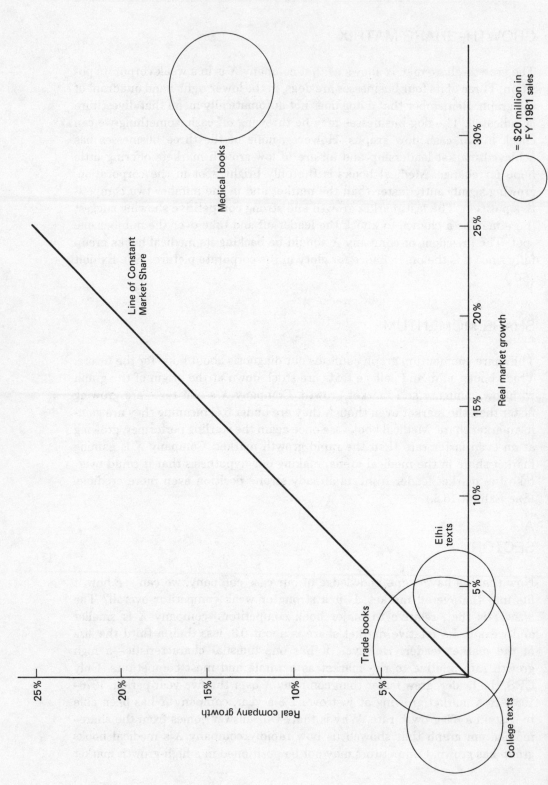

Exhibit 16.2 Company Y, FY 1977–1981, Share Momentum.

like medical books and therefore are stuck at or below the industry growth rate.

How attractive is the industry for new competitors? Not very, according to the sector graph. Not only is the industry growing slowly, but a mass of competitors are struggling for market share from about the same point of relative market share. There are different amounts of vested interest in the industry as shown by the percentage operating income of the corporation represented by books. Company X and SFN, with 100% of their income from books, are a lot more tied to the fortunes of the industry than Time, Inc., with 15.6% of operating income, CBS with 11%, or Times Mirror with 16%. If company X were going to make a move against a competitor, it would do well to choose one of the low-vested-interest companies that operates in its sphere. (See Exhibit 16.3.)

RETURN ON ASSETS

We are showing three LOBs on the financial graphs instead of the four LOBs on the market graphs because financial data were unable to be broken out into four groups. The three groups are general books (trade), educational (college and elhi texts, and professional (medical) books. Return on assets was lowest for the medical books group. General books and educational texts were almost the same on this measure, between 15% and 20%. These findings are not inconsistent with our findings on growth. A high-growth business needs greater investment and a higher asset base than a low-growth business, and we therefore expect return on assets to be lower (the same profit with a higher asset base leads to lower return on assets). The graph shows that the lower return on assets is a combination of factors, both lower operating margin and lower asset turnover. (See Exhibit 16.4.)

ASSETS VERSUS OPERATING INCOME

Despite the lower return on assets shown by the medical books group in the last graph, company X's asset investment in the group is in line with its contribution to corporate operating income. This graph shows that all three LOBs are virtually on the center line of equal contribution. Our first reaction may be to laud the wisdom of the corporation to not invest its dollars where there is no return, but we reconsider on second look. If the corporation is investing proportionately to current returns, how is it going to fund professional/medical books sufficiently to overtake the market leader and really perform? The approach of investing only to the limit of income is overly conservative when it is applied across the board without regard to differing strategies for different businesses. We can hypothesize that company X is not managing its LOBs strategically. (See Exhibit 16.5.)

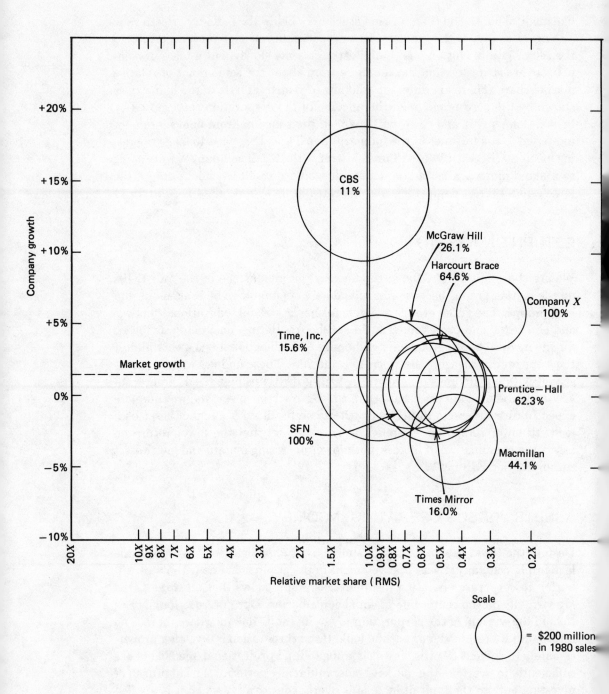

Exhibit 16.3 Book Publishing Sector Graph, 1976–1980.

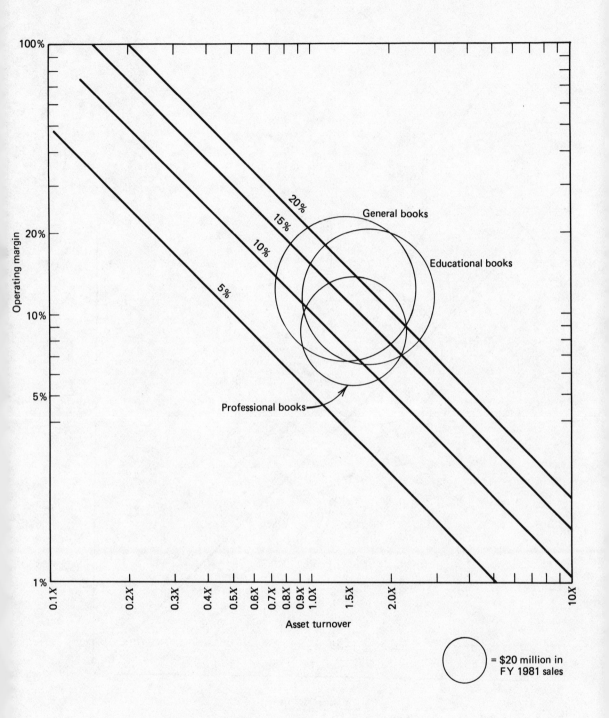

Exhibit 16.4 Company *X*, Return on Assets FY 1981.

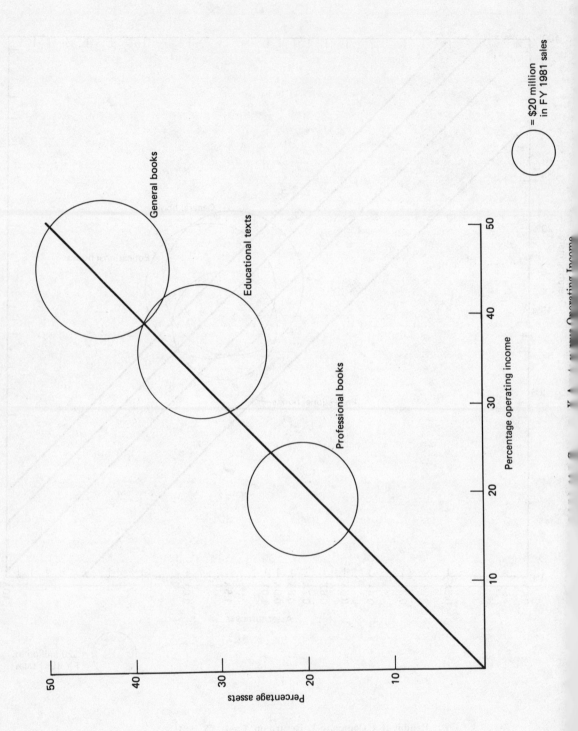

Percentage operating income

Percentage assets

General books

Educational texts

Professional books

◯ = $20 million in FY 1981 sales

248

INVESTMENT TENDENCIES

Assets represent the historical investment in a business. Capital expenditures represent current investment. The investment tendencies graph shows us that company X is investing most aggressively in educational texts as compared with the past. Professional/medical books are getting no favoritism, receiving almost exactly the same investment in fiscal 1981 as their historical asset investment. What does the company have in mind? Why are educational texts getting funded—a low-growth business with unspectacular market share? Reading the annual report's explanation of the LOBs does not provide an answer. The report paints a bleak picture of the market outlook for elhi texts, with declining budgets and Proposition 2½ in Massachusetts but states that, "Despite these economic conditions and the revenue downturn of the division this past year, we remain optimistic that significant inroads can be made—if we broaden our product line and build upon our existing strengths." College texts declined in real growth in fiscal 1981, not supplying a reason for investment either. The graph raises a flag and tells us we have uncovered an inconsistency that needs more information, either from industry sources or from the company itself. (See Exhibit 16.6.)

LONG-TERM TREND

The long-term trend graph shows unspectacular performance for company X over the past five years, not just in fiscal 1981. While the company recovered from a profitability valley in 1979 and 1980 by 1981, it did not reach attractive levels in absolute terms. Return on equity was under 10% in 1981, lower than a money market fund that year. Return on sales was between 3% and 4%, suggesting the need to analyze operations and find a place to do belt tightening. The company was slightly less leveraged in 1981 than in 1979 and 1980, probably a wise move in view of its lackluster performance, although it still had a high proportion of debt to equity. It started to lower dividend payout in 1980 and again in 1981, recognizing the need to conserve cash. All of these financial trends are summarized nicely in the market-to-book ratio, which dropped from 1979 to 1980, rose slightly in 1981, but was still quite low in 1981. Market value of the company was only about half of the book value in 1981.

Company X had a difficult five years between 1977 and 1981. Nowhere in the period did it regain the profitability of 1977. The market noted the amount of leverage in its capital structure, along with lackluster performance, and devalued the stock. The company needs a star business to effect a turnaround—yet it did not invest in its one chance to succeed: professional/medical books. (See Exhibit 16.7.)

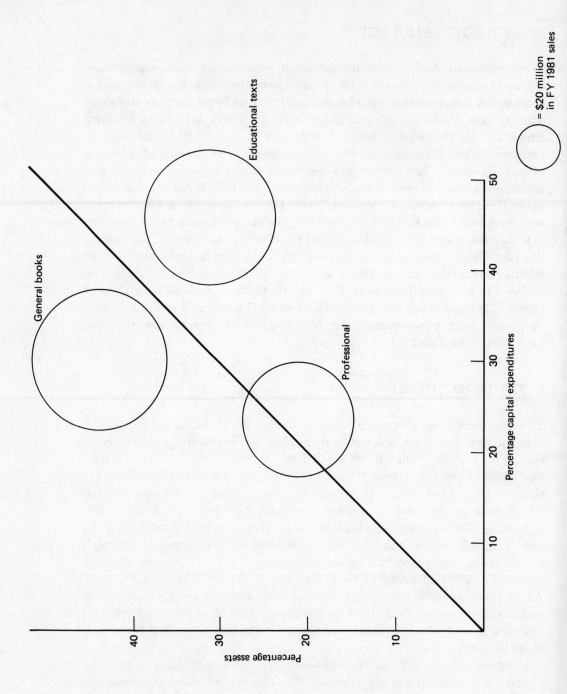

General books

Educational texts

Professional

Percentage capital expenditures

Percentage assets

○ = $20 million
in FY 1981 sales

50

40

30

20

10

40

30

20

10

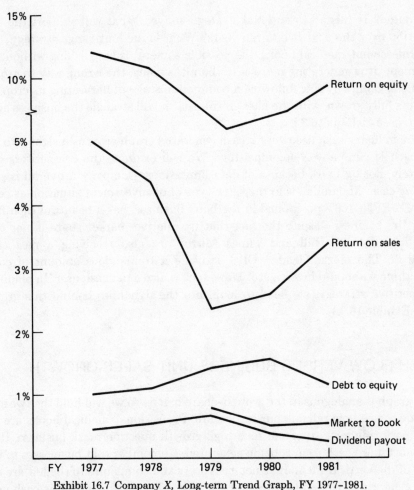

Exhibit 16.7 Company X, Long-term Trend Graph, FY 1977–1981.

CASH USED VERSUS CASH GENERATED

We have talked about the theory that a business must serve one of two purposes: providing growth or providing cash. Since only professional/medical
books is providing company X with growth, we must look at the amount of cash
the other businesses are contributing. The situation shown by the graph is very
interesting. General books and educational texts are indeed well positioned on
the cash-generating side of the center diagonal but are footnoted as a special
case. They are not really generating cash in the sense of net income but rather
in the sense of liquidation of assets. They show a negative change in assets from
year end to year end, meaning that the company is selling off assets in the business. We know from the investment tendencies graph that capital expenditures
are being made, but apparently they are not as great as the amount of assets
being liquidated. Again, this raises questions. Why are these businesses being

liquidated? Is this an intentional strategic move? What will support the corporation over the next five to ten years? What is the long-range strategy?

Professional/medical books, the possible saviour, is languishing without investment. It is generating more cash than it is using, the wrong way to grow a business. Company X is following a common mistake of harvesting its crop before it's fully grown, with the likely result that it will strangle the business at its roots. (See Exhibit 16.8.)

The industry cash used versus cash generated graph gives us insight into the strength of company X's competitors. We will examine the competitors corporately, not by LOB, because of data limitations. Company X overall is generating cash. Macmillan is in the same type of disinvestment situation as company X. SFN, 100% positioned in the book business, has a beautiful cash flow from the business despite the fact that its relative market share is not outstanding. Prentice-Hall and Times Mirror are also receiving a nice cash throwoff. The market leader, CBS, is using a tremendous amount of cash, something we should investigate. Time, Inc., is also a net cash user. In planning competitive strategy, we need to look into the dynamics behind this graph. (See Exhibit 16.9.)

CASH FLOW VERSUS BUSINESS UNIT SALES GROWTH

This graph is analogous to the growth–share matrix so we will hold the two side by side to see how reliable our results are. Professional/medical books are indeed performing as expected. As a high-growth question mark business, they are using more cash than is being generated. Remember that businesses to the right of the vertical 1.0 line are net cash users and companies to the left are net cash generators. General books and educational texts are shown as cash generators. This is in line with recent findings that dog businesses may generate attractive amounts of cash. In this case, the businesses are generating cash by liquidating assets, a hint that company X does not see them with a long-term future. Unfortunately, they represent the majority of company X's sales and income, so they will have to be replaced somehow. (See Exhibits 16.10 and 16.11.)

Let's add it all up.

1. Company X has no market leaders—a weak portfolio.
2. Professional/medical books offers the only opportunity to grow and possibly gain market leadership the way the company is now structured.
3. Company X is not managing strategically. It is not providing funding to its medical books group and is actually taking cash *out* of the high-growth business that should be *using* cash.

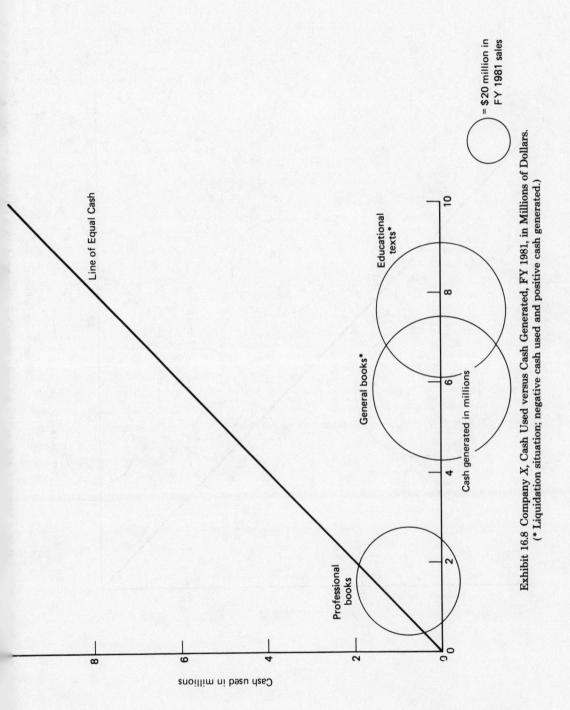

Exhibit 16.8 Company X, Cash Used versus Cash Generated, FY 1981, in Millions of Dollars. (* Liquidation situation; negative cash used and positive cash generated.)

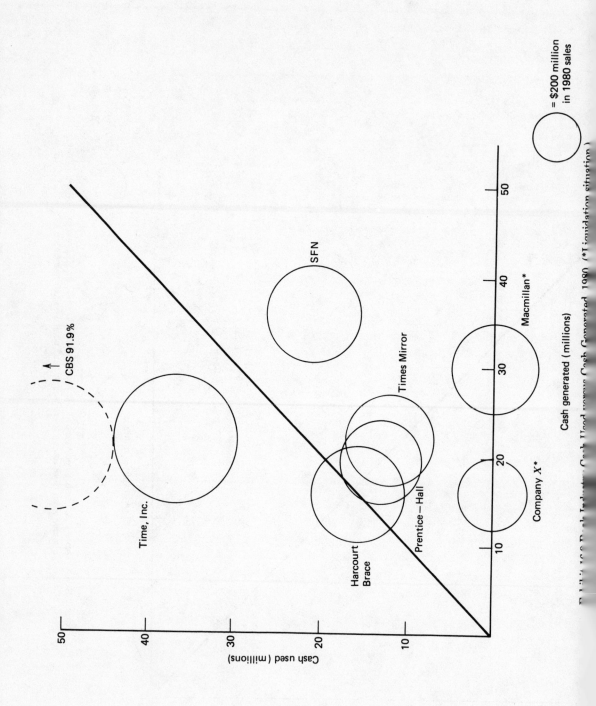

Exhibit 2 Publishing: Cash Used versus Cash Generated, 1980. (*Liquidation situation.)

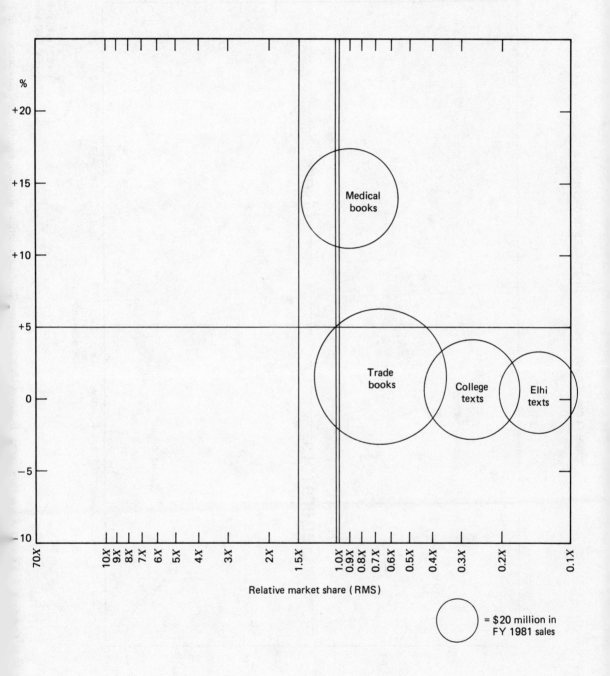

Exhibit 16.10 Company *X*, Growth Share Matrix, FY 1981.

255

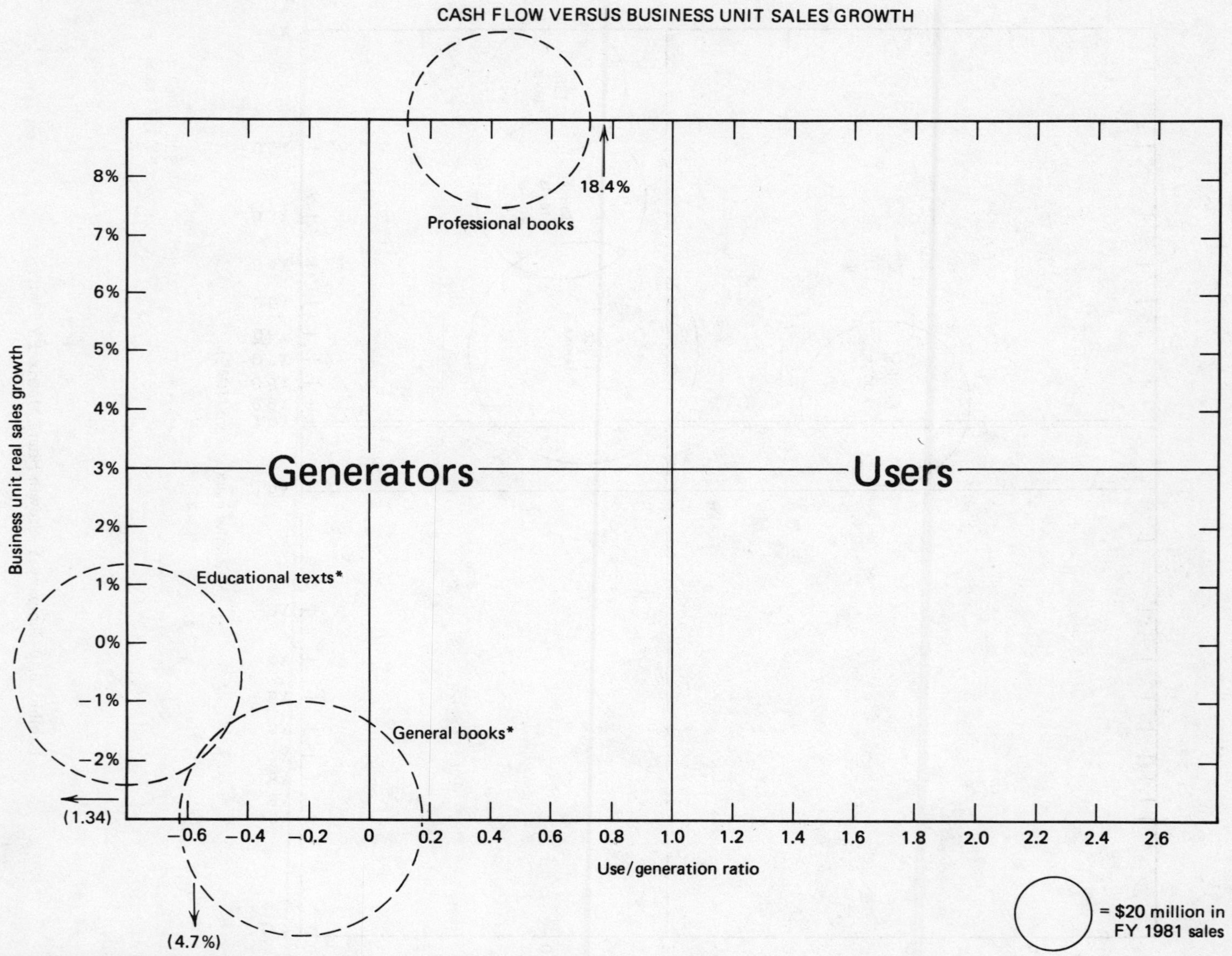

CASH FLOW VERSUS BUSINESS UNIT SALES GROWTH

Exhibit 16.11 Company X FY 1981 Cash Flow versus Business Unit Sales Growth. (* Liquidation situation; negative use/generation ratio.)

4.   Company X is totally dependent on the book industry, unlike most of its competitors, and it is a weak player overall.

Our limited graphic situation analysis has permitted us to focus in on the major strategic issues facing company X. We can draw many more graphs on the industry and individual competitors to round out the data. If the calculations are computerized, it is a simple process to create tons of graphs, cutting the data in every possible way to see if any new insights can be obtained from different vantage points. When dealing with a large number of graphs, it can be helpful to pin them up on a wall and stare at them for a while, hoping that the big picture may emerge. Interpretation is where the real skill comes in, especially where one graph seemingly contradicts another. In that case, you need to draw upon your knowledge of the industry, the company, and strategy to make sense of the puzzle.

Graphic analysis is step one in the strategy-planning process (remember our five steps—situation, objectives, strategy, tactics, and control). It is a vital step, from which sound objectives and strategy can be developed. Our graphs will also be useful when we come to strategy, allowing us to graphically project the effect of a given strategy on the competitive picture and our own portfolio. We can play "what if" games with the data, such as:

What if our strategy increases our market share by x and causes competitor A to lose share by x? How will the sector graph look then? What about competitor A's share momentum? Will it change our growth–share matrix to a more favorable outlook?

What if we abdicate market 1 and make a strong play in market 3? What is competitor A's likely response in market 3? How will that affect its growth–share matrix? Are we threatening one of its businesses that is important to corporate profitability, as shown in the return on assets graph? Will the competitor invest more to protect its position, as indicated on the investment tendencies graph?

What if we do nothing different but competitor B continues to gain share in our base business? How will our growth–share matrix look? What about the sector? The share momentum?

The uses of projected graphs in strategy development are endless. They give realism to our articulated strategies. The impact of a strategy can be put to the test through graphics.

What is the next step? Graphic analysis has given us the ability to ask a lot of questions and challenge common knowledge. Now we must build and develop the most informed possible strategies for success, a creative challenge for the management team. Graphs are a tool for understanding; now we must take the input and exercise judgment.

17

Tools of the Trade

You have now read background about planning, practiced the calculations, and seen how the graphs fit together in analysis. The remaining challenge is to apply the techniques to your own company and industry. We have brought together in one place the formulas, worksheets, and shell graphs to make things easier. The information is organized by original chapter and graph title. You will find four items under each chapter head:

1. A list of formulas used in developing the data
2. The type of graph paper you need to draw the graph
3. Worksheets
4. A shell graph

Of course, you can always return to the original chapter if you have forgotten the meaning of a term or how to do a calculation.

The last portion of the chapter includes an explanation of log paper along with some samples and the name and address of a supply source for templates with which to draw circles. Everything you need to do a complete analysis is here, except the data themselves.

CHAPTER 6: THE GROWTH–SHARE MATRIX

Relative market share versus market growth

FORMULAS:

1. Relative market share

$$\text{Market leader} = \frac{\text{Market leader share/sales}}{\text{Second largest company share/sales}}$$

$$\text{Not market leader} = \frac{\text{Other company share/sales}}{\text{Market leader share/sales}}$$

2. Deflating to real dollars

$$\text{Real dollars} = \frac{\text{Nominal dollars}}{\text{Deflator}} \times 100$$

3. Compound annual growth rate
    Calculator:
       Insert present value, future value, number of years minus 1, and solve for percentage interest

$$\text{Formula: } FV = PV\,(1 + i)^n$$
$$\text{Solve for } i$$

4. Linear regression growth rate

    1. Calculate regression line.
    2. Check fit.
    3. Find data for two years on the regression line.
    4. Calculate CAGR.

5. Circle size

$$\text{mm factor } \sqrt{\frac{\text{LOB/SBU sales}}{\text{Index}}}$$

6. Circle size key

$$\frac{\text{Index circle size}}{\text{Index sales}} = \frac{\text{Scale circle size}}{\text{Small sales dollars}}$$

Paper: 3 cycle log/linear

EXHIBIT 17.1. Growth–Share Matrix Data Sheet

Company: _____
Years: _____

Market Growth

SBU/LOB	Market	Year 1		Year 2			Year 3			Year 4			Year 5		
		Nominal Sales	De-flator	Real Sales	Nominal Sales	De-flator	Real Sales	Nominal Sales	De-flator	Real Sales	Nominal Sales	De-flator	Real Sales	Nominal Sales	De-flator	Real Sales

Growth Rate, Years 1–5: _____

Exhibit 17.1 Three-Cycle Log/Linear.

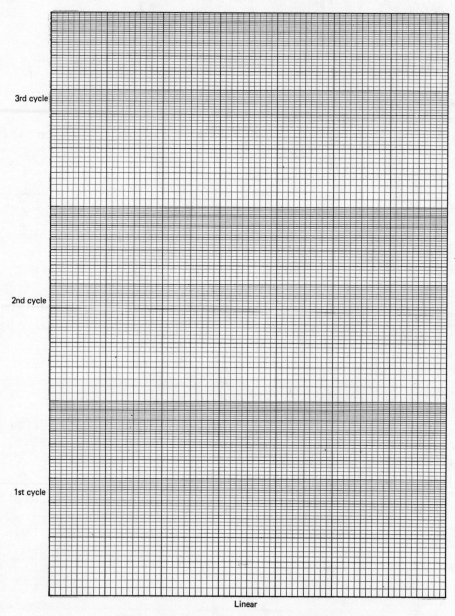

3rd cycle

2nd cycle

1st cycle

Linear

Exhibit 17.1 Three-Cycle Log Linear. (*Continued*)

EXHIBIT 17.1. Growth–Share Matrix Data Sheet (Continued)

Company: _____
Year: _____

Relative Market Share

SBU/LOB	Current Year Sales	Current Year Sales of Market Leader	RMS

Exhibit 17.1 Three-Cycle Log Linear. (*Continued*)

EXHIBIT 17.1. Growth–Share Matrix Data Sheet (*Continued*)

Summary Table

Company: _____ _____
Years: _____ _____

Market growth calculation method: _____

Circle size scale: $ _____ = _____ mm.
Circle size key: $ _____ = _____ mm.

SBU/LOB	RMS	Real Market Growth	Circle Size

Exhibit 17.1 Three-Cycle Log Linear. (*Continued*)

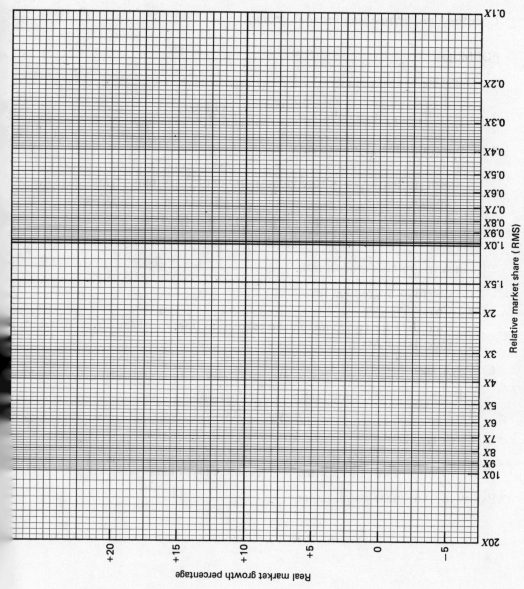

Relative market share (RMS)

Real market growth percentage

Exhibit 17.2 Growth–Share Matrix Shell Graph.

CHAPTER 7: THE SHARE MOMENTUM

Company growth versus market growth

FORMULAS:

1. Deflating to real dollars

$$\text{Real dollars} = \frac{\text{Nominal dollars}}{\text{Deflator}} \times 100$$

2. Compound annual growth rate
   Calculator:
      Insert present value, future value, number of years minus 1, and solve for percentage interest

$$\text{Formula: FV} = \text{PV } (1 + i)^{n}$$
$$\text{Solve for } i$$

3. Linear regression growth rate

   1. Calculate regression line.
   2. Check fit.
   3. Find data for two years on the regression line.
   4. Calculate CAGR.

4. Circle size

$$\text{mm factor } \sqrt{\frac{\text{LOB/SBU sales}}{\text{Index}}}$$

5. Circle size key

$$\frac{\text{Index circle size}}{\text{Index sales}} = \frac{\text{Scale circle size}}{\text{Small sales dollars}}$$

Paper: regular linear graph paper.

EXHIBIT 17.3. Share–Momentum Data Sheet

Company: _____
Years: _____

Company Growth

SBU/LOB	Year 1			Year 2			Year 3			Year 4			Year 5		
	Nominal Sales	De-flator	Real Sales	Nominal Sales	De-flator	Real Sales	Nominal Sales	De-flator	Real Sales	Nominal Sales	De-flator	Real Sales	Nominal Sales	De-flator	Real Sales

Growth Rate, Years 1–5: _____

Exhibit 17.3

EXHIBIT 17.3. Share–Momentum Data Sheet (*Continued*)

Market Growth

Company: _____
Years: _____

SBU/LOB	Year 1			Year 2			Year 3			Year 4			Year 5		
	Nominal Sales	De-flator	Real Sales	Nominal Sales	De-flator	Real Sales	Nominal Sales	De-flator	Real Sales	Nominal Sales	De-flator	Real Sales	Nominal Sales	De-flator	Real Sales

Growth Rate, Years 1–5: _____

Exhibit 17.3 (*Continued*)

EXHIBIT 17.3. Share–Momentum Data Sheet (*Continued*)

Summary Table

Company: _____
Years: _____

Growth calculation method:

Circle size scale: $ ____ = ____ mm.
Circle size key: $ ____ = ____ mm.

SBU/LOB	Real Company Growth	Real Market Growth	Circle Size

Exhibit 17.3 (*Continued*)

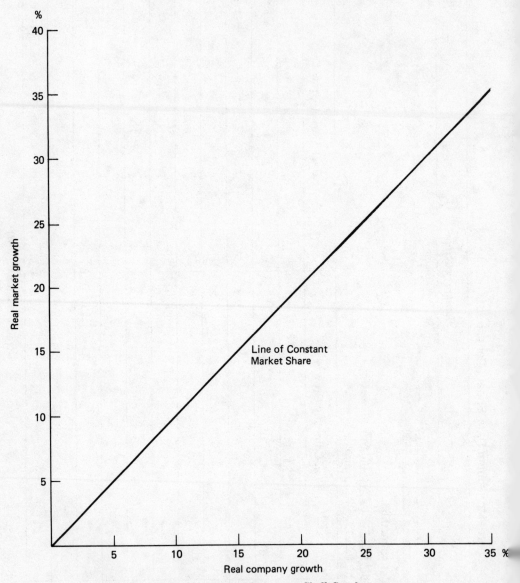

Exhibit 17.4 Share Momentum Shell Graph.

CHAPTER 8: THE SECTOR GRAPH

Relative market share versus company growth

FORMULAS:

1. Relative market share

$$\text{Market leader} = \frac{\text{Market leader share/sales}}{\text{Second largest company share/sales}}$$

$$\text{Not market leader} = \frac{\text{Other company share/sales}}{\text{Market leader share/sales}}$$

2. Deflating to real dollars

$$\text{Real dollars} = \frac{\text{Nominal dollars}}{\text{Deflator}} \times 100$$

3. Compound annual growth rate
   Calculator:
   Insert present value, future value, number of years minus 1, and solve for percentage interest

$$\text{Formula: } FV = PV\ (1 + i)^{n}$$
$$\text{Solve for } i$$

4. Linear regression growth rate

   1. Calculate regression line.
   2. Check fit.
   3. Find data for two years on the regression line.
   4. Calculate CAGR.

5. Circle size

$$\text{mm factor} \sqrt{\frac{\text{LOB/SBU sales}}{\text{Index}}}$$

6. Circle size key

$$\frac{\text{Index circle size}}{\text{Index sales}} = \frac{\text{Scale circle size}}{\text{Small sales dollars}}$$

Paper: 3 cycle log/linear.

EXHIBIT 17.5. Sector Data Sheet

Company and Market Growth

Market: _____
Years: _____

SBU/LOB	Year 1			Year 2			Year 3			Year 4			Year 5		
	Nominal Sales	De-flator	Real Sales	Nominal Sales	De-flator	Real Sales	Nominal Sales	De-flator	Real Sales	Nominal Sales	De-flator	Real Sales	Nominal Sales	De-flator	Real Sales

Growth Rate, Years 1–5: _____

Exhibit 17.5

EXHIBIT 17.5. Sector Data Sheet (Continued)

Market Growth

	Nominal Sales	Deflator	Real Sales
Year 1			
Year 2			
Year 3			
Year 4			
Year 5			

Exhibit 17.5 (*Continued*)

EXHIBIT 17.5. Sector Data Sheet (*Continued*)

Market: _____
Year: _____

Relative Market Share

Company	Current Year Sales	Current Year Sales of Market Leader	RMS

Exhibit 17.5 (*Continued*)

EXHIBIT 17.5. Sector Data Sheet (*Continued*)

Company	LOB Profitability		LOB as Percentage of Total
	LOB Operating Income	Total Company Operating Income	

Exhibit 17.5 (*Continued*)

EXHIBIT 17.5. Sector Data Sheet (Continued)

Summary Table

Market:
Years:
Market growth:

Growth calculation method:

Circle size scale: $_____ = _____ mm
Circle size key: $_____ = _____ mm

Company	RMS	Real Company Growth	Circle Size	Percentage of Operating Income

Exhibit 17.5 (Continued)

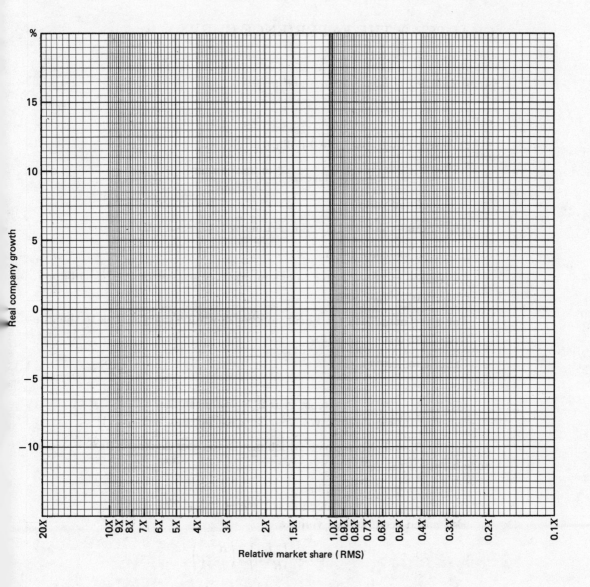

Exhibit 17.6 Sector Graph Shell.

CHAPTER 9: THE EXPERIENCE CURVE

Accumulated volume versus cost or price

FORMULAS:

1. Deflating cost/price to real dollars

$$\text{Real dollars} = \frac{\text{Nominal dollars}}{\text{Deflator}} \times 100$$

2. Accumulated volume

    Add annual volumes and take a running total each year

3. Linear to log conversion

    Calculator method: Enter linear number: press buttons on calculator to convert to a logarithm.

    Table method: Read the linear number down the margin: look to the interior of the table for the log.

4. Experience curve

    2^{α}

$$\alpha = \frac{\log (\text{cost year 2}) - \log (\text{cost year 1})}{\log (\text{accum. vol. year 2}) - \log (\text{accum. vol. year 1})}$$

$2^{\alpha} = a$ _____% experience curve, which means the cost decline is 100% − experience curve percentage. For example,

$$2^{\alpha} = 70\%$$
$$\text{Cost decline} = 100\% - 70\% = 30\%$$

5. Estimated accumulated volume

$$\text{EV} = \left(\frac{L}{R^{N-1}} \right) \left(\frac{R^{N-1}}{R-1} \right)$$

EXHIBIT 17.7.   Experience Curve Data Sheet

Product: _____
Years: _____

Year	Annual Volume	Accumulated Volume		Nominal Unit Cost/Price	Deflator	Real Unit Cost/Price	
		Linear	Log			Linear	Log

Exhibit 17.7

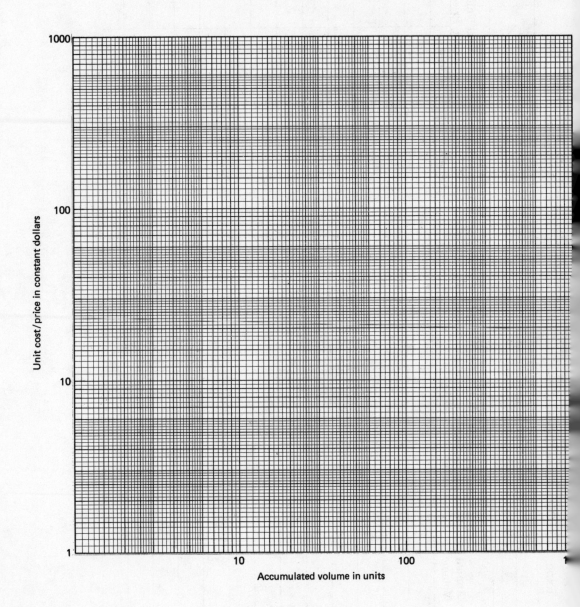

Exhibit 17.8 Experience Curve Shell Graph.

CHAPTER 12: THE PROFITABILITY GRAPHS

I. *Return on assets—asset turnover versus operating margin*

FORMULAS:

1. Asset turnover $= \dfrac{\text{Sales}}{\text{Two-year average assets}}$

2. Operating margin $= \dfrac{\text{Operating profit}}{\text{Sales}}$

3. Circle size

$$\text{mm factor} \sqrt{\dfrac{\text{LOB/SBU sales}}{\text{Index}}}$$

4. Circle size key

$$\dfrac{\text{Index circle size}}{\text{Index sales}} = \dfrac{\text{Scale circle size}}{\text{Small sales dollars}}$$

Paper: 2 x 2 cycle log.

II. *Assets versus income*

LOB percentage of assets versus LOB percentage operating income

1. LOB percentage of assets $= \dfrac{\text{LOB assets}}{\text{Total corporate assets}}$

2. LOB percentage of operating income $= \dfrac{\text{LOB operating income}}{\text{Total operating income}}$

3. Circle size

$$\text{mm factor} \sqrt{\dfrac{\text{LOB/SBU sales}}{\text{Index}}}$$

4. Circle size key

$$\dfrac{\text{Index circle size}}{\text{Index sales}} = \dfrac{\text{Scale circle size}}{\text{Small sales dollars}}$$

Paper: regular linear graph paper.

EXHIBIT 17.9. Return on Assets Data Sheet

Company: _____

Year: _____

LOB	Sales	Year 1	Assets Year 2	Aver.	Asset Turnover	Operating Income	Operating Margin

Exhibit 17.9

EXHIBIT 17.10.   Return on Assets Summary

Company: _____
Year: _____

LOB	Asset Turnover	Operating Margin	Circle Size

Exhibit 17.10

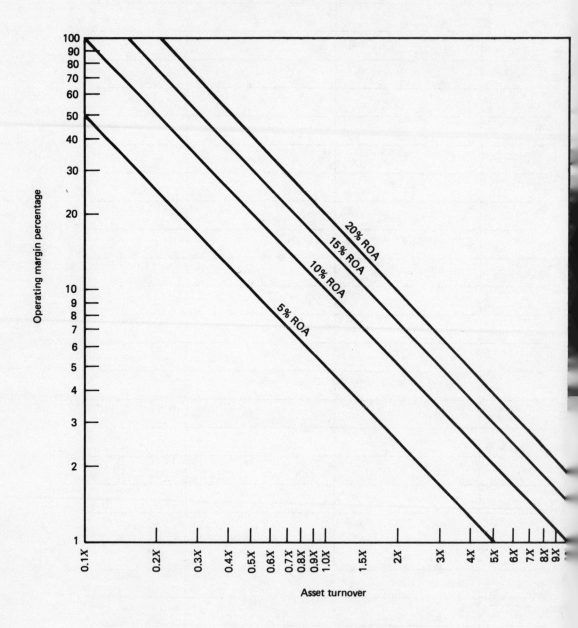

Exhibit 17.11 Return on Assets Graph.

EXHIBIT 17.12.   Assets versus Income Data Sheet

LOB	Operating Income	Percentage of Total	Assets	Percentage of Total

Exhibit 17.12

EXHIBIT 17.13.   Assets versus Income Summary

LOB	Percentage Operating Income	Percentage Assets	Circle Size

Exhibit 17.13

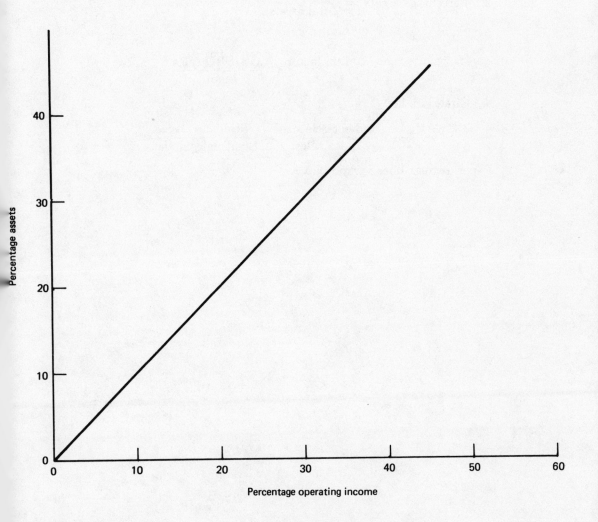

Exhibit 17.14 Assets versus Operating Income Shell Graph.

CHAPTER 13: INVESTMENT TENDENCIES

FORMULAS:

1. Percentage capital expenditures $= \dfrac{\text{LOB capital expenditures}}{\text{Total capital expenditures}}$

2. Percentage assets $= \dfrac{\text{LOB assets}}{\text{Total assets}}$

3. Circle size

$$\text{mm factor} \sqrt{\dfrac{\text{LOB/SBU sales}}{\text{Index}}}$$

4. Circle size key

$$\dfrac{\text{Index circle size}}{\text{Index sales}} = \dfrac{\text{Scale circle size}}{\text{Small sales dollars}}$$

Paper: regular linear graph paper.

EXHIBIT 17.15. Investment Tendencies Data Sheet

LOB	Capital Expenditures	Percentage of Total	Assets	Percentage of Total

Exhibit 17.15

EXHIBIT 17.16. Investment Tendencies Summary Table

LOB	Percentage Capital Expenditures	Percentage Assets	Circle Size

Exhibit 17.16

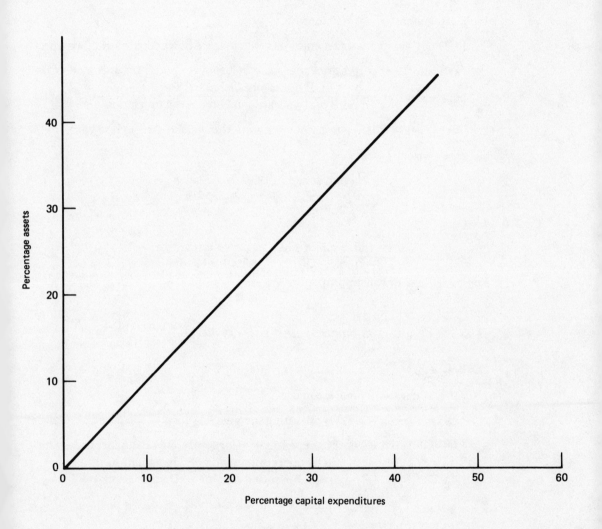

Exhibit 17.17 Investment Tendencies, Shell Graph.

CHAPTER 14: CASH FLOW

I. Cash used/generated

FORMULAS:

1. Cash generated $=$ Net income

    LOB net income = LOB operating income $-$ Allocated corporate expenses

    LOB allocated corporate expenses = (Corporate operating income $-$ Corporate net income) $\times \dfrac{\text{LOB operating income} + \text{Depreciation}}{\text{Total operating income} + \text{Depreciation}}$

2. Cash used = Change in assets = Assets this year $-$ Assets last year

3. Circle size

$$\text{mm factor} \sqrt{\frac{\text{LOB/SBU sales}}{\text{Index}}}$$

4. Circle size key

$$\frac{\text{Index circle size}}{\text{Index sales}} = \frac{\text{Scale circle size}}{\text{Small sales dollars}}$$

Paper: regular linear graph paper.

II. Cash flow versus business unit sales growth

FORMULAS:

1. Cash generated = net income

    LOB net income = LOB operating income $-$ Allocated corporate expenses

    LOB allocated corporate expenses = (Corporate operating income $-$ Corporate net income) $\times \dfrac{\text{LOB operating income} + \text{Depreciation}}{\text{Total operating income} + \text{Depreciation}}$

2. Cash used = Change in assets = Assets this year $-$ Assets last year

3. Use/generation ratio $= \dfrac{\text{Cash used}}{\text{Cash generated}}$

4. Deflating to real dollars

$$\text{Real dollars} = \frac{\text{Nominal dollars}}{\text{Deflator}} \times 100$$

5. Compound annual growth rate
    Calculator:
      Insert present value, future value, number of years minus 1, and solve for percentage interest

$$\text{Formula: } FV = PV\,(1 + i)^n$$
$$\text{Solve for } i$$

6. Linear regression growth rate

    1. Calculate regression line.
    2. Check fit.
    3. Find data for two years on the regression line.
    4. Calculate CAGR.

7. Circle size

$$\text{mm factor }\sqrt{\frac{\text{LOB/SBU sales}}{\text{Index}}}$$

8. Circle size key

$$\frac{\text{Index circle size}}{\text{Index sales}} = \frac{\text{Scale circle size}}{\text{Small sales dollars}}$$

Paper: regular linear graph paper.

EXHIBIT 17.18. Cash Used/Generated Data Sheet

Company: _____
Year: _____

LOB	Operating Income	Depreciation	Operating Income + Depreciation	Percentage Cash	Percentage Cash × Expenses to Be Allocated	Net Income	Assets		Change in Assets
							Year 1	Year 2	

Exhibit 17.18

EXHIBIT 17.19. Cash Used/Generated Summary Table

LOB	Net Income (Cash Used)	Change in Assets (Cash Generated)	Circle Size

Exhibit 17.19

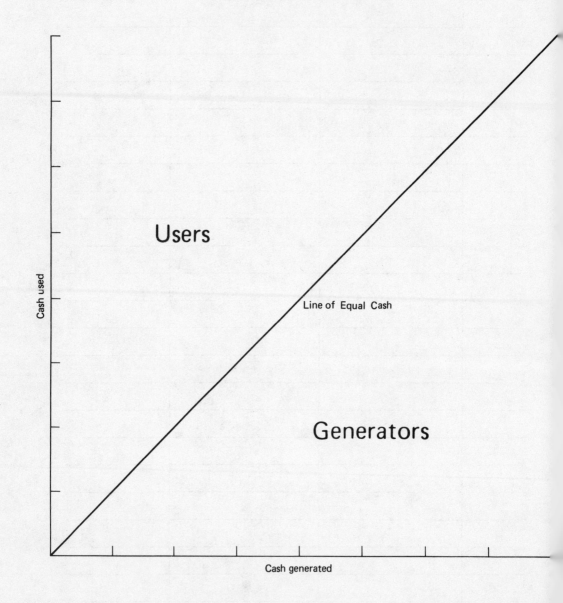

Users

Generators

Line of Equal Cash

Cash used

Cash generated

Exhibit 17.20 Cash Used versus Cash Generated, Shell Graph.

EXHIBIT 17.21. Cash Flow versus Sales Growth Data Sheet

Used/Generated Ratio

LOB	Cash Used	Cash Generated	Used/Generated Ratio

Exhibit 17.21

EXHIBIT 17.21. Cash Flow versus Sales Growth Data Sheet (Continued)

Company: _____
Years: _____

Line of Business Growth

LOB	Year 1		Year 2		Year 3		Year 4		Year 5	
	Nominal Sales	De-flator	Real Sales	Nominal Sales	De-flator	Real Sales	Nominal Sales	De-flator	Real Sales	Nominal Sales	De-flator	Real Sales	Nominal Sales	De-flator	Real Sales

Growth Rate, Years 1–5: _____

Exhibit 17.21 (*Continued*)

EXHIBIT 17.22.   Cash Flow versus Sales Summary Table

Company: _____
Years: _____

Growth calculation method:

Circle size scale: $_____ = _____ mm
Circle size key: $_____ = _____ mm

LOB	Use/Generation Ratio	Growth Rate	Circle Size

Exhibit 17.22

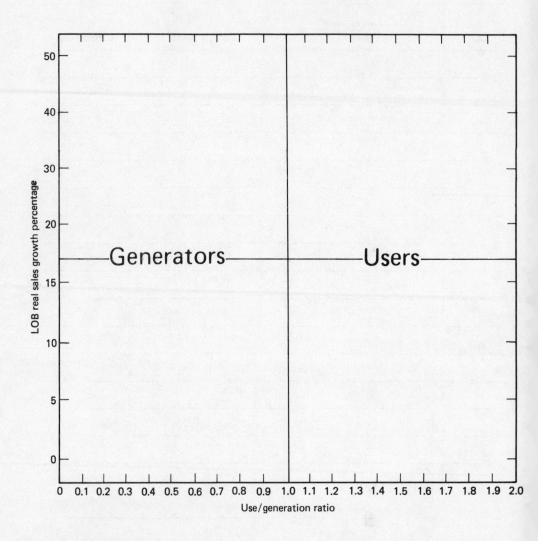

Exhibit 17.23 Cash Flow versus Business Unit Sales Growth, Shell Graph.

CHAPTER 15: LONG-TERM TRENDS

FORMULAS:

1. Debt to equity:

   Current liabilities + Long-term liabilities = Total debt

   $$\text{Debt to equity} = \frac{\text{Total debt}}{\text{Two-year average equity}}$$

2. $\text{Return on equity} = \dfrac{\text{Net income}}{\text{Two-year average equity}}$

3. $\text{Return on sales} = \dfrac{\text{Net income}}{\text{Sales}}$

4. $\text{Dividend payout} = \dfrac{\text{Dividends per share}}{\text{Earnings per share}}$

5. $\text{Market to book value} = \dfrac{\text{Market value per share}}{\text{Book value per share}}$

   $$\text{Market value per share} = \text{Average stock price} = \frac{\text{High} - \text{Low for year}}{2}$$

   $$\text{Book value per share} = \frac{\text{Two-year average stockholders' equity}}{\text{Shares outstanding}}$$

Paper: regular linear graph paper.

EXHIBIT 17.24. Long-Term Trends Data Sheet

Company: _____
Years: _____

	Year 1	Year 2	Year 3	Year 4	Year 5
Current liabilities					
Long-term liabilities					
Total debt					
This year's equity					
Last year's equity					
Average equity					
Debt-to-equity ratio					
Net income					
Average equity					
Return on equity					
Sales					
Return on sales					
Dividends per share					
Earnings per share					
Dividend payout ratio					
Average shares outstanding					
Average equity					
Equity/shares outstanding					
Stock price high					
low					
Average					
Market-to-book ratio					

Exhibit 17.24

Exhibit 17.25 Long-Term Trend, Shell Graph.

USING LOGARITHMIC PAPER

Straight lines that are named "curves," such as the experience curve, result from the use of a nonlinear scale. Logarithmic (log) paper shows *percentage* changes as equal spaces rather than *unit* changes as equal spaces. On linear graph paper, the distance from 1 to 2 is the same as the distance from 3 to 4, yet the percentage change is 100% in the first case and 25% in the second case. By representing equal proportions as equal spaces on log paper, a curve appears as a straight line. This is important because we need linearity to perform some of the analysis.

Log paper is divided into cycles based on 10. Each cycle represents numbers within the range of a power of 10. Remember that all numbers can be rewritten in a form that gives a power of 10.

$$10 = 1 \times 10^1$$
$$100 = 1 \times 10^2$$
$$1000 = 1 \times 10^3$$
$$1523 = 1.523 \times 10^3 \text{ or } 15.23 \times 10^2$$

Follow this procedure to determine the number of cycles your data span. Assume your data are sales of 370, 1,585, and 20,030.

STEP 1.   Take the smallest number in the data and move the decimal point until the number fits between 1 and 10.

   Smallest number = 370

   Change to 3.70 (move decimal two places to the left)

STEP 2.   Take the largest number and move the decimal point the same number of places.

   Largest number = 20,030

   Change to 200.30 (move decimal two places to the left)

STEP 3.   Read the number of cycles from the table below.

If the largest number is between:	The number of cycles is:
1 and 10	1
11 and 100	2
101 and 1,000	3
1,001 and 10,000	4

Since 200.30 is between 101 and 1000, the number of cycles is 3.

STEP 4.   Forget what we did with the data in steps 1 and 2. Move the decimal point back to normal and work with the original data.

When you label the log paper with numbers, remember that each cycle represents a power of 10. You may begin at the origin with any power of 10; it is not necessary to start with 1. If we were graphing the example data, 370, 1,585 and 20,030, we would label the first cycle from 100 to 1,000, the second cycle from 1,000 to 10,000, and the third cycle from 10,000 to 100,000.

It is possible to buy paper that has a different number of cycles on the *x* axis from the *y* axis. You can buy 2 X 3 cycles, which means two cycles on one axis and three cycles on the other. A variety of other combinations are possible: 1⅓ × 2, 3 × 3, 1 × 1, and so on. Remember that your data determines the number of cycles needed. Some log paper samples are shown in Exhibits 17.26, 17.27, 17.28, and 17.29.

Let us examine the data we are working with to determine the type of log paper we will use.

Integrated Circuits*

	Cumulative Volume	Unit Price, Constant 1972 Dollars
1964	2.2	25.41
1965	11.7	11.20
1966	41.1	6.57
1967	109.7	4.20
1968	243.6	2.82
1969	497.2	1.92
1970	797.2	1.63
1971	1,160.2	1.32
1972	1,763.8	1.03

* Source: Electronic Industries Association.

We will follow the four-step procedure to determine the number of cycles for accumulated volume, the *x* axis.

STEP 1.   Take the smallest number and move the decimal point until the number fits between 1 to 10.

Smallest number = 2.2 million

The decimal point is already in the proper place so no movement is needed.

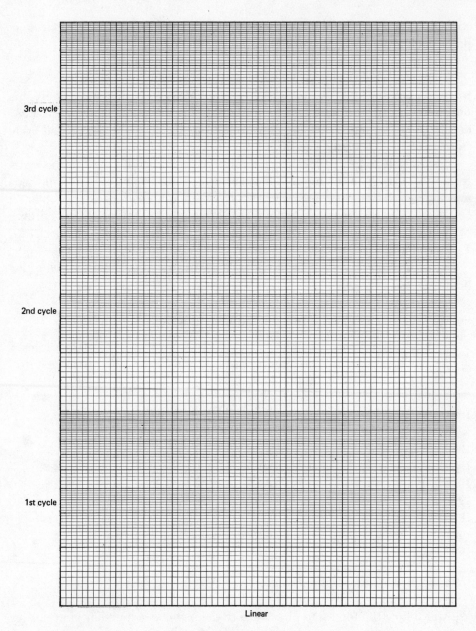

Linear

Exhibit 17.26 Three-Cycle Log/Linear.

STEP 2.   Take the largest number and move the decimal point the same number of places.

Largest number = 1,763.8

Again, no movement is needed because we did not change the decimal on the smallest number.

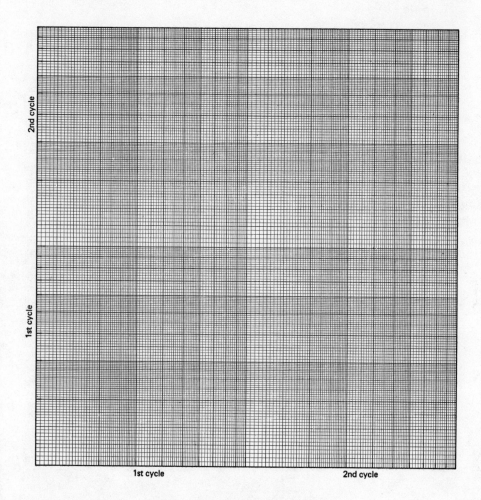

Exhibit 17.27 Log/Log, 2 × 2 Cycles.

STEP 3. Read the number of cycles from the table below. The largest number is between 1,001 and 10,000, so 4 cycles are needed.

If the largest number is between:	The number of cycles is:
1 and 10	1
11 and 100	2
101 and 1,000	3
1,001 and 10,000	4

Step 4. Moving the decimal points back to normal is not needed since we did not make any changes.

We must repeat the procedure on the unit price data to determine the number of cycles on the y axis.

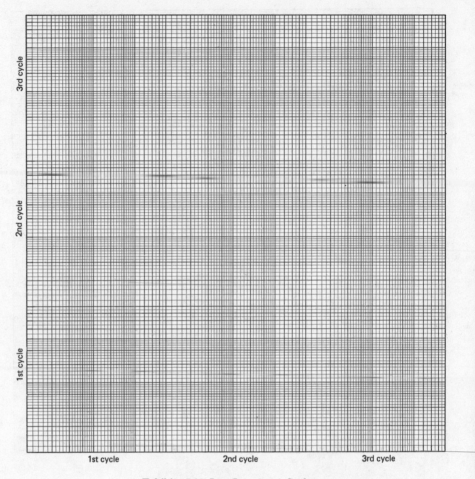

Exhibit 17.28 Log/Log, 3 × 3 Cycles.

Smallest number = 1.03
Largest number = 25.41

The largest number is between 11 and 100, so 2 cycles are needed for the y axis to display unit price. Our required log paper is 2 × 4 cycles.

Be certain you have purchased log/log paper, not semilog or log/linear. Semilog paper uses a logarithmic scale on one axis and a linear scale on the other.

In case you are still a bit confused about log paper and linear data, remember that all the paper is doing is changing the graphic scale, not the data themselves. When you read off a data point from the graph, the numbers are still our regular linear numbers. Label the linear numbers along each axis.

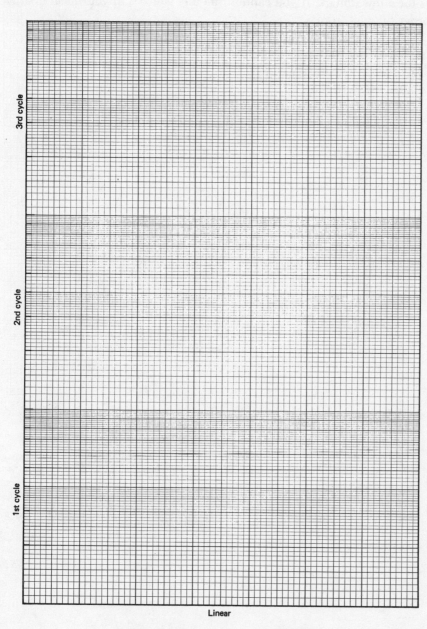

Linear

Exhibit 17.29 Log/Linear, 3 Cycles × Linear.

WHERE TO GET SUPPLIES

Templates for drawing circles are available in stationery and graphics supplies stores for a few dollars. If you cannot find any sources in your local area, you can order by mail from:

Charrette Corporation
31 Olympia Avenue
Woburn, Mass. 01888

Charrette publishes a full catalogue of graphics supplies.

Appendix 17A Natural Logarithms of Numbers between 1.0 and 4.99

N	0	1	2	3	4	5	6	7	8	9
1.0	0.00000	.00995	.01980	.02956	.03922	.04879	.05827	.06766	.07696	.08618
.1	.09531	.10436	.11333	.12222	.13103	.13976	.14842	.15700	.16551	.17395
.2	.18232	.19062	.19885	.20701	.21511	.22314	.23111	.23902	.24686	.25464
.3	.26236	.27003	.27763	.28518	.29267	.30010	.30748	.31481	.32208	.32930
.4	.33647	.34359	.35066	.35767	.36464	.37156	.37844	.38526	.39204	.39878
.5	.40547	.41211	.41871	.42527	.43178	.43825	.44469	.45108	.45742	.46373
.6	.47000	.47623	.48243	.48858	.49470	.50078	.50682	.51282	.51879	.52473
.7	.53063	.53649	.54232	.54812	.55389	.55962	.56531	.57098	.57661	.58222
.8	.58779	.59333	.59884	.60432	.60977	.61519	.62058	.62594	.63127	.63658
.9	.64185	.64710	.65233	.65752	.66269	.66783	.67294	.67803	.68310	.68813
2.0	0.69315	.69813	.70310	.70804	.71295	.71784	.72271	.72755	.73237	.73716
.1	.74194	.74669	.75142	.75612	.76081	.76547	.77011	.77473	.77932	.78390
.2	.78846	.79299	.79751	.80200	.80648	.81093	.81536	.81978	.82418	.82855
.3	.83291	.83725	.84157	.84587	.85015	.85422	.85866	.86289	.86710	.87129
.4	.87547	.87963	.88377	.88789	.89200	.89609	.90016	.90422	.90826	.91228
.5	.91629	.92028	.92426	.92822	.93216	.93609	.94001	.04391	.94779	.95166
.6	.95551	.95935	.96317	.96698	.97078	.97456	.97833	.98208	.98582	.98954
.7	.99325	.99695	.00063[a]	.00430[a]	.00796[a]	.01160[a]	.01523[a]	.01885[a]	.02245[a]	.02604[a]
.8	1.02962	.03318[a]	.03674	.04028	.04380	.04732	.05082	.05431	.05779	.06126
.9	.06471	.06815	.07158	.07500	.07841	.08181	.08519	.08856	.09192	.09527
3.0	1.09861	.10194	.10526	.10856	.11186	.11514	.11841	.12168	.12493	.12817
.1	.13140	.13462	.13783	.14103	.14422	.14740	.15057	.15373	.15688	.16002
.2	.16315	.16627	.16938	.17248	.17557	.17865	.18173	.18479	.18784	.19089
.3	.19392	.19695	.19996	.20297	.20597	.20896	.21194	.21491	.21788	.22083
.4	.22378	.22671	.22964	.23256	.23547	.23837	.24127	.24415	.24703	.24990
.5	.25276	.25562	.25846	.26130	.26413	.26695	.26976	.27257	.27536	.27815
.6	.28093	.28371	.28647	.28923	.29198	.29473	.29746	.30019	.30291	.30563
.7	.30833	.31103	.31372	.31641	.31909	.32176	.32442	.32708	.32972	.33237
.8	.33500	.33763	.34025	.34286	.34547	.34807	.35067	.35325	.35584	.35841
.9	.36098	.36354	.36609	.36864	.37118	.37372	.37624	.37877	.38128	.38379
4.0	1.38629	.38879	.39128	.39377	.39624	.39872	.40118	.40364	.40610	.40854
.1	.41099	.41342	.41585	.41828	.42070	.42311	.42552	.42792	.43031	.43270
.2	.43508	.43746	.43984	.44220	.44456	.44692	.44927	.45161	.45395	.45629
.3	.45862	.46094	.46326	.46557	.46787	.47018	.47247	.47476	.47705	.47933
.4	.48160	.48387	.48614	.48840	.49065	.49290	.49515	.49739	.49962	.50185
.5	.50408	.50630	.50851	.51072	.51293	.51513	.51732	.51951	.52170	.52388
.6	.52606	.52823	.53039	.53256	.53471	.53687	.53902	.54116	.54330	.54543
.7	.54756	.54969	.55181	.55393	.55604	.55814	.56025	.56235	.56444	.56653
.8	.56862	.57070	.57277	.57485	.57691	.57898	.58104	.58309	.58515	.58719
.9	.58924	.59127	.59331	.59534	.59737	.59939	.60141	.60342	.60543	.60744

[a] Add 1.0 to indicated figure.

Source: J. Fred Weston and Eugene F. Brigham, *Managerial Finance* (Hinsdale, Ill.: Dryden Press, 1981).

18

Use of Consultants: Make versus Buy

What is a chapter on consultants doing in a book that is supposed to provide you with the techniques to do analysis yourself? For a variety of reasons, not everyone will want to develop their own graphs. Luckily, there is a flourishing group of consultants who provide you with an option to buy the service. Now that you have read the book and perhaps even worked through some of your own data, you should have a good sense of what is involved in producing a graphics analysis. The task may be exactly what you have the time, resources, and inclination to do. If so, great, go to it! On the other hand, you may be lacking a critical piece of the pie—time, for instance. You would love to have help but cannot justify adding to staff. A consultant may be the answer.

There are other reasons why people use consultants, some of which do not relate at all to time, staff, or desire:

Objectivity.   Consultants can bring an independent, impartial viewpoint to the situation, unbiased by company history, culture, politics, organization, and predispositions.

Experience.   Consultants have dealt with parallel situations, industries, or companies over their consulting career even though the problem may occur only once in a decade in a given company, and they bring cross-fertilization of ideas from other industries.

Problem-solving/analytical skill.   Consultants are trained in finding the *real* problem, analyzing its causes, and looking for a solution.

Catalyst role.   Consultants can surface ideas already existing in the organization, give them air space, and move them along for implementation; they can help to structure the *process* properly.

Concentration. Consultants can spend full-time on a problem that would fall between the cracks in a normal manager's schedule.

Political acceptance.   Consultants can make statements to senior management that would be unacceptable from an internal source.

Any of these reasons may make it more than worthwhile to hire an outsider. Let us take one example from the list above to illustrate the point. Suppose you are the planning executive in a company headed on a path to disaster. Your management has stubbornly clung to an outmoded strategy, and competition is chopping off pieces of market share year after year. You have tried to dramatize the problem but it is not in the corporate culture to accept the fact that the golden years are over and the situation is not reversing itself. What to do? Call in the most prestigious and expensive consultants you can find under the pretext of a "strategic audit" or "helping us with planning." Send them out to study the market and report back on their findings. Gather the management group together for a presentation, having planted the seeds ahead of time that the initial results do not look positive (no one likes surprises). Let the consultants present their findings, replete with graphs, that tell the story you have been trying to get across for months. This tactic is not infallible, but if the consultants have high credibility before they begin their assignment and their use is supported by the key players, it will be pretty difficult for the mucky mucks to turn their backs on the report. Besides, they paid a lot of money to hear the facts, a strong incentive not to disregard them. It is a lot easier to ignore an executive whose salary is lost in overhead than to ignore a $50,000 study. The price of $50,000 may seem high to communicate what you would have said for free, but it is insignificant if it stops the company from throwing away millions of dollars in lost profitability.

TYPES OF CONSULTANTS

Consultants operate in a number of different roles. The *expert* consultant provides specialized knowledge or technical skill that the client lacks in his or her organization but does not need enough to hire a full-time individual or devote a staff person to learning the skill. The *resource* consultant helps the client do a task or solve a problem but does not do it for him or her as the expert would. A *process* consultant works on *how* the problem gets solved or the task is accomplished, not on *doing* the task or finding a solution. These three roles are not necessarily pure; you may have a consultant who acts in both resource and expert roles or any other combination.

We can contrast the three types of consultants as they would relate to a corporate planning assignment. The expert would gather data from the organization, the external environment, and market, and return with a report to the client summarizing his or her findings and recommendations. The resource consultant might put together a "case team" comprised of client people and himself or herself and work interactively on the study, holding frequent meetings with other members of the company to be certain of their involvement in developing a joint solution. The process consultant would put the onus on the client to develop the data and analysis but focus on structuring meetings, getting the client to define and diagnose the situation, and involving the appropriate players. The case team would be 100% client staff, with the consultant acting as a catalyst and facilitator to make certain goals were accomplished.

Which of these roles makes sense for your situation? Some of the questions to ask are:

1. How well-defined is the problem? A well-defined problem lends itself to the resource consultant, while a poorly defined problem might fit the expert or process roles.

2. How much time pressure is there? If you have two months to decide on making an acquisition and no staff time available, the expert route is preferable. Resource and process roles take longer because of client involvement.

3. How important is it for the rest of the organization to "buy in" to the findings? The greatest commitment is developed where the client organization actively participates and takes responsibility for the recommendations, when a resource or process approach is used.

4. Is this a one-time situation or might it recur? If you are trying to establish corporate planning in your company, you need to start training your organization on how to do it. The process role works well here.

Sometimes the situation presents only one role option. I was once desperately recruited to run a planning session only a day before the actual meeting, leaving no opportunity for me to learn about the business. The situation gave me only one choice: to act as a process consultant and stimulate the managers to present their industry knowledge in a systematic manner and think strategically about the product, market, and competition. I could contribute nothing to the knowledge base so could hardly bill myself as an expert, but I served what turned out to be a critical function in the development of strategy. The facilitator role was perfect because the group managers had internalized all of the needed information for situational analysis but had previously lacked the structure and discipline to organize it.

Sometimes it is appropriate to combine roles, switching tactics at different stages of the study. An expert might do the background situation assessment as a starting point for the planning system, and then change to a resource or process role as the strategy development phase begins. A resource consultant may work through the entire plan the first time; then a process consultant works with the organization in the second go-round to train the people involved, with the goal of eventual self-sufficiency. There is no one answer to the question of the "best" type of consultant for your needs. The answer depends on your organization's current situation and long-term goals.

HOW A CONSULTANT WORKS

Proposals

Let us suppose you have decided upon the type of consultant role that makes sense and have focused on one or a few consultants who might satisfy your needs. The next step is to meet with the consultants to provide background on the situation and the scope of the assignment you are considering. The consultants will probe with many questions to get a better sense of you, your company, the situation, and your specific needs. You may wish to conduct this meeting alone or in conjunction with others in your organization who will be involved in the project. Your objective is to impart information and get a feel for the consultants' chemistry and approach; the consultants' objective is to take away enough information so they can write a formal proposal, as well as to get a feel for the flavor of the organization and personal chemistry.

A formal proposal normally consists of a section outlining the background, scope of the project, objectives, methodology or work plan, qualifications, time, and cost. Background reiterates the consultants' understanding of the situation at hand and the assumptions upon which they are basing their proposal. This provides an opportunity for you to assess their grasp of the situation and whether full communication occurred in your meeting. The scope or objectives section lays out the proposal of the study, questions to be answered, or problems to be solved. Again, this is a chance to check on the communication that happened between you and the consultants. The methodology section presents the means by which the consultants plan to locate information and otherwise proceed to fulfill study objectives. Qualifications to conduct the assignment are found in a portion that details the firm's background and capabilities and biographies of the key case team members. Most firms will assign a small group rather than one individual to work on an assignment or case. The last section will present costs of the assignment and timing for various phases and to completion. Costs should specify whether a complete written report and/or an oral presentation will be provided.

The proposal may serve as a contract when you are ready to proceed and comes complete with caveats about guaranteeing specific results and other legalistic hedges. These are standard boilerplate, and there is little you can do to eliminate them when dealing with a large consulting organization. Never sign a proposal unless you are happy with its restatement of your situation and the understanding you have with the consultants, or you may find yourself legally bound to something you don't want to do.

Formal proposals as outlined are not universal. A friend who works for a major consulting firm loves to write what he calls a "Dear Bob" proposal. This flies only when there is a well-established, trusting relationship between client and consultant, the kind in which the client can pick up the phone, call the consultant, and say, "The CEO just announced a reorganization this afternoon. Can you fly up here tomorrow? I want your advice." With this kind of relationship, there may not be a need for a formal assignment proposal, and a "Dear Bob" letter suffices. It goes like this:

Dear Bob:

Thank you for lunch last week. I would be pleased to advise on your reorganization situation. Our usual retainer relationship will apply and we will bill you monthly.

I am looking forward to helping out on this one. See you on the 15th.

Cordially,

(Consultant)

As convenient as the "Dear Bob" letter is for a consultant, there are not many situations where it applies. The need to state written objectives and common understanding is high, whether you are talking about an in-house project or an external consulting relationship. A document serves the purpose of allowing everyone to check their perceptions about the project.

The Assignment

The consultant is ready to begin the assignment once the proposal has been accepted. At this stage, interaction with the client is extremely important. The quality of the consultant–client relationship and joint expectations can make or break a study. A client who expects that the consultants will find a solution and implement it in the organization is going to be dissatisfied when the consultants tell him or her that implementation is not part of their job. The consultants who expect easy access to line management are going to be frustrated when they are told the line is off-limits. Communication, trust, and understanding between parties are absolutely critical.

The client and staff should be prepared to spend a significant amount of time with the consultants at the start of the assignment even if the consultants have been brought in as experts. A common misconception is, "If they're such experts, I don't need to tell them anything—they know it all!" This *may* be true about strategic planning or even industry knowledge but a new consultant cannot possibly know your company in depth. The consultants must be openly given full knowledge of the client company, its perception of the industry, and competition. They should have access to written information, as well as attending company meetings to gain exposure to the issues and personalities. Many clients who have not used consultants before worry that their confidential information will fall into competitors' hands. If they have done their homework in choosing a consultant and checked the firm's or individual's reputation, there is no reason for concern. Consultants make their living by dealing with and creating confidential information and they would rapidly be out of business if they revealed that knowledge. Information is a consultant's only currency.

It is difficult to generalize about how a strategic study might progress because of the large number of different approaches taken. Let us talk about the case where the consultant is playing an expert role and evaluating the market prior to strategy development. The consultant generally begins a strategic study by collecting secondary material on the company, industry, and competitors and by learning about the client company from internal company contacts. Field work is the next step after the preliminaries have been covered; sometimes this is done simultaneously with the background material development. It typically consists of personal and/or telephone interviews with key market participants such as competitors, customers, and suppliers, and industry sources such as trade associations and other industry experts. The consultant will have estimated the number of interviews to be conducted when pricing the assignment but may change his or her mind midstream after learning about the market first-hand. A good rule of thumb in consulting is to keep doing interviews until you start to hear the same information again and again and again, then quit because you will not benefit from additional field work. Sometimes this takes fewer interviews than was initially anticipated because the consultant has tried to be conservative in constructing the sample. In other cases, field work shows the problem to be something different from the assumption going-in and the entire study plan must be reworked to probe the real problem.

Analysis begins during the information-gathering process but becomes the focus after all the field work is completed. It is likely that the consultant began with some hypotheses to be proved or disproved in the field after a close look at the client situation. The field work phase allows him or her to accept, reject, or alter those hypotheses. Analysis is the final synthesis of the situation, given all of the background now available.

The last phase is development of recommendations. Somewhere between analysis and the final presentation it may be useful to have a client–consultant meeting for the consultant to try out his or her thinking on the client. The client may be able to communicate ways in which the findings and considered recommendations can be made palatable to management, and the consultant will be able to check that he or she has properly covered the relevant information sources. If the findings are going to shock the client, it is important for the consultant to prepare the client gradually for what is coming.

The client must judge whether greater acceptance for the findings will come from the consultant presenting directly to management or from the client's own presentation. It is frequently very effective to have the consultant make an oral presentation to a management group, after being well coached about sensitive areas ahead of time. Consultants can say things to the CEO with a disarming impartiality that a company manager could never say.

How do you evaluate the consultant after the fact? The criteria range from hard dollars to soft judgments:

Was the study on time and on budget?

Was the relationship between the consultant and the client good? Between the consultant and other members of your organization?

Were the findings and recommendations useful? Were they communicated well?

Would you hire the consultant again?

A consulting relationship will work smoothly as long as three conditions are satisfied:

1. The project must be defined well from the start. If you do not know what you really want and the consultant does not hammer down the definition, chances are you will be disappointed in the results.

2. The consultant must be selected with care. Know what capabilities and approach you are buying. If the consultant uses a specific theoretical framework, such as the BCG approach, be certain you understand the assumptions since the framework will color the results achieved.

3. Interaction must be frequent to be certain you understand who will take what responsibility in the study, that the assignment is not going off on an irrelevant tangent, and that the consultant has all of your company insights needed to do a good job.

FEES

Never buy a consultant wholesale. Good consultants charge hefty fees for their services just as good doctors or lawyers do. You will find that different levels of professionals are billed out at roughly comparable amounts across major consulting firms. Differences in costs among firms for the same proposal are generally based on the way in which they conceptualize the amount of work needed rather than on daily billing rates.

Consultants may charge for their services in several ways: a retainer, flat fee for the assignment, monthly fee, per diem for the number of days spent, a not-to-exceed amount, or a combination of these. Retainers are used when you want a long-term relationship with a consultant and guaranteed accessibility for some number of days each month. They are a nice way to avoid the frustration of "I'm sorry, she's traveling for the next two weeks overseas. I'll have her call you when she's back but she's pretty well tied up until next month."

Probably the most common arrangement for a strategic planning study is the flat fee, developed for the scope of work and methodology to be used on the assignment. The consultant estimates the number of days it will take to complete that scope of work, the levels of individuals on the case team who will contribute to the assignment, and their billing rates. Billing rates are salary marked up by an overhead factor, usually between three and four times. As the client, you will see only the final figure, which will probably include a fudge factor on top of staff time for the inevitable problems that occur. Expenses are billed separately and may be marked up a small percentage for accounting time. A sample consultant's costing sheet might look like this:

Number of Days

	Secondary Research	Field Work	Analysis	Client Meetings	Total Days	Billing Rate	Total Cost
Bill	1	10	2	3	16	$450	$ 7,200
Sue	0.5	7	2	3	12.5	600	7,500
Chris	8	—	1	—	9	300	2,700
Case leader	1	3	5	6	15	900	13,500
							30,900
					15% contigency		4,635
							$35,535

A case leader might bill between $600 and $1,200 a day, a senior consultant between $500 and $700, and a research assistant between $200 and $300. You will never see these rates published but they will be reflected in the overall estimate for your assignment. The only number you, the client, will see is the bottom line, rounded to the nearest $1,000 or $5,000 (some consultants feel that fees must be rounded to the nearest $5,000 to have the right "panache"). The sample cost sheet above, for example, might become a quote of $36,000 or $40,000, depending on the consultant's philosophy.

A variant of the flat fee is the flat fee per month, such as $20,000 a month for three to six months. This type of fee may be quoted when the project cannot be clearly defined up-front but a level of effort is anticipated for its duration. The $20,000 provides a certain level of effort for the period of time it takes to complete the assignment.

The last type of fee we will treat is the per diem. Many large consulting firms refuse to work on this basis because they feel either that the client is not fully committed to the study or that they will be underpricing their work. A small or one-person firm may be pleased to price on a per diem basis. The per diem may be useful from the client's perspective for a short-duration assignment such as a three-day training seminar, personal advisement, the odd day of counseling between studies, or other intermittent needs. This structure is generally inappropriate for a major consulting assignment because it is too open-ended. Per diem rates can be higher than the full case rates above because the consultant needs a premium for the short duration of the assignment. Depending on the consultant's reputation, the per diem can go as high as thousands of dollars or as low as $300.

Remember that you get what you pay for. Multimillion-dollar decisions deserve the best possible input, and a few thousand dollars more in consulting fees will get lost in the rounding. As one writer said, "A man facing trial on a serious charge does not shop for an attorney on the basis of price alone."*

TYPES OF FIRMS

There are literally thousands of consulting firms in existence, ranging all the way from the one-person firm to those that employ over 1,000 consultants. Arthur D. Little in Cambridge, Massachusetts, is the largest U.S. firm, with revenues well over $100 million.

Firms can be divided into two categories: generalists and specialists. The generalist firm consults in a large number of different functional and/or industry areas, while the specialist focuses on one small segment of the business world, either by industry, by function, or both. We will be concerned with firms that specialize in strategic planning and generalists that cover planning as one of their many functions. Firms may be international, national, or regional.

There are advantages and disadvantages to each type of firm. A generalist firm allows you to draw on a number of diverse backgrounds. You may go in thinking you have a marketing problem only to find out it is a manufacturing problem after the study has progressed. A generalist firm will be able to add manufacturing expertise to your assignment, while a marketing specialist firm will be stymied. A specialist firm, on the other hand, will have more depth of knowledge in your area of concern. You may get added value by dealing with specialists who have seen a similar situation dozens of times and can apply some of the problem-solving techniques developed in other settings to your issues.

Industry specialization can be a plus because the firm already knows your business well, saving time in learning the industry, but at the same time specialization fosters a parochial approach. Just as an industry can become too in-

* Alfred Hunt, *The Management Consultant,* New York: Ronald Press Company, 1977, pp. 30–85.

bred and fail to innovate with methods that have worked successfully in other industries, an industry consultant can suffer the same narrowness of vision. An approach taken by some generalists is to compose the case team jointly with functional and industry specialists.

Which is the best type of firm for you? As you might guess, there is no right answer. Furthermore, the answer will change as your company's circumstances change. Large, well-publicized firms offer a degree of safety since you are dealing with known quantities, but at times their work may be uneven and quality control may be nonexistent. There are many small firms, with one to 10 or 20 people, that have excellent capabilities. They may be splinter groups from the large firms and therefore have the same training in techniques without big-name overhead structures, or university B school professors with interesting new approaches, or seasoned senior businesspeople who can provide a depth of business experience that those who have been consultants all their lives cannot. In dealing with a small firm, the key is to know the people. Look at their backgrounds, talk to other clients, and check satisfaction with their work. Listen to the firm's philosophy of business and consulting style. You may find that the individual consultant or small firm who values your business greatly gives you high-caliber work with a level of personal attention that a large firm cannot. On the other hand, you may prefer the assurance and credibility that a "name" firm provides. Companies involved in litigation who want a consultant to provide expert testimony always hire the most prestigious name around. While you may not have any lawsuits on your hands, your company culture or the CEO may be impressed by a name firm.

ANATOMY OF AN ASSIGNMENT

Consulting firms normally are divided into three or more levels, each of which performs a specific function. It is important to assess the backgrounds and experience of the people who will actually do the work, as well as the people trotted out to see you in the initial selling stage.

You will at first meet consulting firm people from the highest level if you are a sizable potential client. They will probably be firm officers or they may be experienced consultants who have gained enough credibility with senior management that their primary function now is prospecting and smoothing client relationships. These people are sometimes known as the "gray hairs," a term derived from the common wisdom that it takes a gray-haired, experienced consultant to relate well to a gray-haired, experienced CEO. There are, of course, exceptions, especially in the newer boutique consulting firms where the average age is 28 and the founders are in their thirties.

In some firms, the rule of thumb is that the person who sells the work leads the case, but more frequently the sellers are separated from the doers except when the case runs into trouble or client relationships need to be reinforced.

When the sellers and doers are different people, the case or engagement leader has project responsibility. This person may write the proposal, staff the assignment, do the pricing, and supervise execution. He or she normally participates in some field work to get a flavor for the situation, interacts regularly with case team members, sets direction, synthesizes, analyzes, prepares presentations, and meets with the client. From your perspective, the case leader is the key player because he or she has the most impact on quality of the work, cost, and timing.

The case leader may be able to choose the case team freely or may be dictated to by the firm's management based on availability of people or other criteria. The case team can be broken down into two components: those who do field work and those who do desk research. The more senior consultants are sent out into the field to do interviewing or to work with the client firm's personnel, depending on the type of assignment. Junior consultants, sometimes called research assistants, typically lack the all-important MBA and earn their keep by doing literature searches of published material or telephone interviews. They act as support staff to the senior consultants in the field.

The case leader's responsibility is to structure the assignment so each level of consultant is put to best use. There is no point in billing a senior consultant's rate to do a literature search, or in using a case leader to do most of the field work. High billing rates are normally preserved for organizing, supervising, and client meetings.

THE STRATEGY CONSULTING BUSINESS

Strategy consulting is a relatively new specialty emerging from general management consulting. Boston Consulting Group was the first of the "strategy boutiques" when it started in 1963, and it has since spawned several other firms. BCG's revenues are almost $30 million in 1978, making it the fifteenth largest consulting firm in the United States.* The business grew as much as 70% a year in the late 1970s. Today, some of the generalist firms use their strategy practice as a loss leader because of its image-building qualities.

Who are the main players in strategy consulting? We can characterize them by their emphasis on concept—the content of developing strategy—versus process—the dynamics of developing strategy—and their degree of specialization in strategy versus other business disciplines. Mike Porter, a Harvard Business School professior, developed a perceptual map of the leading strategy firms on those two dimensions. The boutiques cluster in the lower left-hand corner, emphasizing concept and strategy work only. Bain stands alone in the lower right, a strategy-only firm that focuses on process. McKinsey is squarely in the middle. Booz Allen and ADL are generalists, with Booz strong on concept and ADL strong on process. (See Exhibit 18.1.)

* "The New Shape of Management Consulting," *Business Week,* May 21, 1979, p. 99.

EXHIBIT 18.1.   Leading Strategy Firms

General	Booz, Allen, Hamilton	Arthur D. Little
	McKinsey	Temple, Barker, Sloan
Strategy only	Boston Consulting Group Strategic Planning Associates Braxton Associates Marakon	Bain
	Concept	Process

Source: Michael Porter, Harvard Business School.

SELECTED CONSULTING FIRMS

There are a few firms that stand out in the quality of their strategic planning services, which will be briefly described here. This is by no means an exhaustive review of everyone who does planning consulting, but rather a cherry-picked list of some of the best.

Boston Consulting Group, Boston, Mass.   We must start with this famed granddaddy of the strategic consulting business, from whom much application and development of new theory evolved. BCG maintains U.S. offices in Chicago and Menlo Park, California, in addition to its Boston headquarters, three European offices, and one in Tokyo. The practice is now divided equally between domestic and foreign clients. BCG tells very little about itself but we can get a peek into its philosophy through the statement it makes in a recruiting book used at Harvard Business School, a rich source of new consultants:

> The Boston Consulting Group (BCG) specializes in competitive strategy. Such strategy requires the commitment of major resources in forms that are essentially irreversible. For this reason, BCG's practice is focused upon the most critical and far-reaching of management decisions. These

decisions must be made with detailed assessment of competitive reactions and capabilities.

Clients turn to BCG for strategy assistance in individual businesses and with entire corporate portfolios. Our practice ranges from broad issues of resource deployment, financial policy, and international competition, to specific questions of pricing, product and market focus, manufacturing structure, and sales policy. BCG's clients seek counsel on strategy issues in industrial and consumer products, and in financial, insurance, retail, and other services. Most clients are large corporations with whom BCG has continuing relationships, involving assistance in executing and monitoring the strategies we design. . . . BCG's real growth constraint has been and continues to be the availability of top-caliber consultants.

BCG considers the case team its main organizational unit. There are four professional levels in the firm: vice-president, manager, consultant, and associate. A case team contains individuals from each level.

The company sees its strengths as creativity and making changes happen through the consulting process. Its consultants are not focused on any particular industry and consider themselves to be management generalists specializing in planning.

Bain and Company, Boston, Mass. If BCG is quiet about itself, Bain is even quieter. Having splintered from BCG in 1973, Bill Bain founded a company that is now a formidable competitor. The company claims to have grown more than 30% annually since 1973 and to have the "largest corporate strategic practice in the United States," a statement BCG might dispute.

Bain focuses on long-term relationships with clients that emphasize improved performance. Company policy is not to release information about its proprietary approach to anyone outside current or potential clients, so little is known about Bain's method of operation even in the close-knit Boston consulting community. One can assume that its BCG heritage had a major influence on the style and method of work. It may take even a client three to six months of interacting with Bain to understand the approach.

Bain never works for more than one company in an industry because of possible conflicts of interest; this is a common consulting practice. It uses a typical case team approach in which the person who sells the work also acts as case leader. There are five offices—Boston, Menlo Park, London, Tokyo, and Munich—staffed by almost 400 consultants. Like many of the other boutique firms, it does heavy recruiting at the Harvard Business School for bright, raw material to work up through the ranks.

Arthur D. Little, Cambridge, Mass. Arthur D. Little (ADL) is probably best known as a scientific and technical consulting firm, much to the distress of the management consulting group that is equal to a medium-sized consulting firm and possesses first-rate capabilities. Strategy work is conducted by about 50 people worldwide. The strategy group within the management counseling section, ADL's nontechnical management experts, focuses on process consulting. A technique used is the profiling session, in which a business's senior management meets for three to four days to lay out the situational analysis and talk about strategy concepts. This intensive beginning may be followed by up to three to six months of work to translate the concepts explored and decisions made into action programs. The profiling technique is a powerful means to do data collection and gain management interaction, often obtaining results that surprise the participants and to which they buy in because of their role in forming the information. Besides profiling, ADL may train client company employees in planning if the company already has a well-developed planning system, or they may actually write a corporate plan for a client.

ADL differentiates itself from other firms by its ability to combine planning methodology with implementation and industry expertise, drawing from the vast range of industry experts on its staff. A typical case team consists of three to four people, led by a person with 10 to 20 years of business experience. The composition of team skills is determined by the consultants' assessment of the client's problem.

A profiling assignment costs between $30,000 and $125,000 per SBU, depending on the unit's size and complexity. ADL's planning clients are generally Fortune 1000 companies, most of which have their own planning groups but feel the need for outside help. Sixty percent of the business is from prior clients, a strong vote of confidence for the value of the work performed.

Strategic Planning Institute, Cambridge, Mass. The Strategic Planning Institute's claim to fame is its PIMS program, the data base that tells clients what strategy produces what results under given conditions. SPI began as an internal project at General Electric, was established at Harvard Business School in 1972–74 for further development, and became an autonomous institute in 1975. It is a unique resource in the business world but is far better known in academia than among practitioners. The concept is for a client company to be able to test a strategy's results without going "live," using the experience of similar businesses as a surrogate. The advantages of having a computerized pretest without incurring market response are enormous.

More than 200 companies have joined SPI in order to both contribute data to the data base and to obtain results from other companies' experience. The Strategic Analysis Report computes the consequences of a strategic move in terms of profit-and-loss impact, investment, and cash flow. Strategic moves may be broad based, such as market share and capital intensity, or they may be more specific. Member companies also receive reports on the return on investment that is normal for the business, an optimum strategy report that suggests the combination of strategic moves that are most effective, and a report on "look alike" businesses, their strategic and operating characteristics that allowed them to achieve an objective. SPI can provide consultants from its own staff to help you analyze these reports and do strategy consulting.

Membership fees vary by company size and range from roughly $15,000 for a small company to more than $25,000 for a large one. There is an additional startup fee the first year. Members are required to contribute data about their businesses. Conferences are offered to members to discuss strategy and techniques, as well as to explain how PIMS works.

There are other fine consulting firms that do strategy consulting. McKinsey and Company, a general management consultant based in New York, certainly belongs on the list. Strategic Planning Associates in Washington, D.C., is well-known for its strategy practice. There are directories of consultants that can provide a more complete list of firms in your area.

APPENDIX: READINGS FOR STRATEGY PRACTITIONERS

Here is a list of the four most readable planning books for practitioners. The focus is on the pragmatic, not on the theoretical. There are many other books on the shelves that provide useful information, but following are my personal favorites:

BUSINESS POLICY AND STRATEGY: CONCEPTS AND READINGS. *Daniel J. McCarthy, Robert J. Minichello, and Joseph R. Curran.* Published by Richard D. Irwin, Homewood, Ill., 1979.

A collection of readable articles in the area of corporate strategy and planning from which you can pick and choose according to your interest. Titles ranges from "strategic responses to technological threats" to "formulating strategy in small companies" to "defining corporate strengths and weaknesses." A good overview because it exposes you to a number of different authors' thinking.

COMPETITIVE STRATEGY. *Michael E. Porter.* Published by the Free Press, New York, N.Y., 1980.

Porter's book was one of the hottest strategic planning books to hit in a long time when it was published in 1980. Corporate planning circles were abuzz with his "generic strategies" for coping with different industry structures. Even though he is a Harvard professor, he has managed to write a book that is nonacademic in tone and designed for the practitioner. Porter's focus is on developing competitive strategy in different types of industry environments and at different stages of maturity in the life cycle. There are excellent sections on how to perform competitive analysis and industry studies.

STRATEGIC MARKET PLANNING. *Derek F. Abell* and *John S. Hammond.* Published by Prentice-Hall, Englewood Cliffs, N.J., 1979.

A combination text and case book, this is one of the more readable overviews of corporate planning, touching on everything from how to do analysis to formal planning methods and the planning process. Chapter 2, on "Analyzing Market Opportunity and Assessing Company Capability," is an excellent presentation of situation analysis, complete with lists of questions to be asked, that can serve as the framework for an in-house planning session. You can skip over the case portions (Abell used to teach at Harvard Business School) and zero in on the text for maximum return on your time.

STRATEGY FORMULATION: ANALYTICAL CONCEPTS. *Charles W. Hofer* and *Dan Schendel. Published by West Publishing Company, St. Paul, Minn., 1978.*

Hofer and Schendel's book focuses on the development of strategy and provides a variety of frameworks to accomplish the task. There is enough theory so you know why you are looking at a particular factor to develop strategy, but the book is basically pragmatic in approach. It is an excellent stimulus for ideas on strategy formulation, both at the corporate and business unit levels. There are lots of charts and grids that provide visual input for the concepts, and the text is written in a highly readable style.

The JOURNAL OF BUSINESS STRATEGY has interesting articles aimed at practitioners. If you find yourself involved in the design of a corporate planning organization, you may want to read Peter Loranges's CORPORATE PLANNING: AN EXECUTIVE VIEWPOINT (Prentice-Hall, 1980). It's heavier going than the books above but presents important concepts in organizational design. Kenneth Andrews's THE CONCEPT OF STRATEGY is on the theoretical side but makes interesting reading for people who want more than just application of theory. Bruce Henderson's ON CORPORATE STRATEGY is a compendium of essays that his Boston Consulting Group published in its "Perspectives" series sent to clients. It contains some concepts that have become part of consulting world jargon.

Bibliography

Abell, Derek F. *Defining the Business: The Starting Point of Strategic Planning*. Englewood Cliffs, N.J.: Prentice-Hall, 1980.

Abell, Derek F., and John S. Hammond. *Strategic Market Planning*. Englewood Cliffs, N.J.: Prentice-Hall, 1979.

Albert, Kenneth J. *How to be Your Own Management Consultant*. New York: McGraw-Hill, 1978.

Allio, Robert J., and Malcolm W. Pennington. *Corporate Planning: Techniques and Applications*. New York: AMACOM 1979.

Ansoff, H. Igor. *Corporate Strategy*. New York: McGraw-Hill, 1965.

Argenti, John. "Corporate Planning: Getting to Grips with Your Company's Destiny." *Director,* April 1979, 61.

Boston Consulting Group. *Growth and Financial Strategies: Special Commentary*. 1971 (pamphlet).

Buzzell, Robert D., Bradley T. Gale, and Ralph G.M. Sultan. "Market Share—A Key to Profitability." *Harvard Business Review,* January–February 1975.

Cannon, J. Thomas. "Auditing and Competitive Environment." In John W. Bongi and Bruce P. Coleman, eds., *Concepts for Corporate Strategy*. New York: Macmillan, 1972.

Cohen, Kalman J., and Richard M. Cyert. "Strategy: Formulation, Implementation and Monitoring." In Robert R. Rothberg, ed. *Corporate Strategy and Product Innovation*. New York: Free Press, 1981.

The Conference Board. *Planning and the Corporate Planning Director*. Report 627, 1974.

Conley, Patrick. "Experience Curves as a Planning Tool." In Britt and Boyd, ed., *Marketing Management and Administrative Action*. New York, McGraw-Hill, 1978.

Daniells, Lorna M. *Business Information Sources*. Berkeley: University of California Press, 1976.

Day, George S. "Diagnosing the Product Portfolio." In Robert R. Rothberg, ed., *Corporate Strategy and Product Innovation*. New York: Free Press, 1981.

———. "A Strategic Perspective on Product Planning." In Britt and Boyd, eds., *Marketing Management and Administrative Action*. New York: McGraw-Hill, 1978.

Denning, Basil W., ed. *Corporate Planning*. London: McGraw-Hill, 1971.

Drucker, Peter F. "Long-Range Planning Means Risk-Taking." In David W. Ewing, ed., *Long-Range Planning for Management*. New York: Harper & Row, 1972.

Figueroa, Oscar, and Charles Winkler. *A Business Information Guidebook,* New York: AMACOM, 1980.

Fuchs, Jerome H. *Making the Most of Management Consulting Services*. New York: AMACOM, 1975.

Gale, Bradley T., and Ben Branch. "Cash Flow Analysis: More Important than Ever." *Harvard Business Review,* July–August, 1981.

Gluck, Frederick, Stephen Kaufman, and A. Steven Walleck. "The Four Phases of Strategic Management." *Journal of Business Strategy,* 2 (3): 9.

———. "Strategic Management for Competitive Advantage." *Harvard Business Review,* July–August 1980, 154–161.

Gordon, Robert J. *Macroeconomics*. Boston: Little, Brown, 1981.

Hall, Dan. "Managing the Management Consultant." *New England Business,* October 4, 1982, 49–51.

Hall, William K. "Survival Strategies in a Hostile Environment." *Harvard Business Review,* September–October 1980.

Hambrick, Donald C. and Ian C. Macmillan. "On the Product Portfolio and Man's Best Friend." Unpublished paper.

Hambrick, Donald C., Ian C. Macmillan, and Diana L. Day. "Strategic Attributes and Performance in the Four Cells of the BCG Matrix—A PIMS-Based Analysis of Industrial/Product Businesses." Unpublished paper.

Harvard Business School. "A Note on the Boston Consulting Group Concept of Competitive Analysis and Corporate Strategy." Cambridge, Mass.: Intercollegiate Clearing House, June 1976.

Haspeslagh, Philippe. "Portfolio Planning: Uses and Limits." *Harvard Business Review,* January–February 1982, 58.

Henderson, Bruce. "Experience Curve—Reviewed." Boston Consulting Group Perspectives, 1974.

Hertzberg, Daniel, and Jill Bettner. "Spotting Early Symptoms of Sick Companies Is Easy if Investors Know What to Look For." *Wall Street Journal,* August 16, 1982, 32.

Hunt, Alfred. *The Management Consultant*. New York: Ronald Press, 1977.

"Improving Consultant-Client Communications." Proceedings from the North American Conference of Management Consultants, New York, 1975.

Kiechel, Walter III. "The Decline of the Experience Curve." *Fortune,* October 5, 1981, 139–146.

———. "Oh Where, Oh Where Has My Little Dog Gone? Or My Cash Cow? Or My Star?" *Fortune,* November 2, 1981, 148–154.

———. "Three (or Four, or More) Ways to Win." *Fortune,* October 19, 1981, 181–188.

Kieso, Donald E., and Jerry J. Weygandt. *Intermediate Accounting*. New York: Wiley and Sons, 1980.

Kudla, Ronald J. "The Effects of Strategic Planning on Common Stock Returns." *Academy of Management Journal*, **23**, (1): 1: 5.

Kubr, M., ed. *Management Consulting*. Geneva: International Labour Office, 1976.

Lawton, Tom. *Financial Aspects of Corporate Planning*. London: Institute of Chartered Accountants in England and Wales, 1975.

Leavitt, Russell L. "Strategic Planning and Management at General Electric." Smith Barney Harris Upham & Company Research Report, August 27, 1981.

Linneman, Robert E. *Shirt Sleeve Approach to Long Range Planning for the Small, Growing Corporation*. Englewood Cliffs, N.J.: Prentice-Hall, 1980.

Lorange, Peter. *Corporate Planning*. Englewood Cliffs, N.J.: Prentice-Hall, 1980.

Miller, Ernest C. *Advanced Techniques for Strategic Planning*. AMA Research Study 104, 1971.

Naylor, Thomas H. *Strategic Planning Management*. Planning Executives Institute, Research Series, 1980.

"Planning Is Not Enough." *Business Week,* January 25, 1982, 120.

Porter, Michael E. *Competitive Strategy*. New York: Free Press, 1980.

Sapp, Richard W., and Robert E. Seiler. "The Relationship between Long-Range Planning and Financial Performance of U.S. Commercial Banks." *Managerial Planning*, **30**, (2): 32–33.

Schaffir, Walter B. *Strategic Business Plan: Some Questions for the Chief Executive*. New York: The Presidents Association of American Management Association, Study # 63, 1976.

Schoeffler, Sidney, Robert D. Buzzell, and Donald F. Heany. "Impact of Strategic Planning on Profit Performance." *Harvard Business Review,* March–April 1974.

Shay, Philip W. *How to Get the Best Results from Management Consultants*. New York: Association of Consulting Management Engineers, 1974.

Simmons, W. W. *So You Want to Have a Long-Range Plan*. Oxford, Ohio: Planning Executives Institute Research Series, 1980.

Steele, Fritz. *Role of the Internal Consultant*. Boston: CBI Publishing Company, 1982.

Steiner, George A. *Top Management Planning*. New York: Macmillan, 1969.

———. *Strategic Planning*. New York: Free Press, 1979.

"The New Shape of Management Consulting." *Business Week,* May 21, 1979, 98–104.

Turner, Arthur N. "Consulting Is More Than Giving Advice." *Harvard Business Review,* September–October 1982, 120–129.

Wasserman, Paul, ed. *Encyclopedia of Business Information Sources*. Detroit: Gale Research Company, 1981.

Weston, J. Fred, and Eugene F. Brigham. *Managerial Finance*. Hinsdale, Ill.: Dryden Press, 1981.

Index